'Most Skilful, Most Devious, Most Cunning'

A Political Biography of Bertie Ahern

John Downing

BLACKWATER PRESS

Editor
Antoinette Walker

Design & Layout
Paula Byrne

Cover Design
Melanie Gradtke

ISBN
1-84131-687-3

© John Downing, 2004

Produced in Ireland by Blackwater Press, c/o Folens Publishers, Hibernian Industrial Estate, Tallaght, Dublin 24

Prologue

It was after 2 am but the floodwaters showed no sign of abating. He had resigned himself to being soaked through. The putrid water had risen above his wellington boots more than an hour previously, and as he moved about it was frequently above his knees. His good Crombie coat was a write-off. It was a weird way to spend a Friday night.

Suddenly, he was approached by an elderly lady in considerable distress. He listened carefully to her tale of woe. Her husband, due to have heart surgery the following Monday, was refusing to leave their flooded home. The man had stubbornly rejected all advice and had stayed upstairs, while she had left along with the firemen.

He followed her directions towards the house. At the street corner, a Civil Defence member told him, 'You're not going down that street!'

But he persisted.

'Right then, you go down there – you're on your own,' the official said as he walked past.

As he neared the house number he had been given, the water was yet again above his knees. The house was in darkness as he rapped on the door and then on a window. After a long wait, an upstairs window opened with a loud creak.

'Yes? What do you want?' the old man asked curtly.

He explained about the woman's concerns and the worry over the surgery just days away.

'Would you not come out?' he appealed.

'Amn't I as well off here in that case. I might as well die here as anywhere else,' the old man said unmoved.

He made one last appeal.

The old man was even less impressed.

'You, of all people should have better things to be doin' with yer time,' he snapped, slamming the window shut.

Bertie Ahern, Prime Minister of Ireland, moved back up the street.

Acknowledgements

Thanks to John O'Connor of Blackwater Press for suggesting this project and to Margaret Burns and Blackwater staff for their help and support. My gratitude too goes to the book's editor, Antoinette Walker, for her patience, skill and professionalism.

Many colleagues and friends helped, encouraged and supported. These include Harry McGee, Stephen O'Brien and Liam Mackey. *The Star* editor, Gerard Colleran, and colleagues Michael O'Kane, Cormac Bourke, Terry McGeehan and Catherine Halloran extended a great mix of forbearance and support. Also, Brian Looney, Ryle Dwyer, Michael O'Regan, Fionnán Sheahan, Carl O'Brien, Tommie Gorman and Jim Ivers gave me extra special help and support.

For permission to use a variety of pictures, my thanks goes to Gerard Colleran of *The Star* and special thanks to picture editor, Brian Dowling, for his help.

Both Tim Vaughan, editor of the *Irish Examiner*, and Geraldine Kennedy, editor of *The Irish Times*, kindly allowed me access to their libraries. The staff at these two marvellous resources ably demonstrated that the era of the internet has still left considerable gaps. For similar reasons, I'm also grateful to the staff at the National Library.

This project led to considerable domestic disruption and I'm especially grateful to my wife, Bethan Kilfoil, for her understanding, support and practical help. Thanks also to Mari and Denis for providing welcome comic relief.

Writing about any person still active in their career is an invidious business. I'm grateful to the many politicians and others in public life who spoke to me at a tricky time, especially those in Fianna Fáil who were facing a Cabinet reshuffle. Some spoke on the record, others confidentially, and some in a mix of those modes. I'm extremely grateful to all of them and hope they find I have honoured their trust.

Special thanks to Senator Tony Kett and Cllr Maurice Ahern for their courtesy and friendship. Thanks also to Senator Cyprian Brady, Joe Lennon and Mandy Johnston.

John Downing
Dublin & Droichead Nua, November 2004

Contents

Introduction

On Friday afternoon, 18 October 1991, Bertie Ahern was in the Cabinet room at Government Buildings in Dublin, patiently explaining a renewed coalition deal to three Sunday newspaper journalists. The door opened quietly and suddenly the beaming face of Charlie Haughey appeared.

'He's the man. He's the best, the most skilful, the most devious, and the most cunning of them all,' an exuberant Haughey proclaimed, pointing at Ahern. When Charlie Haughey left the room, Bertie Ahern looked at the three journalists resignedly and muttered, 'God, that's all I need.'

Haughey's summation of his protégé and most-trusted lieutenant is frequently quoted, though not often in context. Admirers cite it to show how able and reliable Ahern is; detractors use it to argue how a trickster lurks behind his good-natured face; and members of the public often strive to recall it when social conversation turns to politics. Ahern supporters believe that coming from Charlie Haughey, who was an extremely able politician, the citation was high praise indeed. His adversaries argue that the provenance of those words copperfastens their arguments about the Ahern potential for treachery.

Bartholomew Patrick Ahern has led Ireland's biggest political organisation, Fianna Fáil, for 10 years. By now he is also Ireland's longest-serving Taoiseach with the exception of Éamon de Valera who was, after all, an icon of Fianna Fáil and the new Irish State.

But how did this determinedly ordinary lower middle class Dubliner come to be leader of the modern Irish nation? How does he get power, keep power and use power? How did he reunite Fianna Fáil after 29 years of internal war and steer them to win an election at a time when scandalous revelations were emerging about key party figures? How did he defy the odds and keep a minority coalition government on track for a five-year term at a time of further non-stop revelations of sleaze concerning key Fianna Fáil figures, some of whom were closely connected with himself? How did he regain power with an enhanced majority at the end of that first five-year term?

Along the way, how did he help cajole a major breakthrough on ending the 400-year-old Northern Ireland conflict? And what of his work on achieving national consensus with unions, bosses and the other social partners? Was his proclaimed success heading Ireland's EU Presidency in 2004 merely public relations hype? Did he have a real chance of becoming President of the European Commission? What about the likelihood now of his confounding the pundits and creating a modern record by becoming Taoiseach for a third consecutive term? Are all these doings the product of his cunning and deviousness as outlined by Charlie Haughey? And what toll have 27 years of political exertions taken on his family and private life?

This book aims to address all of these issues.

~ ~ ~ ~ ~

The circumstances surrounding Charlie Haughey's appraisal of Bertie Ahern are rarely remembered now. In October 1991, Fianna Fáil's first-ever coalition deal had long passed the deadline for mid-term renewal. In fact, Haughey had breached a core party value in June 1989 by coalescing with the Progressive Democrats (PDs). Led by Haughey's arch-enemy, Des O'Malley, the PDs were a party which drew much of their founding motivation from profound objections to the leadership style and politics of Charlie Haughey. But Dáil arithmetic and a mutual need for political survival brought about their symbiotic alliance. In effect, both parties showed considerable pragmatism and for over two years the Government worked.

But by the middle of 1991 Charlie Haughey's public problems were mounting up. Privately, he had been saved by the munificence of several 'friends' from heavy debt caused by an extravagant lifestyle and the ambition to acquire a large property portfolio. However, that was not to become public for another five years.

Bertie Ahern had already helped Haughey fend off three leadership heaves in the years 1982/83. By autumn 1991 there was another such heave pending. Yet at the start of October, again with Ahern's help, Haughey saw off the first rumblings of a challenge to materialise in eight years. There were several scandals afflicting his Government and mutterings that the PDs would cut and run. Difficulties were compounded by a view among some within Fianna Fáil, including Albert Reynolds, that it was time to stand up to the PDs. But again Ahern mollified the Fianna Fáil hardliners and helped negotiate a mid-term renewal of the coalition deal with the PDs. For a brief time in October 1991 Charlie Haughey felt invulnerable and extremely grateful to Bertie Ahern for that. This is what lay behind that surprisingly effusive affirmation of his protégé.

~ ~ ~ ~ ~

The pair worked very closely together for 15 years and there is no doubt whatsoever about Ahern's total loyalty to Haughey from start to finish. Haughey's sheer presence and force of character coupled with the extraordinary events of his career make it difficult to stop this work about Bertie Ahern being dominated by him.

Indeed, Ahern had a number of reasons to be grateful to Charlie Haughey. He gave the young aspiring politician his first break in 1982 by appointing him Government Chief Whip in a coalition that lasted just nine months. Bertie Ahern was then barely 30-years-old and it was just over four years since he had been first elected to Dáil Éireann. The appointment, which allowed him attend but not vote at Cabinet, gave him a very valuable insight.

In the cauldron that was Irish politics through the 1980s Ahern was to learn many lessons from Charlie Haughey, who was at his best when cornered and boxing off the ropes. There is also evidence that he learnt a good deal from Haughey's errors, as he has not repeated many of them, especially avoiding limiting his political options.

There were many discernible similarities between the two men, despite a considerable age gap of 26 years. Indeed the age gap suited both men, as it led to an understanding that Ahern had time on his side to achieve future ambitions and could in the meantime learn his political trade from the master. Both men were northside Dubliners reared in frugal circumstances in lower middle class families. They also shared an interest in sport. Each was educated by the Irish Christian Brothers and had a flair for mathematics and figures. Haughey seems to have been more academically able; however, Ahern made up for this by his huge work rate. They shared similar views on Northern Ireland, but had the pragmatism to adapt and modify these when the need arose. Each was ambitious to see Ireland prosper and committed to availing of the European Union to achieve this aim.

Ahern's unswerving loyalty was a boon to Haughey who fought many political battles. Time and again Haughey would call upon his protégé to help him survive. But astonishingly, Ahern achieved the feat of being an ultra-Haughey loyalist without antagonising the anti-Haughey faction in Fianna Fáil at a time when the party was deeply fractured. This characteristic was to stand him in good stead as he tried to reunite the party after he became leader in 1994.

The long association with Haughey came at a heavy price, however. Some of Ahern's colleagues argue that Haughey kept him too long as Chief Whip because of the internal Fianna Fáil strife, and later kept him too long in the Department of Labour because he wanted to bed down social consensus. In fact, Bertie Ahern had barely three years' experience in any government job other than Chief Whip or Labour Minister when he became Taoiseach.

This may have some relevance, but ultimately does not seem to matter because Bertie Ahern went on to become a very successful Taoiseach.

Even so, it is clear that Haughey also left a very bitter legacy for Bertie Ahern. Soon after Ahern assumed the Fianna Fáil leadership in late 1994, the most damning revelations about Haughey began to emerge. The extent to which Haughey was financed by the great and the good of business through gifts amounting to some IR£9m (€11.5m) over the years raised serious public concerns. These touched a nerve with the public, reviving doubts about the ethics of Fianna Fáil's links to big business, which went back to the notorious days of its fundraising arm, Taca, in the 1960s.

Ahern had to deal with these issues by a mix of measures. First, he largely airbrushed Charlie Haughey out of the picture for a time and denounced his old boss's actions. Second, he set up an ethics regime within Fianna Fáil. Third, once he won power, he effectively parked the allegations of scandal by setting up tribunals of inquiry and also introducing ethics legislation.

~ ~ ~ ~ ~

Even trenchant Ahern opponents and critics must acknowledge that he is not corrupt. A decade of tribunals and other inquiries have so far yielded not a shred of evidence to the contrary. Equally, his own modest lifestyle and evidence of his very limited interest in money also testify to his integrity. None the less, Bertie Ahern was very close to some people who failed to uphold the high standards expected of those in public life. This has led opponents to contend that he is either a knave or a fool – with little evidence of any foolishness.

Charlie Haughey has already been mentioned – Ray Burke was another. Burke was deemed to have acted corruptly by the Flood Tribunal's second interim report in September 2002. Over the years, Burke was a key supporter who encouraged Ahern to seek the leadership in 1992 and again backed him in 1994 when he succeeded Albert Reynolds. Throughout the 31 months Ahern served as leader of the Opposition, Burke was one of his most-trusted men and elaborated Fianna Fáil foreign policy.

In each case, Ahern himself, his friends, supporters and most Fianna Fáil activists strongly reject these claims as calumnious innuendoes not grounded in fact. In summary, their argument runs that few people were aware of Haughey's real financial position prior to the mid-1990s and some years after his retirement from public life. How could Bertie Ahern have been expected to know? The general assumption, also held by many who worked with him for years, was that Haughey was wealthy having made money on land speculation in the 1950s and 1960s, which he then shrewdly invested.

On Burke, the argument is that Ahern did not really know anything beyond persistent rumours. He had some enquiries made before appointing him Foreign Affairs Minister in June 1997 but felt if he failed to appoint Burke, he would be condemning him without any chance to defend himself.

But, pragmatic as ever, Ahern's Fianna Fáil still maintains close links to business in general and the building trade in particular. Ahern himself has ruled out banning commercial donations to the political parties and instituting a system of total party Exchequer funding. This is in spite of calls from many leading party members to do so.

~ ~ ~ ~ ~

Bertie Ahern stole onto the national stage in 1977 and worked quietly building up an unparalleled constituency organisation, which he still meticulously tends. He worked discreetly below the line as Chief Whip and it was almost a decade before he was recognised as a potential Fianna Fáil leader for the 1990s.

Even then there were grave doubts about his ability to fill Haughey's big shoes. The image of 'anorakman' and his clumsy use of language were cited as reasons why he did not have the qualities required for the big job. These doubts persisted even after he took over the Fianna Fáil leadership in 1994. It is now clear that Bertie Ahern was greatly underestimated for the longest time. The skill alluded to by Charlie Haughey is, and always has been, there in abundance. Ahern succeeded because he applied himself meticulously to the task in hand. And like many driven career people, success has come at a personal cost.

Contemporaries are astonished by Ahern's work rate, which sees him toil from 7 am until midnight most weekdays. He usually puts in a more ordinary eight-hour day on Saturdays and Sundays. His only diversions are spending time with family and friends, watching sport, and drinking a few pints of his trademark tipple, draught Bass ale. These days he likes to spend as much time as he can with his two daughters, Georgina and Cecilia. At Georgina's wedding in France in August 2003, he spoke frankly of his own perceived shortcomings as a parent, and more recently he has confessed that his personal life has on occasion been lonely. Bertie Ahern married a Drumcondra neighbour, Miriam Kelly, in September 1975 on the day of his 24th birthday. The couple separated in 1987 and for some 16 years he had a much-publicised relationship with a long-time friend and political collaborator, Celia Larkin, which ended in the spring of 2003.

Despite his marital situation, Ahern has remained a devout Catholic who attends daily Mass during Lent, frequently also giving up alcohol at this time and during the month of November. There is strong anecdotal evidence to suggest that his family issues have enhanced the affection which many Irish people have for him as their 'Mr Everyman'.

However, he has only rarely and very sparingly commented in any way on personal matters. These days Bertie Ahern cuts something of a lonely figure, spending long periods in his constituency headquarters, St Luke's in Drumcondra, reading through government documentation. As a party leader and chairman of his Cabinet, he remains affable and approachable but ultimately rather aloof. He confides in some ministers about some issues and shares confidences with all of them on one issue or another. But ultimately they do not really know the man.

This writer first encountered Bertie Ahern in 1986 when he was Lord Mayor of Dublin. Our paths crossed during the years I worked in Brussels, where he attended various meetings as a Cabinet Minister and later as Taoiseach. For the past five years, I have observed him in my work as a political journalist at Leinster House.

At time of writing, Bertie Ahern has led Fianna Fáil for precisely 10 years and is already the longest serving Taoiseach since Éamon de Valera. He has also declared his intention to seek a third consecutive term as Taoiseach, which would be something of a modern record.

For this reason, this book does not claim to be the definitive biography. Even so, it is timely to take a close look at the work of Bertie Ahern as a person who has touched the lives of many Irish citizens, and by and large left a favourable impression. Despite the perceived shortcomings of deviousness and cunning, there is no doubt that he has skill in abundance and has enjoyed a remarkable political career.

1

Paranoia is Total Awareness

Bertie Ahern once lived at St Luke's. It was during a troubled time in his life, after separation from his wife Miriam, that he occupied the flat on the first floor, which is still maintained but now only occasionally used. The house itself has the feel of an oddball, small country hotel, though the name, St Luke's, dates from a time when it was a doctor's surgery. These days it has all the hallmarks of a shrine to Bertie Ahern with wall upon wall of photographs of various shapes and sizes. It is at St Luke's that Bertie Ahern begins most days before 8 am and it is frequently where he concludes his day around midnight or 1 am. He likes to pop in and out at weekends and spends hours there reading government reports, briefs and files. Over Christmas, when the two permanent constituency staff are on holiday, he spends a good deal of time there and regularly checks the answering machine.

From the outside, the house is a smart but modest redbrick building set back at a jaunty angle from one of Dublin's busiest traffic routes linking the airport to the city centre. It has no garage but there is parking in a yard at the rear. Constituents and regular travellers on the Drumcondra Road can often monitor the Taoiseach's attendance by the presence or absence of a black shiny Mercedes car parked outside.

Inside, as a medical surgery turned into a political surgery, the house is a curious hybrid. There is a constituency office and a private office on either side of the large entrance hall and stairwell. There is a bar just to the rear of these which is used for occasional entertaining and for periodic constituency organisation cheese-and-wine evenings. It is principally this bar that gives the place its quaint country-hotel aspect. The pumps on the bar counter include his own favourite trademark tipple, Bass. Why is he one of the few people left in Ireland who drinks draught Bass?

'He's a creature of habit,' constituency office manager Senator Cyprian Brady reveals.

Behind the bar there is a small kitchen area. Beyond that again is a large extended meeting hall with chairs stacked up ready for use. Against the window there is a large trestle table also used for meetings. The back door opens on to a large yard with flowerbeds and hanging baskets on the walls. Here the office staff can occasionally find the incongruous sight of the pinstripe-suited Bertie Ahern pulling weeds and tending flowers. This anecdote has become a point of almost irritation for Cyprian Brady. A magazine feature on the Taoiseach and his hanging baskets drew scornful reaction from the Opposition, partly driven by jealousy at his ability to attract invaluable soft-focus coverage in the run-up to the 2002 general election. When questioned with undue scepticism about the Taoiseach's green fingers and love of hanging baskets, Brady shrugs, 'Go on – have it your own way.'

All fripperies aside, St Luke's is the essential hub of Bertie Ahern's power source in Dublin Central. From there he has advanced on to the national and international stage. Before Bertie Ahern moved his political business there, he operated just across the street in an office above Fagan's pub while St Luke's served as a doctor's surgery. Increasingly nowadays, most TDs have stand-alone public offices with the days of supplicant constituents tramping through representatives' family homes becoming less and less prevalent. But few, if any, have such commanding, permanent and well-appointed premises from which to conduct their clinics.

St Luke's is at least a curiosity and so in the recent past has been a target for critics. In 1998, there was controversy over how it was to be treated under the new mandatory registration of political donations, including those given as benefit-in-kind. These include the use of property. Initially, the Ahern camp felt it was exempt from the relevant legislation as it was used by the Fianna Fáil organisation in Dublin Central. For the past two years, St Luke's has been registered with the Standards in Public Offices Commission as worth €12,000 per year in benefit-in-kind donations to Bertie Ahern. The registered donors to Taoiseach Bertie Ahern are cited as 'Fianna Fáil St Luke's'. Officially at least, its political value-in-use to the Taoiseach is put at just €240 per week.

The building was bought in 1988 for €71,000 (£56,000), largely with borrowed money guaranteed by a number of well-off backers. Another large sum of money was borrowed soon afterwards to remedy a serious structural defect and to carry out other works. Once stamp duty and taxes were factored in, the outlay was put at over €127,000 (£100,000).

The Fianna Fáil O'Donovan Rossa Cumann also organises a huge fundraising dinner each year with tables taken by the great and the good at some €200 per head. Proceeds go to cover St Luke's expenses. Formally, St Luke's is managed by five named trustees, including Ahern's old friend and neighbour, Joe Burke, and Des Richardson, on behalf of the Fianna Fáil Party and this group also ensures the mortgage payments are made along with other details.

'When he goes, it will either go to the new incumbent, or Fianna Fáil will sell it and proceeds will revert to the party coffers,' says Tony Kett, a friend, confidant and political collaborator of 30 years.

Cyprian Brady, named by his boss as one of the Taoiseach's 11 nominated senators in June 2002, had been a civil servant on secondment from the Department of Social Welfare for some 12 years. After accepting the appointment to the Seanad, he was obliged to resign from the Civil Service. He is now paid the senator's salary of €56,000 per year. The other staff member is secretary, Sandra Cullagh, who remains on secondment from the

Civil Service. Bertie Ahern's long-time companion, Celia Larkin, also worked at St Luke's for almost a decade, essentially taking charge of constituency matters. Their long-term relationship was the focus of continuing publicity for over a decade until they separated in the spring of 2003. Ahern was the first political party leader and Taoiseach to be separated from his wife, Miriam, and in a long-term relationship with another woman. This situation at a time of great social change in Ireland, including the introduction of divorce, attracted much coverage.

Whichever way you look at it, this house at 161 Lower Drumcondra Road, Dublin 9, is a focal point. Since June 1997, when Bertie Ahern was first elected Taoiseach, it has grown in national importance and prominence and was the venue for several important national meetings. Thus, while Britain has long had No. 10 Downing Street and France has the Hôtel Matignon as prime ministerial bases, for now at least, Ireland has St Luke's.

~ ~ ~ ~ ~

Bertie Ahern is and always has been obsessed with his constituency.

'The simple reality is that he is paranoid about the constituency,' says one seasoned politician who knows him well. Most successful politicians, and many unsuccessful ones, share this mental condition. Discussion is largely about questions of degree.

'You need a formidable constituency machine to keep the constituency safe if you're to devote time to departmental and government business,' says Fianna Fáil TD for Limerick East, Willie O'Dea, who was appointed Minister for Defence in September 2004.

'That may sound like paranoia – but in this business paranoia is total awareness,' O'Dea adds.

O'Dea himself runs a formidable constituency organisation, pounding the beat in tough areas of Limerick comparable to some of the Taoiseach's own inner-city areas. The Limerick man frequently figures in the top-five vote-getters at election time along with, but usually discreetly behind, the Taoiseach. Like most other Fianna Fáil TDs, O'Dea is a long-time admirer of the Dublin Central operation. The veteran TD recalls being in the Royal Dublin Hotel on O'Connell Street sometime before the June 1981 general election. He inadvertently looked into a function room to find it was packed with people. Later he was told it was a meeting of the largely unknown Ahern constituency organisation.

'There were about 300 people present – at first I thought 'twas a gospel session.'

That was exactly four years after Ahern's first successful bid for a Dáil seat in June 1977. In many ways he had stolen quietly onto the national stage by working intensively and locally.

In June 1977, Bertie Ahern, then aged just 25 years and an accounts clerk at the Mater Hospital in Dublin, first stood for the Dáil in the three-seat constituency of Dublin-Finglas. He had been added to the ticket by the Fianna Fáil National Executive, though pre-election newspaper profiles of the constituency scarcely noticed his existence. The main constituency talking point was whether radical trade union leader Matt Merrigan's decision to stand as an Independent would undermine the chances of Labour's official candidate, Brendan Halligan. In the event, Merrigan's intervention helped somewhat to upset the predicted one-each split between Fianna Fáil, Fine Gael and Labour.

The Fianna Fáil standard-bearer was Deputy Jim Tunney, and the second Fianna Fáil candidate was Cllr Des Bell. Ahern was added by headquarters to sweep up some votes at the southern Drumcondra end of the constituency. The thinking was that he would not take votes from the other Fianna Fáil candidates. Topping the ballot paper, since his name began with 'A', was an added bonus. Maurice Ahern, Bertie's eldest brother, recalls that constituency delegate to headquarters, Ray Walsh, helped secure the addition.

'He was able to say, "Here's a good young lad who'll do well and it will set him up for the next locals." We didn't actually think he was going to win,' Maurice Ahern recalls.

But Ahern was already on a mission and had a fair inkling that Fianna Fáil would oust the four-year-old Fine Gael–Labour Coalition Government. Fianna Fáil, he believed, were poised to end four years in opposition. In fact, Ahern had been involved in Fianna Fáil as a 'poster boy', helping to put up election posters since the 1965 elections. Noel Booth, father of his friend and neighbour, Robin, was chairman of the local Fianna Fáil O'Donovan Rossa Cumann. He roped in the 14-year-old Bertie, almost as tall then as he is now, to put up posters. As a 17-year-old he was again involved with Fianna Fáil in the 1969 general election and was recruited into the O'Donovan Rossa Cumann by Lorraine Booth, Robin's older sister.

Tony Kett recalls Ahern saying that he had been very keen to encourage some one of his other friends to stand in the 1973 general election. At the time, Ahern was not yet 22 years old, reluctant to go himself, and there were no other takers among his friends.

Son of a railway signalman from Ballinasloe, Co Galway, and just three months older than Ahern, Kett began working in the same accounts office with his now lifetime friend at the Mater Hospital in February 1974. The pair, along with others, went on to set up a soccer team, All Hamptons, which played in the Dublin amateur league with some success. It became the nucleus of a sporting and social group around the Drumcondra area often gathering in local bars like Kennedy's or the Cat & Cage. The name, All Hamptons, was a fusion of All Hallows, the Vincentian seminary where the team trained and played, and the nearby Hampton Carmelite convent. Indeed Drumcondra was so replete with religious houses in those times that some Dublin wags referred to the area as the 'Holy Land'. Ahern, like many of his brothers, was extremely keen on sport and was an accomplished runner. But Kett recalls that as time went on Ahern became more an organiser and motivator than a player with All Hamptons.

By the summer of 1977 Bertie Ahern had been around politics on and off for a dozen years. In 1976, Fianna Fáil headquarters began revitalising all its constituency organisations in anticipation of the general election, and Ahern had strategically got himself on the Dublin-Finglas Fianna Fáil reorganisation committee.

One of the reasons for the depth of his involvement was simple and at least partly explains the difficulties of getting people into political parties in these more affluent times. 'It was a great help having no money. I just couldn't do anything that needed cash and that created time,' Ahern recalled in an interview he gave in 1984 as he moved more into national prominence.

'After paying for books, extra tutorials and so on, there was next to nothing left. I lived on nixers, doing the books for shops and pubs. I was part of the black economy,' he said of his days as an accounts clerk, while also studying by night.

Slowly Ahern was being noticed at Fianna Fáil headquarters and had been asked to take part in a television discussion involving members of the party's youth wing along with party leader, Jack Lynch, in 1975. Though he was up against two heavy hitters, Ahern nearly won the Fianna Fáil selection convention and both he and his friends were rightly confident that he would be added to the ticket by headquarters.

'We almost began knocking on doors straight after the selection convention,' Kett recalls.

Ahern was duly added to stand in Dublin-Finglas by the youthful Fianna Fáil general secretary, Seamus Brennan, and the elder statesman, Senator Eoin Ryan. The names and details of each constituency were being combed through and little was left to chance.

Fianna Fáil leader Jack Lynch had put in a lacklustre performance as Opposition leader. But he made up for this by totally reorganising the party ahead of that June 1977 election. Lynch had appointed Seamus Brennan as party general secretary at the young age of 25. He also appointed another young man, Frank Dunlop, a journalist, who now remains in the headlines for less positive reasons concerning his involvement in planning corruption in Dublin in the late 1980s.

What political scientists call the 'friends and neighbours effect' was to play a big part in Ahern's debut campaign. Essentially, Bertie Ahern was from a family of five children who grew up in Drumcondra, where they had gone to school locally and then to St Aidan's CBS in Whitehall. Ahern's father, Con, was a farm manager at nearby All Hallows College. A native of Cork, Con was an Old IRA man interned during the Civil War and a life-long Fianna Fáil supporter, though never an activist.

Con Ahern had come to Dublin from his native Ballyfeard, near Kinsale, Co Cork in the early 1930s. After a brief time studying for the religious life with the Vincentian Order, he transferred temporarily to work for a year on the order's farm at All Hallows in Drumcondra. He was a skilled horseman and farmer and the farm job soon became a more permanent arrangement. Eventually, he would become the farm manager in charge also of other lands in north Dublin. In 1937, Con Ahern married Julia Hourihane, who was a Corkwoman from Castledonovan, near Drimoleague, in the west of the county. In the 1930s she had come to work in Drumcondra as a children's nurse and got to know Con early on. The Ahern marriage produced five children in all: Maurice, Kathleen, Noel, Eileen and Bertie. The youngest was Bertie, who was born on 12 September 1951. He was christened Bartholomew Patrick, an old name from his mother's side of the family, popular in her home territory. With Con's post of farm manager came the modest family home at Church Avenue, Drumcondra, which the Ahern family were in time to buy out. It was here that Bertie Ahern grew up, a sort of country kid in the city and a Dubliner with a staunch Cork background, and from where he launched his first foray into politics. By the 1977 election, the Ahern family had been established in Drumcondra for well over 40 years.

Maurice Ahern, the eldest brother, was active in Clonliffe Harriers Athletics Club and had represented Ireland as a middle-distance runner.

'When I started going round canvassing in 1977, he was known to many people in Drumcondra as my brother. But for a very long time now, I've been known as his brother,' he says.

Maurice also recalls the intense Ahern family pride at Bertie Ahern's candidature. Con Ahern was to live until 1990 and saw his son become a successful government minister. Julia Ahern lived to see him elected Taoiseach and died in April 1998, poignantly in a week when he was negotiating what he rates as his finest achievement, the Good Friday Agreement.

'Though she saw him achieve many other things, it's my own view that nothing matched her pride at seeing his name on those first election posters,' Maurice Ahern admits.

Added to these connections, Bertie Ahern was by then married to the former Miriam Kelly from nearby Clonliffe Road, who worked as a bank clerk. His wife was one of a family of 11 children, most of whom were still based in or around the constituency at that time. They had met through the All Hamptons Club and were married on his 24th birthday in September 1975 by a friend, Fr Martin O'Connor. Both of them had similarly met Fr O'Connor through football club training and playing at All Hallows grounds.

Organisationally, Ahern set up at least three new cumainn, or Fianna Fáil local branches, which were to become the cornerstone of the future Ahern machine. And while he was beginning to get wired into local Fianna Fáil, he also became a little better known at Party HQ. Essentially, his relatives, neighbours, colleagues, football pals and anyone else who wanted, came out and pounded the beat on his behalf in May and June 1977.

There was, however, further evidence that Ahern had made himself known at headquarters. He was chosen to make an input into one of the party's televised political broadcasts.

'We were raw young lads and probably quite politically naïve. But we had energy and enthusiasm. We would do nine hours canvassing with scarcely a break for a sandwich,' Tony Kett recalls. It certainly paid off as Bertie Ahern got over 3,700 first preferences as a 25-year-old young lad starting out, according to Ketts.

Ahern's first-time success was in part the outcome of the so-called 'tullymander' named for the then Meath Labour TD, Jim Tully, and 19th-century Massachusetts Governor Elbridge Gerry. The infamous US politician in his eagerness to cheat created an extraordinary salamander-shaped constituency and gave the English language the word 'gerrymander'. As Environment Minister in the Fine Gael–Labour Coalition, Jim Tully followed the example of predecessors from all parties, and redrew constituency boundaries in 1974 in a way that was expected to maximise Fine Gael and Labour Dáil seats. The calculation was that Fine Gael–Labour was strongest in the east of Ireland and could take two seats in three-seat constituencies with around 50 per cent of the votes. Otherwise he favoured four-seaters, where it was expected his coalition could still take two seats with about 40 per cent of votes. It was a hopeless miscalculation.

In Dublin, Fianna Fáil got almost 47 per cent of the vote and thanks to people like Ahern they took two seats in eight of the three-seaters. By contrast, Fine Gael–Labour's combined Dublin vote was 42 per cent – its lowest share since 1957. One expert reckoned the tullymander backfiring gave Fianna Fáil 16 extra seats in the Dublin area.

There was a huge rush of support to Fianna Fáil under former Taoiseach Jack Lynch in 1977. The voters had wearied of the outgoing government and several ministers, notably Posts and Telegraphs Minister Conor Cruise O'Brien and Finance Minister Richie Ryan, had become national hate figures. In its last year in office, controversy over the Minister for Defence, Paddy Donegan, insulting the President, Cearbhall Ó Dálaigh, proved damaging. Donegan called the President, technically the Army commander-in-chief, a 'thundering disgrace' for referring anti-terrorist legislation to the Supreme Court to test its constitutionality.

But Fianna Fáil offered many election sweeteners that ultimately helped start a trend in political auctions which almost bankrupted the country. These included the abolition of domestic rates and car tax, social employment schemes and the expansion of the public sector to bring unemployment below 100,000.

The 'tullymander' actually compounded the outgoing coalition's problems. It also resulted in a respected politician and union leader's name being added to the Irish political lexicon for all the wrong reasons. In three-seat Dublin-Finglas, Fianna Fáil took two out of three seats with the distribution of Jim Tunney's surplus and Bell's elimination carrying Ahern home. The result was replicated in many other constituencies.

The term tullymander became a byword for a botched gerrymander or failed unfair constituency manipulation. From 1977 onwards, in keeping with a Fianna Fáil promise, the redrawing of constituency boundaries became the periodic job of an independent commission headed by a High Court judge. The Electoral Commission was to radically redraw boundaries with considerable consequences for Ahern and others around him after 1977. That first independent Electoral Commission review, chaired by Mr Justice Brian Walsh, saw Ahern move to five-seat Dublin Central by the next election in June 1981, which has been his political home ever since. In the ensuing 20 years, this Commission's workings have been continually monitored by Bertie Ahern, in common with all other TDs and Dáil hopefuls, as he jealously guards his voter heartland of Drumcondra. When hardy comes to hardy, this defence extends to brushes with the Taoiseach's own brother.

By 17 June 1977, Bertie Ahern was one of 148 TDs in Dáil Éireann. Eighty-four of them were Fianna Fáil deputies under Jack Lynch, who had a 23-seat majority. The TD's job carried a yearly salary of £5,322 (€6,760).

Bertie Ahern TD had begun his political journey but Ireland was also heading into very turbulent political and economic times. A huge number of first-time Fianna Fáil TDs were elected alongside him and some were to become household names in Irish politics in the succeeding decades – not always for the best of reasons. Ahern's fellow first-timers in that 'Class of 77' included Albert Reynolds, Seán Doherty, Charlie McCreevy, Joe Walsh, Pádraig Flynn, Michael Woods, Liam Lawlor, Vincent Brady, Martin O'Donoghue, Mark Killilea, Seán Keegan, PJ Morley, Jim Fitzsimons, Kit Ahern and Terry Leyden.

At the Dublin count centre, journalist and future *Irish Times* editor, Geraldine Kennedy, met an exultant Charlie Haughey. She was surprised to find him in such good form as it seemed his chances of ousting the new 'uncrowned King of Ireland', Jack Lynch, were buried by this landslide win which had given Fianna Fáil almost 51 per cent of the national poll. Haughey was even more bullish when she broached the issue of his leadership ambitions.

'But they're all my people. Now I'll be leader,' Haughey correctly predicted.

Even in the first flush of victory, Jack Lynch conceded on RTÉ television that he would have preferred a smaller majority and he pledged his government to behaving modestly. In typical Lynch style he declared, 'You just can't alienate people'.

Jack Lynch was just two years away from departing the leadership to be replaced by his old rival Charlie Haughey, the man Lynch had sacked in 1970 for alleged involvement in importing IRA arms. Soon Haughey and Ahern's careers would be inextricably linked for considerable good and for some ill effects.

The reality was that Fianna Fáil's magnificent June 1977 election victory, which also launched Bertie Ahern on the 20-year road towards becoming Taoiseach, actually sowed the seeds of instability. Soon a deep split was to be opened up in Fianna Fáil which persisted through two decades. All these events were to have a profound impact on Bertie Ahern and his political progress.

~ ~ ~ ~ ~

Bertie Ahern's habit of mooching around St Luke's over Christmas and frequently checking the answering machine has at times produced some bizarre results. During the 1999 Christmas break, he picked up a message on the machine from a man called Peadar Byrne, whose neighbours had been separated from their luggage on a Ryanair flight. The man was gobsmacked when the Taoiseach returned his call and first suspected it was a 'wind-up'.

'Mr Ahern was very nice to us and said he would do all that he could,' Mr Byrne explained later. Oddly enough, they soon received calls from a Ryanair supervisor and a manager at the airport authority, Aer Rianta. The bags duly arrived soon after by courier.

'He's an incredible local politician for a Taoiseach. No prime minister in the world would do what he's doing,' says rival Dublin Central TD, Joe Costello of Labour. Does Costello suspect that this attention to constituency detail is somehow bogus?

'No, I don't for a moment think it's bogus. I think it's his preferred way of life. He likes power but not the pomp and circumstance of power.

'He is essentially a local politician who keeps close to his power base. He almost hankers after it,' Costello believes.

Cyprian Brady argues that something much simpler is afoot. According to him, Bertie Ahern is invariably around at Christmas time and ever-mindful of the season he always says 'if somebody is looking for us, they probably have a real problem'.

Viewed through a rival's eyes the Taoiseach's constituency organisation is a formidable machine. It is also the product of 27 years of studied development and careful maintenance dating from his successful Dáil debut in June 1977. These days there are two

Fianna Fáil TDs, Bertie Ahern and Dr Dermot Fitzpatrick; two senators, Cyprian Brady and Tony Kett; and three councillors, his elder brother, Maurice, Mary Fitzpatrick and Tom Stafford. Then there is an inner core of trusted loyal lieutenants, which include some of the elected representatives.

Ahern's original 'Drumcondra mafia' in 1977 included his Mater Hospital workmate, Tony Kett, who has been a senator in his own right, elected on the administrative panel since 1997. Kett was to be eventually co-opted to Dublin Corporation after Ahern joined the Cabinet in 1988 and he served until the ending of the dual mandate in 2003, which banned TDs and senators from local councils. Though he is one of Ahern's closest friends, he is also very much his own person. Others on that original Ahern team included Paul Kiely who had worked with Ahern in an earlier clerical job with Bord Bainne; Chris Wall, a pharmaceutical executive with Wellcome Ireland; Daithí Ó Broin, a teacher; and his brother, Noel Ahern, who was then a clerk with CIÉ and later became a TD in his own right in neighbouring Dublin North-West. Another was Joe Burke, a Donegal-born builder who lived beside Bertie Ahern in a house he bought in Artane in 1974. Though in reality Ahern lived in Artane, to all intents and purposes his political domicile was his parents' home in Church Avenue, Drumcondra.

Beyond that inner core there is the much storied 'ward boss system'. Having worked in Ahern's constituency office for 14 years, Cyprian Brady says the ward boss system is very simple as he rattles off a random sheaf of statistics. There are 33 council wards in Dublin Central, which is now a four-seat Dáil constituency. There are about 38,000 households that vary from inner-city flats to very expensive homes on the Navan Road and every type of household in between. According to Brady, the ward boss system is borrowed from the US Democratic Party. Quite simply, it's a man or woman, known in their locality, who is a contact point with St Luke's, and with a small team of people around them. It all makes for a potential Bertie Ahern constituency team of 200 to 300 people. That is a formidable political machine.

Brady reckons the constituency office at St Luke's deals with 500 to 700 representational letters each week. He explains this as he completes a pre-printed constituency representation sheet which has slots for all the relevant details of the voter's problem, address, phone and other details in summary.

'These deal with everything from a burst pipe to a broken window right up to big ones like someone at risk of losing their home,' Brady explains.

The representations are made by letter to the relevant authority on headed notepaper from the Taoiseach's constituency office. This fact alone has led to controversy, raising questions beyond heart-warming Christmas stories of the Taoiseach reuniting fretful travellers with their luggage. In December 2003, it emerged that a letter was sent in the Taoiseach's name to a Roscommon County Council planning official asking the Council to hold off action against a quarry owner. The request was made on humanitarian grounds to allow the quarry owner time to complete a course of cancer treatment. The quarry was operating illegally and there was an enforcement order against its owners requiring them to stop. The Taoiseach's involvement came through a request from the quarry owner's brother, a constituent in Dublin Central, who called to the clinic at St Luke's and met Cyprian Brady. Brady sent out the letter to Roscommon County Council on the Taoiseach's behalf. The Opposition seized upon the issue and castigated the Taoiseach's unwarranted intervention in a planning matter. The Roscommon County Manager, John Tiernan, insisted that the Taoiseach's intervention changed nothing, as planning rule enforcement was under law entirely a matter for council officials.

'Representations per se from politicians do not as a rule hold any standing in the process, unless they contain some information or detail relevant to the matters being prosecuted,' the Roscommon manager said.

But Mr Tiernan noted that the Taoiseach's letter might more properly have been addressed to himself as County Manager. Ahern issued a detailed statement utterly rejecting criticisms of his representations in the matter. He also rushed back to the Dáil, on its last day before the Christmas holidays, to make an unscheduled appearance and deliver a robust defence of his actions. The Taoiseach accused Fine Gael of making a political football out of the issue. Moreover, he stressed that it was a humanitarian gesture and a legitimate part of the democratic process.

Cyprian Brady's first appearance in the national media spotlight came as he publicly defended the Roscommon quarry case. He insists the incident was blown out of all proportion.

'We put out between 500 and 700 representational letters each week for constituents. I think journalists – even quite senior journalists – have no real idea of what happens in a constituency office and how the representational process works,' he says.

For some people it was a genuine human response from a big-hearted man. For others it was an example of the continuing political clientelism which is central to the way Irish people do politics. Bertie Ahern built his power base on constituency service and he continues to work that same method of retaining power very assiduously. Clearly, it is a system of politics that works; it is what Irish people want.

~ ~ ~ ~ ~

Bertie Ahern's close supporters point out that he was the first politician to begin knocking on doors outside election time. A story now in the folklore, but widely accepted as true, is that a young man returned to Dublin in 1977 and sought the help of Bertie Ahern, the new Dublin-Finglas TD, in getting a job. Ahern made representations to what was then the Department of Posts and Telegraphs on his behalf. But in the event the man succeeded in getting another job elsewhere. Four years later, when Ahern had moved to the new constituency of Dublin Central, the young man received a letter from the TD. It noted that since the man lived in Finglas he could not vote for Ahern. But it went on to say that he might have relatives and friends residing in Dublin Central who could vote for Ahern.

'Yes, you can bet that that story is true. We kept records and went back to the people we had helped. We never gave up,' admits Tony Kett.

It was in the new base of Dublin Central, an amalgam of several old constituencies, that the upstart Ahern camp first encountered George Colley. A solicitor and son of a former Fianna Fáil TD, Colley had been in Dáil Éireann since 1961 and was regarded as a potential Taoiseach. In fact, Colley had stood for the leadership when Seán Lemass retired in 1966. His nemesis, Charlie Haughey, also thought of contesting but had been prevailed upon to withdraw at the last minute. In the event, Jack Lynch came through the middle as the compromise candidate to become Fianna Fáil leader and Taoiseach.

The legendary Colley–Haughey feud lasted 16 more years and only ended with Colley's untimely death in September 1983. Friends of Colley such as the former veteran Senator Des Hanafin stress the man's affable nature, kindness and integrity. But Colley is also remembered for dealing with constituency matters at some remove. One veteran Fianna Fáil TD who knew Colley well sums things up with a phrase from a much older Fianna Fáil grandee, Frank Aiken.

'Aiken used to say at election time, "I never canvassed much and if I start now they'll think I'm on the way out". Well, Colley didn't go that far – but he was definitely old-style in his constituency dealings.'

The Colley–Ahern contrast was marked. One was a patrician figure, slightly aloof, elegant and well spoken. The other looked and sounded like the rest of the constituents and was, in theory at least, very much one of them. None the less, politics in Ireland was changing and Bertie Ahern saw himself in the vanguard of that change.

2

Short Fellow and Hail Fellow

Bertie Ahern met Charlie Haughey on the stairway of Bolton Street College of Technology in Dublin on the evening of 17 June 1977. Ahern's director of elections, the late Ray Walsh, did the introductions as the Haughey and Ahern groups crossed each other on the stairs at the election count centre. However, Ahern had encountered Haughey once before. In 1965, a 14-year-old Ahern was among the throng of election workers who shook hands with Haughey at a polling booth in Drumcondra. A few days later he was treated to ice-cream, cakes and lemonade at a party thrown by the victorious and munificent local TD for the kids of the election workers.

But this encounter in 1977 was on a far different footing. Haughey took stock of a new neighbouring Dublin northside Fianna Fáil TD, just half his own age. He clearly saw Ahern as another potential ally for the leadership battle he had already spoken about inside the count hall that same day.

'Up to then Bertie Ahern was just beginning to be known to the party hierarchy. But as a new TD it was different,' Tony Kett, who was also in the company that evening, recalls.

Ahern and Haughey were to develop the closest of political, if not personal, relationships over the ensuing 15 years. Soon Ahern was to become a very loyal lieutenant and protégé of Haughey. But first Ahern needed to consolidate his position in politics.

Immediately, he began to create a systematic and professional constituency service which soon became a model of its kind. As we have seen, a constituency database was being developed and elaborated from Ahern's earliest days as TD for Dublin-Finglas. A team of loyal supporters in every part of the constituency was being put together. And certainly the scheme of canvassing outside of election time was unique to Ahern at that time. It was not popular with fellow Fianna Fáil TD, Jim Tunney, any more than it was with rivals outside the party.

'Yes, there were times when Tunney stopped his car, approached us and told us in no uncertain terms to get the hell out of Finglas,' Tony Kett remembers.

However, in April 1980 the report of the first-ever independent constituency boundary review group was published. The team was headed by High Court Judge, Mr Justice Brian Walsh, and it favoured bigger constituencies where the vote dividend for bigger parties was lessened. Its recommendations were enacted in June 1980 by Minister for the Environment, Sylvester Barrett. It was clear that Ahern was bound to return to his own Drumcondra heartland in the new Dublin Central constituency.

The new Dublin Central constituency, which was first used in the June 1981 general election, then had five seats and comprised elements of three old constituencies of Dublin North-Central, Dublin-Finglas and Dublin-Cabra. It stretched from the North Wall to the Phoenix Park, from the Liffey quays to Griffith Avenue, and from Cabra West to the Malahide Road. Ahern's change of constituency suited Jim Tunney who was rightly apprehensive about such an industrious and driven running mate in his Finglas base. But it also cheered Charlie Haughey, who was to see the ambitious Ahern pitted alongside his deadly rival, George Colley.

Inside the Dáil, Ahern was a low-key, diligent backbencher who remained outgoing and friendly.

'I noticed that he knew colleagues' names quite quickly. Some TDs, of all parties, go around for up to 18 months after a new Dáil has been elected, quietly saying, "Who is your man over there?" Bertie was not like that – he got to know people quickly and remembered names,' one veteran Fianna Fáil colleague remembers.

In addition, Ahern's agreeable nature was quite evident, where the colleague recalls that he was 'very hail-fellow-well-met, a good mixer. In fact just a very nice bloke.'

Charlie Haughey had been appointed Minister for Health and Social Welfare, a job which gave him great political scope. It was a big comeback after being sacked by Jack Lynch in 1970 over controversial allegations of involvement in efforts to import IRA arms to defend Northern Ireland nationalists. Lynch deemed that Haughey had purged his indiscretions by behaving himself since his acquittal on the arms importation charges. For several years, Haughey had been quietly ingratiating himself with all elements of the organisation and now he intensified his work on disillusioned backbenchers, who found others in the Lynch Government inaccessible and unhelpful.

Haughey's help was most welcome as Ahern was now devoting most of his energies to working on the ground, consolidating his local base, while health and welfare problems loomed large.

'He was a great local politician. When he got a query, he was like a dog with a bone and he left nothing undone,' Tony Kett again recalls.

In 1978, Ahern had been co-opted to Dublin Corporation to replace the senior constituency TD, Jim Tunney, who was given a junior ministry. He then successfully stood for Dublin Corporation in the 1979 local elections. These were held on the same day as the first European Parliament elections and were also the first major test for Fianna Fáil since their June 1977 landslide win. Across the country the party's local council vote dipped by just 1 per cent. But its European Parliament showing, taking just 35 per cent of votes and five of the 15 seats, was deemed a disaster. In just two years the national mood had swung against the Lynch Government.

There are many reasons for this – not least the start of the breakdown in traditional voting patterns, especially in urban areas. There were also a series of ill-tempered industrial disputes, including a long postal strike which helped turn public opinion against the Government. PAYE workers were also on the march protesting against their unfair tax burden.

A number of crucial issues, including negotiating Brussels grant aid to support Ireland's first-ever break with sterling and entry into the European Community (EC) currency grid – the exchange rate mechanism (ERM) – were mishandled politically. George Colley as Minister for Finance was blamed for this and for infuriating members of the emerging women's movement with a dismissive comment about 'well-heeled articulate women'.

Several backbenchers began meeting to discuss their mutual disenchantment with the Lynch leadership. A repeat of the European Parliament election results would spell the end for many of those first elected in the 1977 landslide. There were various caucus groups and some of these TDs liaised with Charlie Haughey, who had to tread carefully as he was a member of Lynch's Cabinet. There is no evidence of Ahern figuring in these disaffected TDs' meetings. Yet he had many reasons for being on Haughey's side of the emerging divide.

Lynch's difficulties were compounded by a bitter internal Fianna Fáil row over allowing British forces to overfly the Border zone. The party also lost two by-elections in his Cork heartland to Fine Gael that autumn of 1979. One of these by-election defeats was in Lynch's own constituency, where he had taken 20,000 votes and returned in unparalleled triumph in June 1977. The news came to him while on a trip to meet US President Jimmy Carter and was a bitter blow, as he felt few in Fianna Fáil had bothered to canvass properly and had not accepted his preferred candidate.

On 5 December 1979, Lynch announced that he was quitting as Fianna Fáil leader and Taoiseach. He said he had indicated in 1977 that he would cede the leadership some two years ahead of the next expected election to allow his successor time to prepare for that contest.

The extent to which Lynch was 'forced out' by Haughey remains a matter of some dispute. It is undoubtedly true that pro-

Haughey TDs were conspiring with a view to hurrying Lynch's expected departure. Lynch loyalists saw the whole thing as orchestrated by Haughey. But it is also true that George Colley and another minister, Dr Martin O'Donoghue, had persuaded Lynch to go early to catch Haughey unawares in the succession contest, which they were sure Colley could win.

Former Senator Des Hanafin recalls that Colley was sure he would succeed Lynch right up to the start of the Fianna Fáil Parliamentary Party crucial meeting. But when the votes were counted, Charlie Haughey emerged victorious by 44 votes to 38 for Colley.

Colley's campaign was principally run by Des O'Malley, who had only been a backbencher for a year after his election in 1968, and Dr Martin O'Donoghue, a Lynch adviser who had only been elected a TD in 1977 and was instantly appointed to Cabinet. Neither they, nor Colley, knew too many backbenchers well enough to be able to read the signs in a leadership battle, which is often the most treacherous of elections. In most parties and jurisdictions it is common for deputies to promise support to all leadership candidates. Clearly, many backbench Fianna Fáil TDs felt they were voting for their jobs. Haughey had the required magic to turn the ship around – or so they believed.

Of the two Fianna Fáil TDs still representing Dublin-Finglas, Jim Tunney supported Colley, and Bertie Ahern voted for Haughey. But in the coming decade both men were to become central to Charlie Haughey's political survival. Ahern had never been inside the door of Jack Lynch's office and later confessed that the former Taoiseach may not have been even aware of his existence. But the new Taoiseach and Fianna Fáil leader, Charlie Haughey, knew well who Ahern was.

Soon the two men were to get to know each other a great deal more.

~ ~ ~ ~ ~

Charlie Haughey's first Cabinet does show evidence that he was at least trying to deal with the rancour left by the contest to replace Jack Lynch. Haughey retained the bulk of the old Lynch Cabinet, even though it was clear that they had almost all voted for Colley. Four ministers were dropped: Jim Gibbons, his old foe from the Arms Trial days; Bobby Molloy; and Denis Gallagher. Not content with just sacking Martin O'Donoghue, a long-time Lynch adviser, Haughey also abolished his Department of Economic Planning and Development. This had been set up to implement many of the election promises, but Haughey took its functions into the Taoiseach's Department, which was expanded under this and his future governments.

Ray MacSharry, who had been Colley's Junior Finance Minister but proposed Haughey for the Fianna Fáil leadership, became Minister for Agriculture. Albert Reynolds, another firm supporter, was appointed Minister for Posts and Telegraphs and Transport, even though he had only been first elected in 1977.

Colley showed that he retained considerable political force by being appointed Tánaiste and Minister for Energy. Extraordinarily, and demonstrating the long shadow of the 1970 Arms Crisis, Colley also successfully demanded a veto over who would be appointed as Minister for Justice and Minister for Defence.

But within the first week, Colley had publicly stated that he could only give qualified loyalty to Haughey. Colley argued that Haughey had set a precedent for this attitude himself by undermining Lynch. That question would remain a bone of contention for years to come with differing views over the extent to which Haughey may have undermined Lynch. Some Haughey supporters insist that it was Colley who demonstrated the more fundamental disloyalty.

The issue dates right back to the 1966 Fianna Fáil leadership contest to replace Lemass, which saw Lynch come through the middle of a stand-off between Colley and Haughey. Later, in 1969, Colley made a damning public speech about 'low standards in high places', which was taken to be a reference to Fianna Fáil's links with business, epitomised by Charlie Haughey and others.

The day of Haughey's election as Taoiseach also saw a sharp change in the tone of political discourse. Fine Gael leader Garret FitzGerald spoke of Haughey having 'a flawed pedigree' in an unprecedented attack on an incoming Taoiseach.

However, for the moment Ahern continued his work as a backbencher and on developing his constituency organisation ahead of a rapidly approaching tough general election battle. On the national stage the economy was beginning to run into serious difficulty. During this period, Charlie Haughey is remembered as being extremely profligate and determined at all costs to win the upcoming general election and become Taoiseach under his own steam. On 10 January 1980, Haughey appeared on RTÉ television and told the nation that things were looking grim – but without spelling out any remedies.

'As a community we have been living at a rate which is simply not justified by the amount of goods and services which we are producing. To make up the difference we have been borrowing at a rate which just cannot continue,' he said.

Two tribunals of inquiry and several major investigations later, we now know how deeply ironic that pointless lecture was. For all of the previous decade, various executives at Allied Irish Banks (AIB) had been struggling in vain to get Haughey to rein in his extraordinary personal spending, which had mired him in debt. But Charlie Haughey was not just living high on the hog. He was also acquiring a very valuable property portfolio, which included an island, Inishvickillane, off the Kerry coast.

Correspondence relating to his personal finances shows that bank executives were in despair and could find no effective sanctions to bring Haughey to book. In 1976, AIB chief executive Liam St John Devlin noted that a threat to bounce Haughey's cheques was empty because he was politically powerful, popular and a potential Taoiseach. In late 1979 when Charlie Haughey was elected Taoiseach, his bank manager wrote a fawning letter of congratulation which is now part of Irish political and banking lore.

'To say the task you have taken on is daunting is an understatement, but I have every faith in your ability to succeed in restoring confidence in this little nation.'

Charlie Haughey, Taoiseach and leader of Fianna Fáil, then owed Allied Irish Banks almost £1.1m (€1.4m), equivalent to one-eighth of the bank's profit that year. It was a time of recession driven by the second oil crisis of the 1970s. Irish banks were playing hardball with business and personal borrowers struggling to meet their commitments.

Again following two tribunals of inquiry, we now know that the so-called 'Short Fellow' was helped overcome his difficulties through the munificence of builder Patrick Gallagher, who took an option on some Haughey lands at Kinsealy. This was complemented by AIB bosses who first reduced the debt to £750,000 (€950,000), and went on to also magnanimously write off £110,000 (€140,000) in back interest. Nominally, the £110,000 was left on the AIB books as a debt not attracting interest and Haughey later grandly termed it 'a debt of honour'. Everybody knew it was never to be paid. The bank's total write-off was some £400,000 (€508,000).

It was not to be the first time that Haughey was to rely upon a good deal of help from his 'friends' to resolve his heavy debts. All of these developments were to be unexpectedly aired more fully later. Ultimately, Bertie Ahern was to be left with considerable explaining and clearing up to do. Much of this continues to this day.

But on the political agenda of 1980 and 1981 the problems of Northern Ireland began to dominate with initial meetings between Haughey and British Prime Minister Margaret Thatcher. The H-Block hunger strikes by Republican prisoners in the North also evoked a good deal of public support in the South.

On 21 May 1981, Charlie Haughey called a general election to happen precisely within the minimum legally required notice term of three weeks on June 11. Both Fianna Fáil and Haughey were riding high in political opinion polls but the national coffers were seriously depleted. Much of the funds allocated for 1981 had been spent and the Haughey Government had definitely added to the nation's growing economic crisis. Haughey was looking at a potential mini-Budget with raised taxes – all work best done after an election rather than before.

Little did anyone think this would be the first of three elections inside 18 months during the politically fraught years of 1981 and 1982. In all, there were to be five elections during the 1980s and Bertie Ahern was to build on his vote in each one.

~ ~ ~ ~ ~

Bertie Ahern was one of three Fianna Fáil candidates standing in the new five-seat Dublin Central in the June 1981 general election. It was widely expected that his senior running mate, Tánaiste George Colley, would head the poll. Some pundits suggested Bertie Ahern could edge out the other Fianna Fáil candidate, Tom Leonard, to take a second seat for the governing party. Others suggested that Ahern would be a casualty in a very noisy election with voters showing signs of great volatility.

There were other big name contenders in Dublin Central including Michael O'Leary, then deputy Labour Party leader and soon-to-be party leader; and Michael Keating, then of Fine Gael and later to join the Progressive Democrats. Two other candidates on the ballot – Independent Tony Gregory and Alice Glenn of Fine Gael – were to hit the headlines soon afterwards for different reasons. Within a year Gregory was to do a major deal in return for supporting a Haughey Government, while Glenn soon became the *bête noire* of Fine Gael members seeking legislation changes on divorce and related issues.

It was a tough campaign nationally and locally. Charlie Haughey was touring the country by helicopter to maximise exposure. His theme song, 'Charlie's Song' – which was an adaptation of the Scottish folksong about Bonnie Prince Charlie – became a Fianna Fáil anthem for a time. The refrain was predictably 'Rise and Follow Charlie'. In fact, the campaign became increasingly presidential with Garret FitzGerald being pushed forward more and more by Fine Gael.

At the time, Fine Gael had a new general secretary in Peter Prendergast, who helped bring principles of marketing to the FitzGerald campaign. And to Haughey's dismay, Fine Gael were fielding a number of successful and popular women candidates.

The names of nine H-Block prisoners, including hunger strikers, were put forward for election too. Haughey, in common with others from the main parties, faced taunts from H-Block supporters in many towns around the country – the more so as the hunger strikers began to die.

Haughey had promised through his ardent local supporter in Mayo, the then Junior Minister Pádraig Flynn, to build an airport near the religious shrine at Knock. The Taoiseach followed on by playing on the fact that he himself was born in Mayo and had a plaque unveiled in Castlebar to herald it.

Locally, there were tensions for Ahern and his campaign team, which mounted a much more elaborate operation than his debut in June 1977. In fact, his elder brother, Maurice Ahern, recalls that the 1981 election was when they had begun 'a really military operation'. As usual in the Darwinian politics of Fianna Fáil, the battle was as much with Colley as with those outside Fianna Fáil. Indeed there were some tense stand-offs between the Colley and Ahern camps.

'As often happens there was tension between rival groups of supporters, rather than between the candidates themselves. We came back nearly every night to stories about how there were nearly fights between the various groups,' Maurice Ahern says.

There was no doubt that the Ahern camp had some disdain for the Colley camp's more upmarket pitch.

'Sometimes there'd be stories about Colley's pinstriped law library types moving into "our areas" of the inner city. We'd be thinking that might go down all right in areas like Marino or Fairview – but hardly down there,' Maurice Ahern adds.

These tensions were mirrored by similar stand-offs on election day. It was a time before the more recent rules banning canvassers from operating in close proximity to polling stations. Tony Kett looks back on this and the succeeding two elections as a time when Colley realised that he had underestimated Ahern and his young band of supporters.

'I think he initially took us for gillies and believed we were in no way a threat to him. But he could not match our enthusiasm and he couldn't match our energy,' Kett says.

Tony Gregory, an inner-city teacher and Dublin city councillor originally from Charleville Avenue, off the North Strand, recalls early lessons in Fianna Fáil's first-up-best-dressed approach to campaigning. In this or one of the two subsequent elections in 1982 he canvassed a row of houses not long after Ahern. An elderly woman in one household told Gregory that Ahern had advised her to vote number one for himself and number two for Fianna Fáil's other candidate, Tom Leonard.

'But he told us to give you the number three – ahead of George Colley,' she told Gregory, much to his astonishment.

However, Gregory was also to suspect that a political enemy's enemy might not often be a friend. On polling day in June 1981 he got up early only to find posters had appeared overnight in his name, urging support for him as a way of advancing the H-Block prisoners' demands. These were put up in the better-off parts of the constituency where H-Block support was less abundant and a more sceptical view of the whole issue prevailed. Gregory was largely sympathetic to the H-Block issue but had not campaigned on it. On urgent enquiry, Gregory was assured by the H-Block campaigners that they had not erected them. Some circumstantial evidence gave him reason to suspect elements attached to the Ahern campaign. As he recalled the issue for author Katie Hannon over 20 years later, Gregory could clearly remember his anger. He had lost the fifth seat to Alice Glenn of Fine Gael on that occasion. When Gregory confronted Bertie Ahern at the time, he brushed the allegations gently aside.

'Now, Tony do you think I'd do anything like that?' he asked affably.

Gregory vowed to stay up all night on the eve of the next election and bury a hatchet in the head of anyone putting up hoax posters. It was not to be the last Ahern–Gregory encounter.

But the June 1981 election was not all political gamesmanship. As a sitting TD and councillor, Ahern commanded more coverage than on his debut outing in June 1977. His campaigners made much of his range of clinics and round-the-clock availability to constituents. Ahern himself identified employment as the key issue. He told one political journalist he had written 300 letters covering every supermarket in the area, saying he could personally vouch for people he was recommending for jobs. However, he had success in only about 10 cases. He also had some pragmatic, if controversial, advice for young jobseekers from the inner city.

'I positively encourage them to use addresses outside the area, of relatives maybe, because some districts here have a bad name.'

Furthermore, he said that he was liaising with the Gardaí who had some success with problems like curbing vandalism. It was his view that more Gardaí on the beat could curb petty crime because those involved were not hardened criminals. Finally, Ahern declared that the 'real solution is employment'. It was to be a mantra repeated throughout his career in Dublin Central, nationally and at EC meetings in Brussels almost a decade later.

The election count brought very good news for Ahern who headed the poll with 8,738 first preferences. Colley, who scarcely canvassed at all, realised how much he had underestimated his rival as he polled 8,011 votes and took the third seat behind Fine Gael's Michael Keating. Labour's Michael O'Leary took the fourth seat and the fifth went to Alice Glenn of Fine Gael. Two out of five could be deemed a reasonable result for Fianna Fáil in Dublin Central.

At all events, the news nationally was bad for Fianna Fáil and especially for Charlie Haughey, though he had got almost two quotas in his own nearby Dublin North-Central base. Overall, the party polled 45.3 per cent of the first preference vote, taking 78 seats in a Dáil expanded to 166 TDs. This Haughey-led Fianna Fáil result compared with 51 per cent under Jack Lynch in 1977 and 77 out of a total of 148 Dáil seats. Haughey critics had a field day in their unflattering comparisons with Lynch's score.

However, there is strong evidence to suggest that Fianna Fáil support was ebbing before Haughey took the reins. Subsequent voting patterns, including results under Bertie Ahern, also indicate that Charlie Haughey was unfairly loaded with blame after the June 1981 election. These days Fianna Fáil stalwarts dream about a vote of 45 per cent. Under Bertie Ahern, Fianna Fáil took 39 per cent in 1997 and 41 per cent in 2002. The vote was managed much more tightly however with consistent transfers.

By the time the votes were counted on 12 June 1981, the combined forces of Fine Gael and Labour amounted to 80 TDs – just two more than Fianna Fáil. Two H-Block prisoners were elected, Kieran Doherty in Cavan-Monaghan and Paddy Agnew in Louth, who actually headed the poll. Haughey was to attribute these two losses, the impact of the H-Block generally, and a quirk of the electoral system to his loss of power.

The balance of power rested with one Workers' Party deputy, Joe Sherlock from Mallow, and five Independents. Dr Garret FitzGerald was elected Taoiseach by 83 votes to 79 with Sherlock's support and that of most of the Independents.

Just 18 months after being elected Taoiseach and Fianna Fáil leader, Charlie Haughey found himself leading his party in opposition. But Bertie Ahern had meanwhile taken a small but significant step upwards. In late 1980 he had been appointed an assistant party whip. This was not a particularly exalted job and consisted largely of helping the Fianna Fáil Chief Whip, Seán Moore, ensure that all TDs voted. Soon he was doing the lion's share of the work because Moore, a veteran Fianna Fáil TD for

Dublin South-East, was taken ill. The work gave Ahern a complete insider's view of how Dáil procedures worked and also brought him into contact with a wide variety of Fianna Fáil TDs. It also began formal contacts with whips on the Opposition side as they organised so-called 'pairs'; the system which allows deputies from either side not to attend certain Dáil votes and effectively cancel each other out.

Thus, again unnoticed, Bertie Ahern had taken his second step on the ladder.

~ ~ ~ ~ ~

Bertie Ahern and all the other TDs and would-be deputies were once again pounding the election beat just eight months later. Limerick socialist TD Jim Kemmy threw Charlie Haughey an unexpected lifeline on 27 January 1982, by voting against the Fine Gael–Labour Coalition's Budget. The actual issue involved a plan to impose VAT on children's shoes. The vote was effectively a crucial confidence issue and the Government fell.

But other events that evening were to rebound on Fianna Fáil and Bertie Ahern almost nine years later. Charlie Haughey issued a short statement pointing out that the President, Dr Patrick Hillery, had absolute power under Article 13 of the 1937 Constitution to refuse a dissolution of the Dáil. The plan was that, if enough Independents were prepared to support Fianna Fáil to stave off an election they all could ill afford, Haughey could return to government. Even if this government were short-lived, Fianna Fáil would still be fighting the next election from a stronger position as an outgoing administration. Several Fianna Fáil frontbench members – including Haughey – followed up with calls to the President's residence, Áras an Uachtaráin, but failed to get through to Dr Hillery.

President Hillery – a former Fianna Fáil Minister and European Commissioner, confidant of Jack Lynch and definitely no friend of Haughey – was enraged. His anger was added to by his suspicion that Haughey was linked to the spread of rumours about the President having an extramarital affair. Hillery was well aware of his constitutional prerogative and chose not to exercise it. The incident was leaked to the press but it was not to become a major issue until October 1990. Then, almost nine years later and in bizarre circumstances, Fianna Fáil's presidential candidate Brian Lenihan first admitted their actions on the evening of 28 January 1982, and then later denied it all. Ahern was by then Lenihan's director of elections in the teeth of a tough campaign and reaping another portion of the strange Haughey legacy.

Even before the election of February 1982, the cracks in Fianna Fáil were opening up. Kildare TD Charlie McCreevy had very stridently criticised Haughey's leadership in opposition, saying the party seemed to be against everything and for nothing. McCreevy followed on by saying that Irish politics had degenerated into a series of auctions with all parties making promises the country did not have the resources to deliver.

'We are so hell-bent on assuming power that we are prepared to do anything for it,' he said.

Charlie Haughey moved swiftly to have McCreevy expelled from the Fianna Fáil Parliamentary Party but the Kildare TD jumped before he was pushed. When the election was called, McCreevy was confirmed as a Fianna Fáil candidate but he never received promotion of any kind while Haughey led Fianna Fáil over the following 10 years.

Polling day was 18 February 1982, and the outcome saw Ahern consolidate his premier position in Dublin Central. He headed the poll with 8,570 votes and was almost 1,000 votes clear of Colley who was again in third place. Tom Leonard was once more a Fianna Fáil candidate but got fewer than 3,000 votes. There was also a fourth party candidate, Michael J Ward, who got just 600 votes. Fine Gael's Michael Keating was again in second place. Labour leader and Tánaiste in the previous Government, Michael O'Leary, was also re-elected and took the fifth seat. But there was a newcomer in Tony Gregory who had edged out Fine Gael's Alice Glenn this time.

Gregory's arrival on the scene proved to be a double-edged sword for Bertie Ahern in the immediate election aftermath of February/March 1982. He was quickly catapulted to political celebrity at some cost to Ahern's local pride. Against that, Gregory's support for Charlie Haughey also delivered Bertie Ahern's first government job. The political year 1982/83 certainly shaped Irish politics as never before. And it also gave Bertie Ahern a true baptism of political fire.

3

Walking the Line

'As Chief Whip, Bertie Ahern learned to come down the white line and take both sides of the street with him. I don't know how he got away with it.'

Seamus Brennan, the veteran politician, recalls an era he would at times prefer to forget. It was clearly a bitter time of deep and prolonged conflict within Fianna Fáil. Most of that bitter conflict centred on the loved or loathed figure of Charlie Haughey, who was by now Ahern's boss and mentor.

The vast bulk of Fianna Fáil TDs agree about two things regarding Bertie Ahern throughout the decade 1982–92. First is that Ahern was unswervingly loyal to Haughey from start to finish. Second is that, though he was Haughey's most loyal lieutenant, he managed not to antagonise too many people on the other side of the gulf within Fianna Fáil.

The year 1982 brought not just two anti-Haughey leadership heaves but two general elections. There were also allegations of attempted bribery, bugging of ministerial conversations, telephone tapping, interference in Garda matters and other extraordinary happenings. In fact, Fianna Fáil's bitter feuding started even before they could get back into government and just a week after polling day in February 1982.

Ahead of a Fianna Fáil Parliamentary Party meeting on 25 February, Des O'Malley signalled his intention to challenge Haughey's party candidature for Taoiseach. There were days of intense media speculation and some predictions that O'Malley, a close associate of former Taoiseach Jack Lynch, would oust Haughey. Otherwise, there was implausible speculation that Haughey would step down as Fianna Fáil leader. But Haughey faced down the dissidents.

On the day, O'Malley told fellow Fianna Fáil TDs that he would not let his name go forward, and Charlie Haughey was unanimously chosen as Fianna Fáil candidate for Taoiseach. Haughey enjoyed telling political journalists at a subsequent acrimonious press conference just how wrong they were. But that night Jack Lynch issued a statement praising O'Malley and predicting that he would one day lead Fianna Fáil. The leadership heave was not even out of the stocks but Haughey's leadership was far from safe.

Haughey moved on with getting the necessary support outside Fianna Fáil to put together a government. First, he met Ahern's new Dublin Central rival, Tony Gregory, at his inner-city headquarters in Summerhill Parade and was presented with two pages of demands. Over the years, Tony Gregory's election has proved remarkable for a number of reasons. As an Independent socialist TD he has endured through six further elections spanning 22 years and defying all predictions that he was a 'flash in the pan'. Yet Gregory has never again had the pivotal national role he had in February and March 1982. Then he held the balance of power and did a £4m (€5m) inner-city investment deal with Charlie Haughey in return for his support in the vote for Taoiseach. The whole episode was a bitter pill for Bertie Ahern to swallow, seeing as he viewed himself as the emerging kingpin of Dublin Central and the inner city especially.

For Gregory there was extra delight as he recalled his suspicions about bogus H-Block posters, which he claims did him in at the June 1981 general election. He recalls that Bertie Ahern drove Haughey to his headquarters and had to wait outside in the car for over three hours while the deal was worked upon. The Ahern camp remembers that one rather differently.

'Bertie was driving Haughey around to those Gregory meetings in a battered old red Escort he had at the time. After an election campaign it was full of old papers and rubbish and generally in rag order. At one stage Haughey said to him, "God, we'll have to do something about a car for you",' Maurice Ahern recalls.

This was Bertie Ahern's first intimation that he was getting a promotion which merited a State car and eased any misgivings he had about helping the national profile of a constituency rival. Ahern's friends also insist that he saw the 'Gregory deal' as something which was long overdue for Dublin inner city.

'By then it was over 100 years since Gardiner Street parish had a development of any kind. The biggest irony there is that both Haughey and Colley represented that constituency for the longest time,' one of the Ahern camp comments.

It is interesting to note that newspapers, radio or television of the day did not make anything of Ahern's discomfiture over the Gregory deal, clearly indicating that he had yet to register as a potential political force. It is also clear that Ahern helped and facilitated Haughey in every way he could in his dealings with Gregory. In return, Bertie Ahern was able to make some serious advances onto the national stage. When Haughey announced his new government on 9 March 1982, Ahern had made it as far as the Cabinet room as Government Chief Whip.

Tony Kett recalls that the 'Gregory deal' was galling for their camp, which had been working hard in the inner-city part of the constituency since 1977. However, they had to live with it, but also had the consolation that Bertie Ahern was almost a government member.

Charlie Haughey went on to do a deal with the three Workers' Party TDs from the party which had previously been 'Official' Sinn Féin and were now dedicated to developing socialism in Ireland north and south. Both Ahern and incoming Finance Minister Ray MacSharry were involved in these talks. Finally, Haughey won the support of his co-accused in the 1970 IRA arms affair, Neil Blaney, a TD for Donegal since 1948 and an Independent deputy since 1970. In fact, Blaney managed to extract a Taoiseach's Seanad nomination for one of his campaign people in return. This enraged Fianna Fáil people in Donegal, who had been left to battle against Blaney for over a decade.

On 9 March 1982, Charlie Haughey was back in the top political job in the land and formally named his government. The Dáil back-up was not very regular. But it was rather similar to the so-called three-legged stool Bertie Ahern was to fashion with far greater durability for his own first government all of 15 years later. This new Haughey Government did not include Ahern's Dublin Central Fianna Fáil colleague George Colley. Colley had rejected Haughey's appeal for support in the abortive O'Malley challenge and turned down a Cabinet post. MacSharry was Finance Minister and there was a post for another supporter, Albert Reynolds. However, dissidents Des O'Malley and Martin O'Donoghue were also included. The new Attorney General was barrister Patrick Connolly who had been on Haughey's 1970 Arms Trial defence team. Another Haughey supporter, Seán Doherty of Roscommon was the first former Garda to become Minister for Justice. The last two appointments were to cost Haughey dearly.

Daily politics went on in a rather fraught way with Haughey successfully persuading Fine Gael Dublin West TD and former EC Commissioner, Dick Burke, to return to Brussels as Ireland's Commissioner at the end of March 1982. Haughey's hopes of winning the subsequent by-election in May and strengthening his precarious Dáil support did not materialise, however. Fine Gael won against the odds and Haughey's stroke backfired. The net result was that he had given the biggest political plum outside the party and got nothing in return.

Haughey was denounced by the Fianna Fáil-supporting *Sunday Press*. George Colley launched a blistering and thinly veiled attack on Haughey as seeking success and power at any price. Earlier, on April 20, Charlie Haughey's own election agent and good friend,

Pat O'Connor, appeared in court on charges of voting twice during the February general election. The bizarre case failed for lack of definitive evidence but it was publicity the Taoiseach could have done without.

Meanwhile, efforts to make headway on Northern Ireland were bedevilled by lack of trust between Haughey and Margaret Thatcher. Difficulties were further compounded by Argentina's invasion of the Falkland Islands in April 1982 and Haughey's reluctance to support EC trade sanctions against Buenos Aires.

Then in June 1982 Fianna Fáil Galway TD John Callanan died, worsening Haughey's Dáil support problems. This was followed in October by the death of another Fianna Fáil TD, Bill Loughnane of Clare. A day later Haughey's old Arms Trial foe and Kilkenny Fianna Fáil TD, Jim Gibbons, was taken seriously ill with a heart attack and confined to hospital. These two deaths and Gibbons's serious illness turned the job of Chief Whip into a nightmare for Bertie Ahern. He was already contending with the fickle and wavering support offered by the Workers' Party trio of Joe Sherlock, Proinsias De Rossa and Paddy Gallagher and by Tony Gregory, who by now was deemed an epic ingrate by Fianna Fáil and the Ahern camp.

The country's economic problems were piling up, aggravated by the cost of voter sweeteners in the run-up to the Burke by-election in Dublin West. The Government was therefore obliged to impose some belt-tightening measures much to the dismay of the Workers' Party trio.

Fine Gael declared that their mission was to bring down the Government. Labour, in some disarray through these years and riven over whether they should join coalitions, were keen to maximise the Workers' Party's embarrassment as their rivals on the left.

Some writers on the period noted that Bertie Ahern did valuable work for his boss in this instance by using a personal connection with someone on the Workers' Party National

Executive to keep abreast of that party's internal debates on government support. The significance of that link has been played down by other Workers' Party activists from that time. Fianna Fáil veterans of that era also think there was a simpler explanation for Ahern's understanding of the Workers' Party's attitude.

'He had a very good relationship with Joe Sherlock, who was a sort of Worker's Party parliamentary leader. He listened to what Sherlock had to tell him,' one Fianna Fáil TD of that period recalls.

During the month of August 1982, by far the most bizarre episode of an extraordinary time occurred. The prime suspect in two brutal murders, Malcolm Macarthur, was arrested at the home of Attorney General Patrick Connolly. Macarthur was the subject of the biggest manhunt in the State's history. He had travelled with Connolly in his State car and even been introduced to the Garda Commissioner at a big hurling match, where he politely inquired about the investigation progress in 'that dreadful murder'. Connolly had innocently given Macarthur shelter as an old friend down on his luck. However, as Attorney General he was the State's most senior law officer and had to resign.

The succeeding weeks brought more political woe to the Haughey Government. In September 1982, Minister for Justice Seán Doherty's State car was involved in a crash in Kerry. Efforts to hush it up gave rise to all sorts of lurid rumours and the cover-up became the subject of damaging controversy. More alarmingly, on 27 September 1982, an assault case against Seán Doherty's brother-in-law at Dowra District Court, Co Cavan, was dismissed because the complainant was not present. Doherty's brother-in-law was a Garda and the vital witness had been detained by the RUC on the other side of the Border. In a second case, a Garda sergeant in Doherty's native Roscommon successfully resisted attempts to have him transferred for raiding a bar after hours, which was owned by a Doherty supporter. Both of these controversies only came to light after Haughey had been ousted from government. They were investigated by the new Fine Gael–Labour administration and the outcomes were to add considerably to Haughey's ongoing travails.

Haughey himself described the Macarthur affair as 'grotesque, unprecedented, bizarre and unbelievable'. His great rival Conor Cruise O'Brien shortened this to the acronym GUBU and argued that it aptly described this extraordinary period in Irish politics led by Charlie Haughey.

~ ~ ~ ~ ~

October 1982 was a hectic month for Bertie Ahern, barely seven months in his first big job. He worked fending off a second Haughey leadership heave and contemplated a manoeuvre worthy of Houdini to try to keep the Government in place. On Friday, 1 October, Bertie Ahern was the first to be handed a no-confidence motion in Haughey, which was put down by Charlie McCreevy. It was to be discussed at the parliamentary party meeting the following Wednesday.

That meeting was a long and fraught affair with the dissidents failing to get a secret ballot. At a subsequent roll-call vote, Bertie Ahern was first to vote publicly in favour of Charlie Haughey, who won by 58 votes to 22. There were ugly scenes that night at Leinster House as Haughey supporters sought to jostle and assault dissidents like McCreevy and Jim Gibbons.

Members of what were later to be called the 'Club of 22' have no illusions about what Bertie Ahern was doing at this time. Willie O'Dea, a Limerick constituency colleague of Des O'Malley who also opposed Haughey, recalls that Ahern's job was to get the numbers and keep the leader in power. Ahern was busy phoning and talking quietly to those feared to be wavering in support for 'the Boss'.

'But that being said, he was very, very easy to talk to, though you were never in any doubt that he was on the Boss's side,' O'Dea says.

Another member of the 'Club of 22', Seamus Brennan, also remembers how Ahern operated. Brennan had been ousted by Haughey as Fianna Fáil general secretary in 1979. Haughey had specifically canvassed against him and in favour of Síle de Valera in the 1981 general election, which also saw ex-Taoiseach Jack Lynch canvass for Brennan in the Dublin South constituency.

'From the first time I took note of Bertie Ahern, I remember counting him as "not on my side". But, while most of Haughey's supporters thought we were treasonous types who should be shot – and said so – Bertie never did that. He never antagonised us, though we were in no doubt as to whose side he was on,' Brennan adds.

Another veteran Haughey opponent, Michael Smith, recalls that Ahern did a considerable amount of work for Haughey in keeping up his parliamentary party support. According to Smith, Ahern did it quietly and 'without much show'. He also believes that Ahern was 'underestimated for years'.

Albert Reynolds – then on the Haughey side of Fianna Fáil's divided house – was also impressed by Ahern's quietly effective machinations.

'In a tight corner you need to be able to totally trust the guy who's there as Chief Whip. Haughey had that with Ahern.'

Another veteran of the period saw it like this:

'It was during the Haughey heaves that Ahern proved himself most adroit. It was a difficult job and if he wasn't quick and smart, he would have been very quickly exposed.'

It was at this time that Ahern became more widely known nationally as the anorak-wearing, long-haired young man with the soft Dublin city accent who explained procedures to television reporters. Asked after one fractious meeting about specific insults hurled by named Fianna Fáil TDs, Ahern quietly told reporters:

'I don't know – I didn't hear that because I was writing the minutes at the time.'

~ ~ ~ ~ ~

Haughey's creaky minority administration, in office only since March 1982, was doomed. The Government committed itself to a tight-spending regime outlined in a document called 'The Way Forward' and published earlier that summer. Clearly, the Workers' Party TDs were in a dilemma and had been agonising for months. They could ill afford another election. But by their very name, they had grave difficulty supporting Haughey and MacSharry's proposals which especially hit health funding and public service pay.

In June, the Workers' Party TDs had voted against a taxation measure and the Government survived only by the casting vote of the Ceann Comhairle, Dr John O'Connell, an Independent TD. Tony Gregory was in a similar position to the Workers' Party but had the cushion of the 'Gregory deal', which he knew would be a dead letter if Haughey lost power. As Chief Whip, Bertie Ahern made repeated efforts to mollify the Workers' Party deputies. He arranged special meetings with MacSharry and Haughey in efforts to find a formula that could keep them on side.

Ahern was also heavily involved in one last-ditch effort to save the Government in early November 1982, as they faced another knife-edge vote on economic policy. It was a complex matrix which, away from the Leinster House hothouse of that era, seems rather madcap. The survival scheme was linked to a promised referendum banning abortion under the Constitution. Both Fine Gael and Fianna Fáil had promised such a referendum to anti-abortion lobbyists – but Fianna Fáil's pledge seemed the more clear-cut and likely to give anti-abortion campaigners the desired result. Veteran Fine Gael TD Oliver J Flanagan was a proponent of a strong abortion prohibition being written into the Constitution. Charlie Haughey reckoned Flanagan might be prevailed upon to abstain in this economic vote to help Fianna Fáil stay on long enough and deliver that better abortion prohibition.

A strange type of 'pairing' arrangement with Jim Gibbons was envisaged by Haughey and he looked to Ahern to deliver on the details. The initial idea began with Jim Gibbons being transported from his hospital bed in Kilkenny, taken by ambulance to Dublin and by stretcher into the Dáil chamber to vote. But if Gibbons were too ill for this, there were plans for a farcical charade instead: Gibbons could be transported a short distance from the hospital by ambulance and then promptly returned. Ideally, this drama would give Oliver J Flanagan some political cover against potential Fine Gael sanctions if he were to abstain.

Ahern had earlier gone and got the reassurance of Ceann Comhairle Dr John O'Connell that he would give the Government his casting vote in the event of a tied vote. Next Ahern and MacSharry approached the fickle Tony Gregory, urging him not to abstain from the economic cutbacks vote, as he had intended. Gregory was non-committal and said he would have to talk to Flanagan. But in the event the all-too-complex stratagem could not be pulled together. For one thing, Haughey's old foe, Jim Gibbons, was not for budging from his hospital bed in any circumstance.

In the debate, Fine Gael leader Garret FitzGerald played on Fianna Fáil divisions by saying over 100 of the 166 TDs had no confidence in Charlie Haughey as Taoiseach. Ironically, Ray MacSharry insisted that the Government was facing a no-confidence motion because Fianna Fáil refused to do deals with anybody. The vote was decisive and Fianna Fáil lost by 80 to 82. Tony Gregory abstained, the Workers' Party voted with the Opposition, Neil Blaney backed the Government, Oliver J Flanagan voted with his Fine Gael colleagues, and there was no dramatic Gibbons ambulance dash.

Weary politicians were already headed for their third general election in 18 months, fixed for 24 November 1982. Bertie Ahern had tried all imaginable stratagems to keep Fianna Fáil in power. But he knew it was at very best a long shot and he had already made his own arrangements. Within hours of the fall of Ireland's second government of 1982, Dublin Central voters received a handsomely printed circular letter from Bertie Ahern telling them how hard he had worked in the previous nine months. Achievements included securing extra Gardaí and working hard to save jobs at Lemons Sweet Factory.

'Forewarned is forearmed,' commented a columnist in *The Irish Times*.

~ ~ ~ ~ ~

Maurice Ahern says the bitter cold of the February and November 1982 general elections convinced his younger brother that summer is the only time for elections. Even if the weather is not much better, at least the long evenings allow a more thorough canvass. He has vivid memories of 'being frozen cold on the canvass and of being frozen solid at the polling stations' during those 1982 elections.

But it was this election, by now Ahern's fourth, which confirmed him as the Dublin Central kingpin, outstripping all comers. Given the circumstances, there was not even a semblance of Fianna Fáil unity on the constituency canvass. Ahern polled over 10,500 votes to put him in the top slot. In little over five years he had tripled his vote. George Colley took something near half of that total with 5,600 votes, which was enough to get elected. Tom Leonard stood for the third time for Fianna Fáil, getting just under 2,400 votes. Fine Gael's Michael Keating was again in second place with almost 9,000 votes. Tony Gregory reaped benefits from his now defunct inner-city deal, though much of it remained undone, by taking over 6,000 votes. Gregory noted that he was now out of the national limelight by wryly referring to himself as 'Tony Who?' He remained a solid constituency performer but was unlikely to ever again be in the pivotal position he found himself in February 1982. Alice Glenn, who was to be the focus of some controversy in succeeding years, took the second seat for Fine Gael. But there were other big talking points in Dublin Central.

Former Labour leader, Michael O'Leary had abandoned the party when his electoral strategy was rejected at a national conference in October that year. He then enraged Labour activists by joining Fine Gael within a few days and, with Garret FitzGerald's help, he also abandoned Dublin Central, successfully moving cross river to Dublin South-West, where he took a Dáil seat in November 1982.

Colley's disillusionment with the train of things in Fianna Fáil was evident as he remained sullenly on the backbenches. At constituency level there was no evidence of a big campaign. The reality was that his health was failing. Haughey's one-time schoolmate and constituency rival faced what one observer termed 'an uncertain future'. But the sad fact was that Colley was to die within 12 months. George Colley, only a few years previously a hugely popular Fianna Fáil figure and potential Taoiseach, was awaiting heart surgery at a London hospital on 17 September 1983 when he took ill and died, aged just 57. He was mourned by many colleagues who respected and admired him.

Nationally, the November 1982 election campaign had thrown up few issues. Both Fianna Fáil and Fine Gael agreed the economy was in deep trouble. But neither would spell out the tough medicine required to overhaul things. Haughey tried to use a Garret FitzGerald plan for All Ireland courts and police as evidence of Fine Gael's sell-out on the national issue. For their part, Fine Gael worked all they could to play up lack of confidence in Haughey within Fianna Fáil and more generally.

Despite this and GUBUs galore, Charlie Haughey and Fianna Fáil scored 45.2 per cent of the national vote. But this compared to almost 40 per cent for Fine Gael and 9 per cent for Labour. Fianna Fáil had just 75 seats compared to the combined Fine Gael–Labour total of 86 seats. There were just two Workers' Party TDs and three Independents.

Ireland was facing four years of Fine Gael–Labour Government and ever-growing economic turbulence. Fianna Fáil were headed back into opposition to face some bizarre revelations and more vicious infighting which would badly fracture the party. The political education of Bertie Ahern was to intensify as the party faced into its third anti-Haughey heave in 12 months.

~ ~ ~ ~ ~

By Christmas 1982 Charlie Haughey was once more leader of the Opposition. Bertie Ahern was now Fianna Fáil Party Chief Whip and well established among Haughey's most-valued lieutenants. And Haughey's opponents were once more working on efforts to oust him as leader. After all, he had failed in three consecutive elections to deliver an overall majority after inheriting Fianna Fáil's biggest ever majority from Jack Lynch in 1979.

Ministers of the new Fine Gael–Labour Coalition led by Garret FitzGerald were presented with their seals of office by President Hillery on 14 December 1982. The new Tánaiste and Minister for Energy was a 32-year-old Kerry barrister, Dick Spring, who had risen from new TD to Labour Party leader in just 18 months.

Two days later, on 16 December, the new Ceann Comhairle Tom Fitzpatrick wished all 166 TDs 'a Happy Christmas and a well-deserved rest'. All sides felt physically and emotionally drained by the exertions and uncertainties of the previous year.

Christmas was barely over when all hell broke loose again, however. The new Minister for Justice Michael Noonan confirmed reports that the telephones of two journalists, Bruce Arnold and Geraldine Kennedy, had been tapped. Former Minister for Justice Seán Doherty was closely involved in both cases, breaching government guidelines on sensitive procedures authorising telephone taps. Charlie Haughey stressed that he had no knowledge of, or involvement in, these phone taps. That statement was to prove Haughey's undoing all of a decade later.

Days after the news of the phone taps, the Minister for Justice also revealed that the previous October Ray MacSharry had used borrowed Garda equipment to record a private conversation with ministerial colleague, Martin O'Donoghue. MacSharry said he was trying to flush out efforts to offer him money to overcome his debts, and to allow him to feel free to vote against Charlie Haughey.

News of the phone taps and conversation buggings further weakened Haughey's position. He appointed Bertie Ahern to a Fianna Fáil internal committee headed by parliamentary chairman, Jim Tunney, to investigate the claims. The other 'Tunney Committee' members were two barristers, Michael O'Kennedy and David Andrews.

Meanwhile, pretenders to succeed Charlie Haughey grew in numbers. Leading anti-Haughey candidate, Des O'Malley, was joined in the field by his Limerick neighbour, Gerard Collins. Others included Michael O'Kennedy who had abandoned the job of EC Commissioner, and veteran Cavan TD, John Wilson. Some of these were encouraged by Haughey in order to muddy the waters.

Media speculation that Charlie Haughey would quit reached a crescendo. The *Irish Press*, established as the organ of Fianna Fáil by party founder Éamon de Valera, published what amounted to a political obituary, stating Haughey's resignation was inevitable.

The Fianna Fáil Parliamentary Party was due to consider the leadership issue on Wednesday, 2 February. But the previous evening, Donegal South-West TD and Haughey opponent, Clem Coughlan, was killed in a car accident on his way to Dublin. Ahern's former Dublin-Finglas Fianna Fáil colleague, Jim Tunney, adjourned the meeting as a mark of respect to Coughlan without any modicum of discussion. Tunney, the one-time Colley supporter, was now a devoted backer of Charlie Haughey and the adjournment caused some disarray. Enraged deputies successfully petitioned for a prompt re-call and it was fixed for 7 February. But Haughey used the intervening period provided by his party chairman to crank up his defence campaign. Ahern began the 13-hour-long fraught proceedings on 7 February by reading the findings of the Tunney Committee investigation. A few numbered copies of the report were also left in the room for TDs to read.

The Tunney Committee report exonerated Charlie Haughey of any responsibility and placed the major onus of blame for MacSharry recording private conversations on O'Donoghue as a sort of instigator. Committee member David Andrews, a long-time TD for Dún Laoghaire, dissented and said ultimately Haughey must take responsibility. Andrews found that Doherty's involvement in phone tapping was party politically motivated rather than by concerns for national security. Not surprisingly, Andrews never again received promotion until Haughey left office a decade later.

As the meeting proceeded there were lengthy attacks on a partisan and anti-Haughey media and special criticisms of Charlie McCreevy for publicly criticising his party leader. It was to culminate, however, in Haughey seeking to expel both Doherty and O'Donoghue from the Fianna Fáil Parliamentary Party.

Haughey dissidents succeeded in getting a secret ballot. But the outcome was the same as the roll-call vote five months earlier. Charlie Haughey won, this time by 40 votes to 33, and survived the third effort in 12 months to oust him. Though the margin was tight, it should have been clear-cut enough to make peace within the party ranks. And though an uneasy stability was to descend, Fianna Fáil still remained a party at war with itself.

4

The Works Foreman

Bertie Ahern openly defied Charlie Haughey just once – over the choice of a Fianna Fáil candidate in Dublin Central. This was in the by-election which followed George Colley's death in September 1983. Charlie Haughey wanted local funeral undertaker John Stafford, with whom he was friendly, to stand for Fianna Fáil. At that time, however, Bertie Ahern feared Stafford because he had considerable resources and could mount future election campaigns that Ahern might not be able to match. Instead Ahern successfully argued for Tom Leonard who had stood alongside him in three elections and had the good grace to lose in all of them. By all accounts, Leonard did not have the most healthy or robust of appearances and local wags took to cruelly calling him 'the Corpse'. Consequently, the joke in Dublin political circles in late 1983 was that Charlie Haughey couldn't have the Undertaker – but Ahern gave him the Corpse instead!

By tradition, Fianna Fáil policy-makers had respected loyalty and believed in giving struggling stalwarts their turn to stand. But since 1994, under Bertie Ahern's leadership, this climate of opinion has been replaced by a more clinical assessment of one simple premise: the chances of winning the seat.

Given that it was just two months since Colley's death, Fianna Fáil in the constituency was heavily divided along pro- and anti-Haughey lines. However, the Coalition's new £50 (€64) per year domestic service charges and a 19 per cent pay rise for politicians helped augment Government unpopularity.

The by-election vote was taken on 23 November 1983 and Tom Leonard won easily. Fine Gael did not fare so well but Labour, still reeling from the desertion of ex-party leader, Michael O'Leary, was beaten into fifth place behind their enemies; the Workers' Party and Sinn Féin's Christy Burke.

It was also in 1983 that Ahern caused an uncharacteristic stir by giving qualified support to vigilante groups. According to him, crime had dropped in one part of his constituency after known criminals had been kneecapped. Though he condemned such action, Ahern did admit that he could see it was quite effective. At the time Gardaí were saying that Sinn Féin and IRA activists were involved with certain vigilante groups in Dublin. Ahern's comments came as a new IMS survey suggested that Dublin crime levels were higher than those in average US cities. Indeed, Ahern told RTÉ radio presenter, John Bowman, that many people came to him looking for advice on setting up their own vigilante groups.

'I take the Garda line on this – I tell them that that's very dangerous. At the same time, they come back a few months later and tell me how they've succeeded in cutting down crime in the various areas where they have vigilante groups,' Ahern went on. However, he did concede that it was hard to keep saying to them, 'Well, it's not a good idea'.

'In one particular part of the constituency very severe action was taken against known criminals and the area has almost cleaned itself up since,' Ahern concluded. The 'very severe action' was the kneecapping of two youths in Cabra West by self-appointed law enforcers.

Ahern retained his controversial views on law and order, and in an interview with *Hot Press* magazine in June 1986 he maintained his view that the Gardaí had in the recent past been out of touch with the people. He also said he had still to be convinced by Garda claims that they were hampered by court rules and procedures in the fight against organised crime especially. Moreover, he noted that 'when the Gardaí put their minds to it', they enjoyed considerable success and he cited the cases against the notorious Dublin criminal drug-dealing family, the Dunnes.

'There's still a long way to go but there are plenty of people capable of handling the problem,' he told the magazine. The interviewer, Michael O'Higgins – now a leading barrister – pointed out that Ahern had previously advocated that Gardaí be given power to deliver summary justice by 'boxing an offender's ears'. Ahern did not hesitate in reply, 'Yeah, I never withdrew that. I've no intention of doing that now.'

Then he took a nostalgic flight about the notorious amateur boxer and Garda, 'Lugs' Brannigan, who operated his own direct form of justice in the Dublin of the 1940s, 50s and 60s.

'I remember being in discos in Drumcondra and Clontarf when Lugs Brannigan came in and he never arrested anybody – he never did. You respected the police. You didn't have free legal aid or got some TD to raise it in the Dáil.'

Portraying oneself as 'a bit of a lad' in the *Hot Press* political interview had been licensed, if not rendered mandatory, by Charlie Haughey in 1984, when he himself used the 'f word' and talked about sex. Bertie Ahern played his part when asked about his drinking habits. He replied that he had a rule about only drinking Bass; he rarely drank during the day and avoided drinking too late in the evening.

'If there is Bass around, I'm immune to the bloody stuff regardless of the breathalyser. I enjoy a few jars.'

Inevitably, the interviewer wanted to know if he could drink and drive. Ahern laughed and indicated that he did not want to be drawing trouble on himself and replied, 'You'll have them waiting outside for me.' But he went on to agree that he could drink a gallon of Bass and walk a straight line in a Garda station – though he suspected he would fail the breathalyser test in those circumstances.

Ahern revealed that he had been in some tense situations with senior Gardaí over comments he had made about Garda and prison matters. Essentially, he had been questioned by very senior Gardaí following statements arising from matters told to him by ordinary Gardaí and prison officers. In these cases he never once betrayed a confidence, fearing it would lead to someone losing their job. In practice, however, it meant he had to be more careful about alcohol intake and driving for some weeks after such incidents. The interviewer wanted to know how senior were the Gardaí who questioned him.

'Everyone except the Commissioner,' Ahern duly replied.

Along with his Dáil work, Bertie Ahern was also very active on Dublin Corporation. But, just to show that even the big operators have periodic setbacks, he was defeated at the Fianna Fáil selection convention for the 1985 local elections. Fianna Fáil delegates chose John Stafford – the man Ahern shot down for the November 1983 by-election – and Ernie Beggs to contest the Dublin North Inner City ward. Maurice Ahern blames the arcane voting system then used by Fianna Fáil, which allowed two weaker candidates combine far more easily to exclude another. But it was a passing indignity as the Fianna Fáil National Executive's local elections committee promptly added Ahern's name to the candidate list. In fact, the setback further spurred him on in the campaign and he achieved a huge vote.

Something of the Ahern approach to elections had emerged the previous autumn when he was called upon to talk to potential Fianna Fáil women candidates in those forthcoming local elections. Though, given that he later had to be added to the ticket, perhaps he was not following all of his own advice when he approached the 1985 selection convention. Speaking at the women's candidate advice workshop in the Gresham Hotel, Dublin, Ahern had this to say:

> You have to walk the line...take the middle ground...you may hate your TDs but you must do what is required. We all have to swallow humble pie – and I have been doing it for years – but if you keep at it, you can break through and get selected at the convention.

If you do it the other way, you haven't a chance. And if getting there means selling your soul a little bit, there isn't a profession in the world where you don't have to change your principles.

Ahern also frankly told the Fianna Fáil women that his party had a built-in hostility to women. He cited the experience of Mary Mooney, later to be elected a Fianna Fáil councillor in 1985 and a TD for Dublin South-Central in February 1987, who had failed just a day previously to be co-opted to a seat on Dublin Corporation. He told delegates that the national group selecting candidates should have at least one woman on board. But he also offered practical advice for the candidates successfully selected and out on the stump. Furthermore, he warned that in the recent spate of elections, Fine Gael supporters had honed their tactics to delay the Opposition, by saying 'they would vote for you, if you changed your leader'.

The remedy was simple and had already become an Ahern political code of practice: avoid long chats, shake hands, have a word and then move on.

Nationally, the portents of the 1985 local elections were also good for Fianna Fáil, as they collected 45 per cent of the vote compared with a combined Fine Gael–Labour of 38 per cent. Ahern's rival Tony Gregory has a vivid memory of this election, as he was very conscious of talk, especially emanating from Fianna Fáil, that he was a 'flash in the pan'. He recalls that there were signals from the Ahern camp that their man would head the poll and Gregory could forget any such ambition.

'It never entered my mind that I could head the poll. I didn't have those kind of resources. As it turned out, Ahern wiped the floor with me. But I did what I set out to do – I got elected,' Gregory recalls.

Ahern later conceded that he decided to 'stick it to Gregory' because there was talk that he was 'king of the inner city'. So he set out to bury that one for good and soundly defeated Gregory.

'Twenty years on – it seems funny. But it was totally just to sort out who was "king of the inner city". We beat Gregory by two and a half thousand votes – just to sort out who was "king",' one of the Ahern camp recalls.

These days there is the distinct impression of peaceful co-existence between Ahern and Gregory in Dublin Central. According to an Ahern stalwart, apart from those incidents they have 'rarely fought' and really 1985 was the end of it. The fact of the matter is that the voting pattern in the inner city is now 'one Ahern – two Gregory' or vice versa.

Gregory says much the same thing in different words. 'I never see Ahern personally from one end of the year to the other. The myth that we hate each other's guts is just that – a myth. I neither like him nor dislike him. I couldn't say that about too many politicians in this constituency,' he says.

Clearly, the real Dublin Central battles and tensions lie elsewhere these days. But even in 1985, inside the City Council, where Ahern was now Fianna Fáil group leader and with numbers extremely tight, the old conciliatory approach kicked in. Gregory remembers that he tried to see to it that everybody got some committee or other that they wanted. Gregory wanted a council nomination to the Dublin Port and Docks Board because his father had been an employee in the docks. The places were scarce but Ahern helped him secure it and Gregory was impressed with his attitude.

'If he could do it by agreement, he would. If he could make arrangements that would keep everybody happy, he would do it,' Gregory recalls.

Younger Fianna Fáil councillors and aspiring TDs like Mary Hanafin and Eoin Ryan were also grateful that they could get a slice of the Dublin political action. Mary Hanafin, a young teacher, was especially pleased with a nomination to the City of Dublin Vocational Education Committee.

~ ~ ~ ~ ~

Even some of Fianna Fáil's enemies reckoned the party was entitled to a period of stability after the non-stop upheavals of 1982. But, as we have seen, 1983 began with another challenge to Haughey's leadership which he defeated. Despite his demonstration of local defiance through the years 1983 and 1984, Bertie Ahern was to show his unswerving loyalty to Charlie Haughey in myriad practical ways.

Fianna Fáil's woes continued for a time with the revelations about phone-tapping and bugged conversations. There were also accusations by Tánaiste and Labour leader, Dick Spring, that Fianna Fáil's outgoing Minister for the Environment, Ray Burke, had packed the planning appeals authority, An Bord Pleanála, with Fianna Fáil apparatchiks. Publication of a book by journalists Joe Joyce and Peter Murtagh entitled *The Boss* stoked up all of the previous year's GUBU controversies, adding some new detail to each extraordinary controversy. Moreover, the nation remained largely polarised about Haughey, who was deeply offended by the book.

None the less, within Fianna Fáil things were gradually and finally showing signs of settling down. George Colley's tragic death in 1983 removed a potential rallying point for Haughey rivals, and others like Martin O'Donoghue and Jim Gibbons had lost their Dáil seats.

However, Des O'Malley remained a dissident who was increasingly looming into Haughey's sights. O'Malley clashed openly with Haughey about the latter's attitude to the New Ireland Forum set up by Taoiseach Garret FitzGerald to promote new thinking on the Northern Ireland problems. The Forum was the brainchild of SDLP founder, John Hume, and aimed to bring together all nationalist parties opposed to violence in the North. For a time FitzGerald and Haughey collaborated well. But soon a fundamental difference emerged, with Fianna Fáil insisting on Irish reunification as the only long-term option, while Fine Gael stressed peaceful co-existence for the North's communities.

Des O'Malley was a Limerick solicitor who came into politics in 1968 after the sudden death of his uncle, Donogh O'Malley. As Minister for Education, O'Malley senior had written himself into political history as the minister who delivered free secondary school education in 1967. The younger O'Malley was initially a reluctant politician but also a protégé of Jack Lynch, who trusted him enough to appoint him Chief Whip a year after his arrival at Leinster House. Lynch had then appointed O'Malley as Minister for Justice after the 1970 Arms Trial sackings and resignations, which cleared out many of the senior Cabinet members, including Charlie Haughey. It was a big task for a 31-year-old relative political newcomer.

O'Malley showed himself to be a conviction politician and was a tough Minister for Justice, as paramilitary violence exploded in the North and constantly threatened to spread south in the early 1970s. There was no love lost between himself and Haughey and some felt O'Malley, rather than George Colley, should have contested the Fianna Fáil leadership after Lynch's resignation. Instead, O'Malley had helped run Colley's unsuccessful leadership campaign in 1979. He had also been the first to signal a challenge to Haughey's leadership in February 1982 – but he pulled back at the last minute.

On publication of the Forum's report in May 1984, there was some disquiet at the way Haughey announced that Fianna Fáil believed the only solution for the North was the ending of partition. O'Malley warned that Fianna Fáil's Northern Ireland policy was being framed without adequate debate and dictated by Haughey's expedient decisions on positioning the party politically. This time Haughey did not hesitate and within 24 hours his Chief Whip, Bertie Ahern, had summoned a Fianna Fáil Parliamentary Party meeting which expelled O'Malley by 56 votes to 16 on a roll-call vote. But it did not end there.

In February 1985, the Fine Gael–Labour Coalition moved to amend contraceptive legislation framed by Haughey himself in

1978 when he was Minister for Health. Haughey's so-called 'Irish solution to an Irish problem' meant that, in theory at least, non-medical contraceptives such as condoms were available only to married couples with a doctor's prescription. Haughey attacked the Minister for Health, Barry Desmond of Labour, for introducing the freer availability of contraceptives. Furthermore, he sought to exploit misgivings among Government backbenchers, especially given objections by the Catholic bishops.

It fell to Ahern to ensure that all Fianna Fáil TDs voted against Desmond's contraceptive legislation – irrespective of their personal convictions. He did this without apparent demur, despite his knowledge as a 33-year-old man representing one of Ireland's poorest constituencies. By now O'Malley was outside the Fianna Fáil Parliamentary Party but still a member of the organisation. He announced that he would not vote against the contraceptive legislation and made a highly rated Dáil speech explaining why.

This time Haughey summoned a meeting of the Fianna Fáil National Executive and forced a roll-call vote to have O'Malley banished from the entire organisation. It succeeded. In November 1985, Fianna Fáil Dublin South-West TD Mary Harney, another of Lynch's young protégés, was also expelled. Harney's expulsion followed her support for the Anglo-Irish Agreement, which had been signed by Garret FitzGerald and British Prime Minister Margaret Thatcher on 15 November 1985. The deal provided for co-operation on the North between Dublin and London with a permanent council of both governments served by a secretariat based at Maryfield, outside Belfast. It was condemned by the bulk of Unionists. But it was also rejected in the strongest terms by Charlie Haughey on Fianna Fáil's behalf.

For his part, Bertie Ahern had left no doubt about his commitment to orthodox Fianna Fáil Republican values. At the annual commemoration for Old IRA leader, Liam Lynch, in September 1983 in Fermoy, Co Cork, Ahern said Northern nationalists were entitled to full support in their quest for Irish reunification. Addressing the party faithful, who attended the commemoration for the last major anti-Treaty leader to die in the Civil War, Ahern had this to say:

> One could be forgiven, listening to some politicians and commentators, for thinking the whole Republican idea consisted in the liberalisation of laws on contraception, divorce and abortion, instead of being about the removal of the British political and military presence from every part of our country and the assertion of a distinctive national identity.

Ahern stressed several times that violence would achieve nothing but insisted that the political weakness of the Northern state must be challenged. The speech came just five days after Irish people voted for a prohibition on abortion to be written into the Constitution, put forward by the FitzGerald Government but supported by Fianna Fáil. However, Ahern was keen to stress that this development was not evidence of the Republic being a confessional state.

'No Church, be it Catholic or Protestant, will dictate the laws for the Constitution of this State, which will be decided by the people and their representatives in accordance with their own life,' he declared.

When it came to O'Malley's expulsion from the Fianna Fáil Parliamentary Party, Ahern was again to the fore to defend Haughey's prompt action. The Chief Whip appeared on RTÉ television to argue that the issue was not about splits over Northern policy or about leadership challenges. He insisted that O'Malley had to go simply because he had no regard for party discipline. He also rejected O'Malley's argument that Haughey was making Fianna Fáil Northern Ireland policy on the hoof at the New Ireland Forum and said the party also favoured a united Ireland. Furthermore, the Chief Whip said that O'Malley was entitled to say what he liked within the party rooms but he had to support party policy outside of that.

'Everyone was sad that it came to this. But the party leader was left with no option. We had to restore discipline,' Ahern admitted.

A year after O'Malley's expulsion, Ahern told the *Hot Press* magazine interviewer that he liked and respected the Limerick politician. In fact, he respected people of principle who had difficulty following the party line on one issue or another. However, he added, 'But when they start saying that about the weather, then you start wondering, "Is this the political party for that person?" '

Haughey, who had seen off three O'Malley-led leadership challenges, had finally gained strong control over Fianna Fáil almost five years after first taking over the reins. But it soon became clear that this overall control came at a high price. After months of speculation and behind-the-scenes planning, O'Malley, Harney and others launched their new Progressive Democrat Party on 21 December 1985. In the run-up to Christmas 1985, the PDs, as they quickly became known, dominated the headlines and captured the public imagination.

The panel for the last broadcast of the political discussion programme, *Saturday View*, for 1985 included both Bertie Ahern and Haughey loyalist, Brian Lenihan. It was unusual for the panel to include two from the same party, but circumstances conspired to bring it about. The programme was a ruminative look-back at the events of the previous 12 months and made for a less than happy Fianna Fáil retrospective. When the broadcast concluded at 2 pm, Ahern and Lenihan adjourned for a drink. They continued their drinking session until closing time, conducting a maudlin discussion on O'Malley's treachery in breaking with Fianna Fáil. The deep Fianna Fáil split had given Irish politics a new political party. Des O'Malley had insisted the mould of Irish politics – dominated by a cleavage created in 1923 by the Civil War – had been broken.

~ ~ ~ ~ ~

Away from Fianna Fáil's internal travails, Bertie Ahern was beginning to make some considerable political progress in his own right. He began to play a bigger role in the Fianna Fáil Parliamentary Party as Chief Whip in opposition and spokesman on labour affairs and the public service. He organised a committee system for backbenchers to follow policy – though more cynical TDs thought it a form of occupational therapy.

However, veteran politician, Mary O'Rourke, who entered the Dáil in 1982 after a career as teacher and mother, remembers that the party began working well and at least reasonably cohesively. She recalls how Haughey 'tried to create a kind of cabinet-in-exile' where he drove the various spokespeople 'fairly hard', which she found positive.

Ahern thrived on the impossible work schedule. When the Dáil was in session he was at Leinster House until after midnight. Otherwise, there was an endless round of clinics and constituency meetings. By the mid-1980s it was a well-known fact that his operation in Dublin Central generated the biggest volume of representational correspondence of any TD in Ireland. By way of explanation, Ahern argued that his constituency contained some of Ireland's poorest areas and had some of the most pressing problems.

Opposition too brought the small pleasures of mischief making from his pivotal position. As Chief Whip, he cleared every line taken in every Dáil debate, had a say in most party press statements and knew the current state of play with all items of legislation. There was also fun to be had by taking potshots at the slow-moving target of a Government making new laws.

'Haughey will smell something in a Bill and say that's the line to take. He'll probably spot it in the papers and say that's the line to take,' Ahern told an interviewer in 1985 in *The Irish Times*.

'He'll say, "Go for that." I then get the lads on to it. What we do is to get in a view and make them uneasy,' Ahern continued.

Pragmatism was the watchword but it was overlaid by a 'kick

everything' approach to opposition with every stratagem first going through Haughey. Ahern reflected on the *modus operandi* at the time:

> If you're smart enough as a whip, you must get on to the Chief's office first saying, "we should be on this line". I get the timetable of Bills – handling that is not just bureaucratic – it's highly tactical: we may just let one through if it's not contentious.

The one aspect of the job which he did not enjoy was playing works foreman to his fellow TDs, ensuring there was no morning lateness or early skiving off. He told that same interviewer that he was not convinced that this should be the Chief Whip's job. But here again the genial Ahern approach appears to have helped. Mary O'Rourke remembers one occasion when she went off early to do some shopping.

'Well, he cornered me next day and said, "Where were you last night, Mary?" with the most pleasant smile. It was as if to say, "Don't do that again!",' she recalls.

Another backbencher remembers Ahern as very even-tempered and as someone careful not to personalise his work disputes. Rebukes were handed out quickly and then it was on to next business.

'Ten minutes later he smiles at you. It's clear that he's not taking you on personally. And he doesn't seem to have a boiling point. Yet this is a job where you could easily lose your rag,' the backbencher of that era recalls.

There were other aspects of the political personnel function that Ahern found less distasteful. He told the 1986 Fianna Fáil Ard Fheis that TDs' salaries should be fixed by an independent body, and he strongly defended special tax breaks then available to TDs as a tool to help them provide a better constituency service. However, he has not offered much public comment on the theme of political pay and perks during 27 years of public life. But his actions have made it clear that he believes full-time politicians must be paid a good rate for the job. In October 1996, as Fianna

Fáil and Opposition leader preparing for a general election, he reflected on the difficulty for all parties of attracting and keeping quality Dáil candidates:

'All parties have problems in getting good-quality candidates. A salary level of £32,000 per year (€41,000), with limited expenses, isn't that attractive,' he said.

By January 2004, after seven years of Bertie Ahern at the helm of State as Taoiseach, TDs were paid between €80,000 and €86,000 per year with a generous system of expenses and incremental allowances. The rates have been fixed by an independent body and are linked to the salaries of senior civil servants, with the result that politicians automatically get whatever pay rises senior officials get.

~ ~ ~ ~ ~

By the spring of 1986 it was clear that Bertie Ahern had the required support and was on his way to becoming Lord Mayor of Dublin – a post of considerable prestige for a politician whose career is on the rise. On the evening of 7 July 1986, Bertie Ahern was elected Lord Mayor. He defeated Alderman Carmencita Hederman by 27 votes to 24 and took the chain of office from the outgoing Lord Mayor, his old Dáil colleague from Finglas, Jim Tunney. There were 25 Fianna Fáil councillors but the two additional votes from community councillor Brendan Lynch and Labour's Michael O'Halloran were crucial. In fact, there were gasps as O'Halloran announced that he was voting with the Fianna Fáil group.

There was pride and joy in the extended Ahern household, however, as the ordinary boy from Drumcondra would be residing at the Mansion House along with his wife Miriam and two children for the coming 12 months. Lord Mayor Ahern's acceptance speech was short and to the point. He pledged to fight unemployment as best he could, to revitalise the quays and Custom

House dock area and generally use his influence to tackle the blight of dereliction, which afflicted central Dublin.

Although the Lord Mayor can have a great deal of influence, the post has few if any powers. Bertie Ahern used the position to the maximum for what it really offered: huge public exposure across Dublin and the rest of the country. His diary for his first fortnight in office had 140 engagements listed within hours of his election.

He later recalled that he drew on all his reserves of stamina to attend virtually every local and national function to which he was invited. Invitations to events outside Ireland were by and large left to his Deputy Mayor, Joe Burke. His former next-door neighbour was now a Dublin city councillor who was deputed to any overseas functions which came the Lord Mayor's way. The one exception in overseas trips came in November 1986 when Ahern and three city councillors went on a trade mission to San José, California. When Fine Gael councillor Pat Lee criticised the trip and delegation size as excessive, Ahern replied that it was not a holiday – but a trade delegation aimed at opening business links.

Still Bertie Ahern remained one of the lads with scruffy hair, rumpled clothes and unpolished shoes. This description penned in late 1985, though rather snooty, aptly sums up the appearance he presented to the world.

> Bertie Ahern looks as though he has slept in for work and got dressed in a hurry, picking up whatever clothes are within reach. His tie is askew, his shirt collar well fingered, his navy blue pinstripe suit rumpled and badly in need of a brush and a press. And his hair has a mind of its own.

It was the start of a decade of mutterings that Bertie Ahern really did not have the finesse and class to be at the top in politics. And it was also the start of a decade of predictions that he would lead Fianna Fáil and the Irish nation in the 1990s.

Ahern had clearly enjoyed his period as Chief Whip in opposition. But Fianna Fáil had high hopes of regaining power as an election drew ever closer. This time Ahern had the added bonus of being Lord Mayor of Dublin heading into that contest and a solid decade of working the ground in Dublin Central.

Meanwhile, things were going badly for Garret FitzGerald, Dick Spring and the Fine Gael–Labour Coalition. The country was mired in debt and Labour ministers, looking over their shoulders at a fractious membership deeply divided about involvement in coalition, were reluctant about supporting more and more necessary spending cuts. The problem was that the Coalition was reaping the worst of all worlds. It was very unpopular for cutting public spending – but those cuts were nowhere near enough to remedy a dire situation.

Fianna Fáil had opposed the Government on every possible front in a way which would probably not be possible now almost 20 years later. Charlie Haughey is remembered from that period as being against everything and for nothing. At the time, Fianna Fáil posters warning that 'Health cuts hurt the old, the poor and handicapped' were in every corner of the country.

A series of meetings between FitzGerald and Spring failed to resolve serious differences about the 1987 Budget. On Tuesday, 20 January 1987, Labour ministers, Dick Spring, Liam Kavanagh, Barry Desmond and Ruairí Quinn quit the Cabinet. In explanation, Spring said Labour had defended tough and unpopular decisions but the latest Fine Gael plans were just too much.

Next day, the Progressive Democrats announced their candidates and predicted they would take 20 seats. Fianna Fáil had been hit by defections, notably Bobby Molloy in Galway and Pearse Wyse in Cork, but speculation about many other big names leaving came to naught. In fact, there were also defections from Fine Gael, including Ahern's long-time Dublin Central rival Michael Keating. There were well-founded fears within Fine Gael that the new party would do them damage, and another PD recruit, FitzGerald's own constituency organiser Michael McDowell, seemed to symbolise that fear.

Despite the PD threat, Fianna Fáil expected to win an overall majority and some early polls supported that view. Polling day was 17 February 1987, and Ahern was working with the best-ever Dublin Central Fianna Fáil structure, which has not been replicated since that period.

There was a surprise in store for Deputy Tom Leonard at the selection convention. The man favoured by Ahern in the 1983 by-election found he was not automatically on the ticket and subsequently lost out on votes to John Stafford and newcomer Dr Dermot Fitzpatrick from the Navan Road. Bertie Ahern's fears of the wealthy undertaker had abated and the trio worked exceptionally well. The strategy was extremely simple: push Ahern's vote to the maximum and work for the most rigid pattern of transfers.

In the event it worked a treat. Ahern got the biggest personal vote in the entire country with 13,635. Stafford got almost 4,000 and Dr Fitzpatrick under 2,500. All in all it was enough to take three out of five seats for Fianna Fáil.

Other parties within the constituency had suffered serious upheavals, which benefited Ahern and Fianna Fáil. As noted, Michael Keating, disappointed in his ambitions, abandoned Fine Gael for the PDs and the other Fine Gael TD, Alice Glenn, had resigned the party in a split over the divorce referendum. Labour's two candidates were only able to muster 1,400 votes between them and still suffered the fall-out from the departure of ex-leader Michael O'Leary. Tony Gregory had consolidated his position and polled almost 8,000 votes.

However, the result overall proved a major disappointment to Charlie Haughey, who had failed to take an overall majority for the fourth consecutive election. In reality, just hundreds of votes deprived him of four extra Dáil seats but the outcome was a totally hung Dáil. Fianna Fáil had 81 seats, three short of that overall majority; Fine Gael had 51; Progressive Democrats 14; Labour 12; Workers' Party 4 and Independents 4. Weeks of manoeuvrings followed but there was no readiness to make deals such as that with Gregory in February 1982.

The PDs were the big winners having deprived their enemy Haughey of an overall majority. But the way the numbers stacked up, the PDs could not force Haughey out of the Fianna Fáil leadership, and he showed considerable steel in driving onwards to put together a government. There were mutterings of another anti-Haughey heave but he summoned his front bench and laid it on the line that, if necessary, he would fight another election. Haughey gathered party faithfuls like Ahern around him, but it was Ray Burke who was put forward to publicly warn against any further heaves.

The prestigious post of Ceann Comhairle was proffered hither and yon in strategic efforts to take out one anti-Haughey vote and secure a casting vote. Fianna Fáil offered it to Independent Tipperary South TD, Seán Treacy, who duly accepted.

When the Dáil finally convened on 10 March 1987, there was much talk of a potential constitutional crisis. All TDs bar Independents Neil Blaney and Tony Gregory were pledged to vote against Haughey. In the event Ahern's rival, Gregory, abstained and Blaney supported his former Arms Trial colleague. The verdict was 81:81 and Ceann Comhairle Seán Treacy duly obliged Fianna Fáil with his casting vote.

Charlie Haughey became Taoiseach for the third time but by the narrowest possible margin. On RTÉ television news that night Bertie Ahern smilingly reflected that the outcome could not have been tighter.

'Things can't get much closer than the Taoiseach being elected by the casting vote of the Ceann Comhairle. That never happened before – even in the hung Dáils of 1981 and 1982,' Ahern positively beamed at the viewers.

Bertie Ahern had several reasons to sport such an electric smile. He was soon to head to Áras an Uachtaráin to collect a ministerial seal of office for the first time.

Charlie Haughey's Government was not as precariously balanced as it appeared, however. He had pledged to take on board 90 per cent of Fine Gael's 1987 Budget plans and Garret FitzGerald had signalled support in that event. What's more, Charlie Haughey had big plans for his new Minister for Labour. Almost a decade after his name first appeared on an election poster in Drumcondra, Bertie Ahern had taken a big step towards the centre of the political stage.

5

Compulsive Fixer

One Sunday afternoon in the winter of 1992, Bertie Ahern was attending a constituency function in a bar close to Dublin docks. He was intrigued to see that the pub was extremely busy for the middle of a Sunday afternoon with lots of comings and goings. Then a quiet enquiry to the customers resolved the puzzle.

'There were special day-trip fares on the ferry to Holyhead, so they were stocking up on the duty-free before Christmas. But better again, they said there were no customs men on duty on Sunday afternoons, so they had a free run,' he told a group of journalists in Brussels the following day.

'I'm supposed to be the Minister for Finance and I'm in charge of all those things. But I find out about it in a pub down the docks,' he laughed.

The incident also serves well to illustrate how Ahern operated during his period as Minister for Labour, which lasted from March 1987 until he moved to the Department of Finance in November 1991. In fact, traces of that dockland bar incident recur through accounts of his period in charge of labour affairs. One trade union leader of the period recalls Ahern's reaction to a long contribution from a delegation about unemployment and poor welfare payments.

'You come in here telling us all sorts. But I can tell you that there's 20 building companies out there now that can't get labourers,' the trade unionist recalls Ahern saying.

The union leaders always felt they were speaking to someone with the earth wire permanently connected and well aware of the reality on the ground.

This was a period in which Ahern played a crucial role in building the series of all-embracing deals between unions, Government, bosses, farmers and social groups. Moreover, Ahern was to remain committed to these 'national understandings' when he moved on to become Minister for Finance and ultimately Taoiseach. It was also a time during which he intervened again and again to defuse potentially bitter strikes, especially in the public sector. Peter Cassells, who was then general secretary of the Irish Congress of Trade Unions (ICTU), remembers these interventions well. He recalls that Ahern always began in a low-key, low-visibility fashion.

'But he always knew as much, if not more, about the dispute issues as anyone else from the start. He made good contacts on the ground and had a feel for the problem and an eye for the details,' Cassells remembers.

Des Geraghty, then a middle-ranking official with the Irish Transport and General Workers' Union (ITGWU), which he later led in its new incarnation as SIPTU, recalls that Ahern used a ready-made network to tap into what was happening.

'It is too often overlooked that many union activists and shop stewards were traditionally also Fianna Fáil supporters and activists. He could frequently get ready access to all the details of a dispute in this way,' Geraghty says.

Ahern had been preparing for the job of Minister for Labour for many years prior to taking it on in 1987. Two years previously, Charlie Haughey had charged him with forging links with the trade union movement. Relatively quickly, he had established contact with Bill Atlee who was then leader of the Federated Workers' Union of Ireland. Ahern himself had been a member and activist in this union when working as an accounts clerk at the

Mater Hospital and had been a delegate to their national conference. The other key contact he made was Phil Flynn, leader of the Local Government and Public Services Union.

Haughey had in the past enjoyed reasonably good relations with the trade union movement and is remembered as someone who engaged with unions. Haughey and ITGWU leader, Michael Mullen, were on friendly terms and held similar views on the North. In fact, Mullen acted as independent guarantor for the 1982 Gregory deal. Three years earlier, Haughey had been led into his first Ard Fheis as Fianna Fáil leader by an ITGWU band playing 'A Nation Once Again'.

In the late 1970s and early 1980s the thinking within the trade union movement was undergoing radical change. According to Des Geraghty, several officials and activists believed it was time to stop taking example from the British unions.

'In Britain the unions could rely on Labour returning to power at some stage and resolving issues. In Ireland it was most unlikely that you would ever have a Labour government. So, it was necessary to make terms with the government of the day,' he says.

'We were also looking at things like an "ideal wage". The problem was you'd fight a bitter dispute and win a big pay rise. Then a huge chunk of that would go on tax and another huge chunk would be eaten up by inflation. Twelve months later you were worse off,' Geraghty adds.

The Irish unions' need to stop following their British colleagues' lead became even more acute after 1979 and the election of Margaret Thatcher's new-right Conservative government. From then on, the only contact was through a series of wars between the unions on one side, and government and bosses on the other. Thatcher's action in smashing once powerful unions, like the miners and printers, concentrated the minds of Irish trade unionists. An offer of dialogue was a welcome contrast to the British war of attrition.

This new Irish thinking – based on the need to tackle inflation, create jobs and lower taxation – was feeding through the union movement. In 1984, the ICTU produced a document entitled 'Confronting the Jobs Crisis – Framework for a National Plan', which drew a weak response from the Fine Gael–Labour Government. But Charlie Haughey sought a meeting with the ICTU on this and accompanied by his labour affairs spokesman, Bertie Ahern, he went specially to their headquarters on Raglan Road in Dublin in 1986. Peter Cassells says the venue itself was significant.

'It was the first time a major political grouping of any kind came to us rather than the other way around,' he notes.

It was also the starting point for much more significant dialogue. The union leaders' message to Ahern was, if Fianna Fáil in government could produce real action on lowering taxation and creating jobs, then the unions would reciprocate by moderating wage demands. But this had to be formalised in a wide-ranging agreement.

At the same time, employers were reaching a similar conclusion for somewhat different reasons. As centralised wage bargaining broke down in the late 1970s, the then Federated Union of Employers commissioned an expert study on the issue. This concluded that centralised bargaining still had a role but stressed the need for government, both as a major employer and as the driving force of the economy, to be involved. Prophetically, the employers' document entitled 'Pay Policy for the 1980s' noted that national understandings functioned best where they were born out of some form of crisis.

Clearly in 1982, Ireland was broke and stuck with the worst of all worlds. All sides reckoned it was time to think anew and Haughey moved to include the farmers and various other groups.

~ ~ ~ ~ ~

Once in government Ahern moved swiftly to make a national agreement a reality, and what emerged borrowed heavily from practices in Austria and the Nordic countries. Ray MacSharry, who as Minister for Finance had the unenviable task of trying to turn the economy around, recollects that negotiations on what was to be called the Programme for National Recovery moved very quickly. Writing in *The Making of the Celtic Tiger* in 2000, MacSharry paid tribute to Ahern's work.

'On the Government side, Bertie Ahern as a young Minister for Labour was quick to see the significance of the shift in trade union thinking and its importance in securing the foundation of economic recovery,' MacSharry wrote.

Bertie Ahern was on the platform beside Charlie Haughey when the Programme for National Recovery was unveiled in the Burlington Hotel, Dublin, on 16 October 1987. The venue was just down the road from where things had really begun at ICTU headquarters on Raglan Road a year earlier. There was a recurring irony in all of this. Essentially, it was that most union leaders were lifelong Labour Party activists and indeed the party had been set up by the trade unions as their political vehicle. However, relations between Labour in government and the unions were often strained, partly because the party's numeric strength circumscribed its power and money was usually scarce. The Labour Party frequently felt slighted and betrayed by the unions – but union leaders quietly conceded that Fianna Fáil's power, pragmatism and grassroot links to trade unionists sometimes made it easier to do business.

All involved in the various national agreements over the past 17 years are keen to stress that the process has been well served by senior civil servants, notably Pádraig Ó hUiginn, Paddy Teahon and Dermot McCarthy. According to Des Geraghty, Ahern had a great capacity to pick the right officials for the job and to trust them implicitly to get on with the job. Many union officials noted that the bulk of negotiations were done through officials, but there was usually a sense of Ahern's presence and an expectation that he would intervene when the time was right. Critics see this as an unerring capacity to steal the glory; supporters see it as a keen sense of timing in an able politician. Both sides agree that Ahern has learnt to trust and use the huge resources available in the Civil Service.

Even so, Peter Cassells argues that Ahern's record as a reforming Minister for Labour risks being overlooked. Under his term of office there was a major review of Irish industrial relations leading to the 1990 Industrial Relations Act, which was the first overhaul of legislation in this area dating from 1906. A year previously, he put through the Safety, Health and Welfare at Work Act, which led to the creation of the Health and Safety Authority, while also improving the rights of part-time workers. And in 1991, he created the Labour Relations Commission to improve structures for dealing with disputes.

Some of the union leaders are equally adamant that it would be wrong to see Ahern as any kind of 'soft touch' in either the national agreement process or his work trying to resolve strikes. Former ICTU president, Senator Joe O'Toole, puts it like this:

> Bertie Ahern is a deal maker, a person who wants to do deals. But any idea that he is soft or easy is totally wrong. We have all learnt of his sticking points and his capacity to be hard as nails. He also has an ability to oblige ministers to totally reverse their views and abandon hard positions they have taken up, if the need arises.

To this day Bertie Ahern still rates the Programme for National Recovery as his finest achievement and ranked alongside the 1998 Good Friday Agreement in Northern Ireland. The succession of national consensus agreements since 1987 has wobbled and creaked on many occasions and often been condemned as too expensive and as undermining the national parliament. But these deals have provided a framework that helped raise the Irish economy out of a crisis of debt, inflation, unemployment and emigration. Perhaps more importantly, the succession of agreements has provided a forum for dialogue, which recently has been studied by countries like Sweden, providers of the original idea.

~ ~ ~ ~ ~

Bertie Ahern was very definitely the acceptable face of Charlie Haughey's Cabinet. This was in sharp contrast to many of his colleagues. Following on from his first Budget, Minister for Finance Ray MacSharry was predictably dubbed 'Mac the Knife' as he also announced a public service recruitment embargo. Very soon after that, Minister for Health Dr Rory O'Hanlon, a genial GP from Cavan, was pilloried as 'Dr Death'. Minister for Education Mary O'Rourke also had to take considerable flak as funding cuts hit hard.

Still short of 20 years after the event, it is difficult to overplay the enormity of the crisis. In January 1987, the *Economist* magazine, read in many boardrooms across the world, did a feature on Ireland entitled, 'How the Government Spent the People into a Slump'. It noted that Haughey and his 'rural based Fianna Fáil party' were most likely to return to government and would quickly begin lashing out cash again. More contentiously it stated, 'Irish bankers fear that, to their shame, the International Monetary Fund may have to step in to impose stringency that their own politicians cannot muster.'

As things turned out, the only prediction it got right was that Haughey was going to win the election. But the *Economist*'s darkest suggestion quickly became transposed into the popular myth that the IMF was ready and waiting in the wings to seize control of the Irish economy. It was, however, all grist to the mill to Haughey and MacSharry, now working hand in glove. At all events, the situation was dire. Ireland's national debt stood at £25 billion (€32 billion). One in every four pounds in current spending went on interest, which gobbled up one-third of all tax revenue. The interest bill was rising by 20 per cent per year. Not surprisingly, the impact on national morale was immense. Many people had the impression of living in a country that was sinking fast.

MacSharry was soon to be doubly empowered, however. He recalled later that at no stage did Haughey ever second guess his work or do anything that was less than totally supportive. None the less, this Government had been put into office by the casting vote of the Ceann Comhairle and most observers felt it would soon be time for another election. This prognosis gradually changed after Garret FitzGerald resigned as leader of Fine Gael, soon after Haughey's election as Taoiseach. FitzGerald's departure half-closed a chapter in Irish politics that had seen him repeatedly pitted against Charlie Haughey in a series of four closely fought elections. As the Fine Gael leader departed, so too did several of that party's best tacticians, including former general secretary Peter Prendergast, who took a senior post in Brussels.

Kildare TD, Alan Dukes, succeeded FitzGerald as Fine Gael leader. He had been Finance Minister for most of the Fine Gael–Labour Coalition term and had for several years wanted to do exactly what MacSharry was now doing. FitzGerald had already signalled Fine Gael support if MacSharry took the tough budgetary action his party had tried to implement. Dukes slipped into this formula, but later in 1987 he went a little further. In a hitherto unprecedented example of grown-up politics, Alan Dukes addressed Tallaght Chamber of Commerce in Dublin on 2 September 1987, stating:

> When the Government is moving in the right direction, I will not oppose the central thrust of its policy. If it is going in the right direction, I do not believe that it should be deviated from its course, or tripped up on macro-economic issues. Any other policy of opposition would amount simply to a cynical exploitation of short-term political opportunities for a political advantage which would inevitably prove to be equally short-lived. I will not play that game.

Haughey's minority coalition now had the necessary and explicitly stated Dáil backing to do deeply unpopular things. Despite frequent howls of protest as cutbacks kicked in on the ground, there was also a growing level of acquiescence among Irish people that what was now happening was inevitable.

That stance by Dukes, known as 'the Tallaght Strategy', helped the Fianna Fáil Government and the country enormously. But its impact on Fine Gael and Dukes' career as leader was less beneficial, to say the least. MacSharry's courage was rewarded and nowadays he is credited with playing a central role in turning around the nation's fortunes. This says a lot for his force of character because in reality he presented just two Budgets, the first of which was a largely Fine Gael creation, before moving to Brussels in January 1989 as Ireland's EC Commissioner. MacSharry's fortitude was augmented by some good luck in 1987/88 as economic growth picked up and interest rates fell. Though there was a long road ahead, Ireland was quickly starting to turn a dark corner.

~ ~ ~ ~ ~

The dreadful economic climate did, however, make for a very unhappy time in the late 1980s. There were huge strikes and very soon Bertie Ahern became a one-man strike fixer. Seamus Brennan remembers the Minister for Labour very well during that period. For a start he was still the same low-key, friendly bloke he had been for the previous decade around Leinster House.

'He was never seen as a powerful figure in Cabinet. He was not like "Pee" Flynn or Ray Burke – sort of "don't-mess-with-me types" – Bertie was always approachable,' says Brennan.

The Dublin South Fianna Fáil TD was first a junior minister in 1987 and came into the Cabinet as Minister for Tourism and Transport in 1989. He recalls Ahern's strike-fixing days vividly.

Invariably, the pattern was that Ahern would tell colleagues that whatever dispute in question was almost intractable and outline just how polarised the various parties were. Brennan remembers how Ahern would say:

'I don't know, it's going to be very difficult. You see the ITGWU won't talk to the NBU [National Busworkers' Union] and the other union is at total loggerheads with some other crowd. But I've a meeting tonight in a pub and I think we can do something. But this one won't be easy.'

Brennan further recalls how the final resolution would be reached.

'Then there'd be all-night talks – which usually broke down. Then they'd reconvene and finally Bertie would emerge saying something like, "By Jaysus, it's been a long two weeks – but we've done it".'

Brennan stresses that Ahern was extremely effective – and the tasks were often difficult. What he remembers most was that Ahern 'did not try to make things look easy'. According to Brennan, Ahern's style was in contrast to other ministers who would 'go off quietly and do all sorts of things and nobody would know anything about it'. But he also recalls Ahern's technique of intervention as being quite special.

'He always avoided taking a strong position himself and kept his ego out of it. By getting his ego out of the way, he could then become the ringmaster.'

That assessment is borne out by the then ICTU leader Peter Cassells, who had already noted Ahern's unerring skill of finding out as much as possible about a dispute in advance.

'He kept his views to himself. For example, privately he may well have viewed one or other of the parties involved as miscreants. But he didn't let it show,' Cassells notes.

'He showed an incredible ability to absorb what the parties to a dispute were saying and then to find a way out of the problem. He showed a great capacity to absorb the mundane details,' Cassells adds.

Ahern used his knowledge of GAA, football and sport generally as an icebreaker to help relax those involved. Then without any form of judgement, he sought a way of managing the conflict.

'He never came down heavily on one side or the other. His approach was to ask, "How can we manage our way out of this problem?" There never was any talk about "this has to stop",' Cassells says.

Mary O'Rourke, working through her own difficulties as Minister for Education, remembers Bertie Ahern as something of a kindred spirit at Government meetings. She recalls how they did 'a lot of muttering together' at Cabinet and that he had an extraordinary habit of 'cracking his knuckles'. Rather crucially, she remembers a fellow feeling among ministers because of the public reaction to various cutbacks. Ahern was highly rated because he could defuse disputes and strikes without too much cost to the Exchequer.

'There was no money because of the cutbacks. But he showed you can divert anything if you go and talk to people,' she says.

But there were, inevitably, some costs to the Exchequer before a dispute could be settled. Albert Reynolds remembers Ray MacSharry's occasional frustration at being hit with an extra bill just when he had figured out the tightest budgetary arithmetic imaginable.

'It's one thing to settle strikes. But somebody else has to find the money,' Reynolds recalls MacSharry saying on one occasion.

In April and May 1987, a major national power strike was threatened with ESB workers in dispute with management. Some stoppages had already occurred and the situation was poised on a razor-edge as people looked to Bertie Ahern. Mary O'Rourke recalls that she helped Ahern by making an introduction to an ESB group union leader, Joe La Cumbre, who was a neighbour of hers in Athlone. She arranged to bring the union leader to the Mansion House for a meeting with Ahern, still Lord Mayor at the time. The ESB dispute is also remembered by Des Geraghty, who was responsible for the energy sector in the then ITGWU.

'The pressure was intense. The papers were carrying stories about the day-old chicks which would die. There were worries about hospitals and jobs in places like meat factories. Many of these were places where we had members,' he recalls.

Geraghty has abiding memories too of 'the Jesuits making tea for us' as negotiations continued all night in their place in Milltown. There were also constant phone calls through the night to and from Bertie Ahern, with Geraghty and others well aware that the Minister was keeping close tabs on what was happening. Finally, the deal was done and a strike mainly averted through an offer of a free electricity allowance to staff. A whole raft of other lingering problems was dealt with too.

Ahern was also to the fore in trying to find a resolution to a prolonged strike by Dublin Fire Brigade in early 1988. Much of the negotiating on this issue was informally done at Ahern's old office over Fagan's pub in Drumcondra, and across the road from St Luke's. As well as his union contacts, he relied on the skills of Dublin Corporation's head of personnel, Willie Soffe.

When a deal was finally done, it was immediately threatened by a new row over demarcation between Brigade and Eastern Health Board ambulance crews. Bertie Ahern was again on hand to pour oil on troubled waters. He also personally phoned reporters on the two Dublin evening newspapers – including this writer who was then at the *Evening Herald* – to successfully dissuade them from running reports of a renewed dispute. Unsurprisingly, a personal call to a rookie reporter from a minister exuding charm easily did the trick.

'You know, John, I believe we can fix this as well, and it would be better if you didn't run with that. You see, in the long run you'd be wrong,' he said in a confidential, almost fatherly tone.

The story did not run and this final glitch in the firemen's dispute over ambulance cover was resolved.

~ ~ ~ ~ ~

In May 1989, Charlie Haughey decided to take a chance and try to break out of minority government. One Minister in Cabinet at the time recalls that Fine Gael in opposition kept 'yanking their chain' from time to time.

'Many votes were a knife-edge and we lost several less important ones. It was liveable but less than ideal,' the Minister recalls.

Not everyone in the higher ranks of Fianna Fáil felt an election was a good idea. But Pádraig Flynn and Ray Burke persuaded Haughey that an overall majority – something that had eluded him four times – was now possible. The opinion polls of the time showed Fianna Fáil were riding high above 50 per cent. Besides, there was a strong feeling within Fianna Fáil that the upstart PDs had seen the end of their bright flash in the pan.

In hindsight at least two senior ministers from that era believe that Burke, Flynn and indeed Haughey could have had additional reasons for seeing the attractions of an election at this stage.

'More recent revelations from this period show that they were able to raise money at election time and indeed successfully did so around this time in 1989,' one of the former ministers says.

In fact, subsequent tribunal findings have shown that Charlie Haughey got £150,000 (€190,000) from supermarket tycoon, Ben Dunne, two days before that June 1989 election. It was part of £1.3m (€1.7m) in total donations received by Haughey from Dunne between 1987 and 1992. Justice and Communications Minister, Ray Burke, received a total of £95,000 (€121,000) in cash from three sources at this time. Environment Minister Pádraig Flynn received £50,000 from developer Tom Gilmartin, details of which are, at time of writing, being disputed at the Planning Tribunal currently chaired by Judge Alan Mahon. In response to huge controversy, Ahern himself was to establish the Planning Tribunal in October 1997 to investigate alleged planning corruption in Dublin.

Nobody was to know of these things for up to eight more years. But when the details began to dribble out, they were to create a whole series of headaches for Bertie Ahern as the new Fianna Fáil leader facing an election. There were vague mutterings in and around Leinster House about Haughey's finances in June 1989. There was also ongoing speculation about Ray Burke, who had kept responsibility for Communications as he moved across three departments.

But there was evidence too that Haughey was genuinely irked by his Government's situation. He wanted to call an election from April 1989 onwards but was prevailed upon by others, including Albert Reynolds and Bertie Ahern, not to do so.

Ahern has privately confided that he remained totally against the idea of an election in June 1989 but was over-ruled. His determined view was that minority coalitions can survive; his hero Seán Lemass steered one along successfully in the 1960s and managed to make no concessions whatsoever. The 1989 experience and others steeled Ahern's determination to persist with a minority coalition in 1997–2002, which many observers had insisted could at best last only several months.

None the less, Burke, Flynn and Haughey himself were determined to make a break for it and there was nothing Ahern and Reynolds could do to dissuade them. Haughey finally fixed the election for 15 June 1989, which was also the same day as the third direct elections to the European Parliament.

There were signs however that the public could not entirely see the point of being called to the polls at this stage. In his biography of Haughey, *Short Fellow*, historian T Ryle Dwyer notes that in the political year 1988/89, Fine Gael had voted with the Fianna Fáil minority Government on 42 occasions, abstained eight times and voted against only 12 times. Indications from Fine Gael were that they might be able to do a more lasting pact. But Fianna Fáil's initial pre-election poll ratings were 54 per cent. By the time the election was called, they were on 47 per cent and this dropped to 45 per cent a week later. On polling day the party took 41 per cent of the vote and had just 77 TDs. This was four fewer TDs than they had in the previous Dáil. It was seven deputies short of the number required for an overall majority, something Haughey had failed to achieve for a record fifth consecutive time as Fianna Fáil leader. Ryle Dwyer reckons that continuing public suspicion about Haughey's business associations played a small but important role in this and other tightly fought elections. Public annoyance with Haughey for implementing draconian health and other service cuts, which he had condemned in the run-up to the previous election in February 1987, played a bigger role.

On the local front it was a happy outcome for Bertie Ahern and his team in Dublin Central, who again took three out of the five seats. Ahern, by now well ensconced in St Luke's on Lower Drumcondra Road, headed the same team of Dr Dermot Fitzpatrick and John Stafford as fielded for Fianna Fáil in February 1987. Though there were 13 candidates in all, the Fianna Fáil trio between them took almost half the total vote.

But the other two were dwarfed by Ahern's tally of 13,589 votes, which was almost one-third of the entire vote and just a smidgen short of two full quotas. Fitzpatrick and Stafford got 2,500 votes, or about 6 per cent of the total each. The huge imbalance almost cost Fianna Fáil a seat. Labour's Joe Costello came close to taking John Stafford's seat as he picked up transfers right across the board. This time Ahern was the nation's number two overall poll-topper just behind his soon-to-be Cabinet colleague, Seamus Brennan, who attracted the biggest overall vote. Tony Gregory retained his seat in Dublin Central and Dr Pat Lee took a seat for Fine Gael.

The only other party to fare worse than Fianna Fáil was their breakaway group, the Progressive Democrats. They lost eight seats and were reduced to six TDs. Soon a new but enduring irony of Irish politics was to emerge as the PDs signalled that they could find common cause with Charlie Haughey. The major reason for the foundation of the PDs in December 1985 had been the key founders' profound objections to the leadership style and politics of Haughey. Now just four years later, the PDs were looking at going the way of many fledgling Irish political parties before them. They and Charlie Haughey had much to gain from a new symbiotic relationship.

Ireland was also definitively moving to a more mainland Europe model of consensus politics. Fianna Fáil was about to breach a core value and share power for the first time in its 63-year existence. Haughey was now to have his key lieutenant deploy his considerable negotiating skills in another direction. Along with Albert Reynolds, Bertie Ahern was asked to negotiate Fianna Fáil's first-ever coalition deal with people who, just days beforehand, were still Charlie Haughey's sworn enemies.

6

Exit Short Fellow

It was a straight case of public betrayal by Charlie Haughey. On national radio Bertie Ahern and Albert Reynolds were loudly proclaiming that the Progressive Democrats could have only one Cabinet seat. At that very moment, Haughey was with the PD team, conceding two senior posts, one junior and three Seanad nominees.

Some two weeks earlier, it was Bertie Ahern who did the talking for his side at the first Fianna Fáil–Progressive Democrat coalition-negotiating session on 30 June 1989 at the Mansion House in Dublin. Veteran Galway TD Bobby Molloy was insistent that the PDs had to be part of a coalition with seats in Cabinet. However, Ahern told Molloy and the other PD negotiator, newly elected MEP Pat Cox, that they had no mandate to negotiate Cabinet places.

The PDs' essential goal throughout the process, which took until July 12 to complete, was to have Fianna Fáil accept the principle of coalition. If the Government seats were not initially conceded, Fianna Fáil could later collapse negotiations and claim a deal foundered on PD greed for State cars and other perks. Albert Reynolds, negotiating the Fianna Fáil side along with Ahern, was prepared to reluctantly concede coalition, but remained insistent that the PDs could only have one seat in Cabinet. However, Bobby Molloy clung fast to the principle of two PD ministers to preclude a risk of isolation or bullying.

Meanwhile, Haughey was holding a series of meetings with his old foe and PD leader, Des O'Malley, to resolve issues Ahern and the other negotiators could not deal with. But the others did not know that Haughey was also quietly conceding the PD demands on Cabinet seats. There were bitter recriminations among the Fianna Fáil Cabinet members and those most stridently opposed included Pádraig Flynn and Máire Geoghegan-Quinn. Flynn argued that no coalition was a party core value and Geoghegan-Quinn had the added annoyance of seeing constituency rival, Bobby Molloy, in line for a place in government.

But Haughey relied on his force of character to face them down and deftly avoided getting a mandate for negotiations from either Cabinet or the parliamentary party. In his book on Fianna Fáil, *The Power Game*, Stephen Collins cites a comment Haughey made to a Fianna Fáil backbencher in relation to his Cabinet colleagues at this time.

'They're only a crowd of gobshites,' Haughey is quoted as telling the backbencher.

Despite his bravado, Charlie Haughey was also acutely aware that the PDs might successfully demand a change of leader as the price of power for Fianna Fáil. Equally, and more pointedly, he knew he could rely on rank and file Fianna Fáil TDs, and those from all parties, not wanting to face another election.

Ahern and Reynolds negotiated doggedly onwards on a range of policy details. But as the principle of coalition was conceded again, the issue turned to the number of Cabinet seats. Both Fianna Fáil negotiators were equally determined the PDs were entitled to only one minister. Fine Gael and the rest of the Opposition extended time to both parties for negotiations. However, with the Dáil due to return on 12 July, a deal still hung in the balance.

Haughey met the PD team at lunchtime on 12 July and concluded the essential points. The PDs were to have two senior Cabinet posts, one junior and three of the Taoiseach's 11 Seanad nominees. At that very minute, Bertie Ahern and Albert Reynolds each spoke on RTÉ radio and insisted the PDs would get only one minister. Both Ahern and Reynolds were enraged by Haughey's peremptory treatment.

'There was no difficulty about Haughey meeting O'Malley. But Ahern was just as sore as Reynolds about Haughey conceding behind their backs,' a friend of Ahern's recalled recently.

'It really irked Ahern. The PDs had only six TDs – they weren't entitled to two ministers. But once Haughey conceded, it was impossible to go back,' the friend added.

Inevitably, it was to add to Reynolds' ongoing alienation from Haughey. But Ahern got over it and was to remain loyal despite his annoyance. When the Dáil met at 2.30 that afternoon, Charlie Haughey was re-elected Taoiseach by 84 votes to 79. Without a hint of irony, Haughey and O'Malley paid tribute to one another for the conduct of the negotiations.

'Why did you leave so?' one un-named Opposition TD heckled as O'Malley spoke.

Later that evening Charlie Haughey announced his new Cabinet. The two PDs got their places with Des O'Malley named as Minister for Industry and Commerce and Bobby Molloy as Minister for Energy. Brian Lenihan was named as Tánaiste and Minister for Defence, though he frankly admitted that in practice O'Malley was the real number two in Government. The only new appointee was Seamus Brennan as Minister for Transport and Tourism; he had almost joined the PDs in 1985 and was on good personal terms with them still. Three ministers were dropped, Michael Smith of Tipperary North, Michael Noonan of West Limerick and Brendan Daly of Clare. Ahern was still in there as Minister for Labour.

Fifteen years later, Reynolds reflects that Charlie Haughey had kept Ahern too long in his two Government posts thus far.

'In fairness to Ahern, Haughey probably held him too long in that job. But there weren't too many others he could trust so totally,' Reynolds says of Ahern's stint as party and Government Chief Whip.

Reynolds believes that Ahern also probably overstayed as Minister for Labour because of the development of social partnership. Even so, Haughey deemed it wise to keep Ahern there to maintain good trade union links, as the PDs had been making strong noises about privatisation and economic liberalisation.

At all events, the Government settled down reasonably well and surprised many by the pragmatic way the former enemies collaborated. Dáil arithmetic and the political survival imperative worked wonders.

The year 1990 saw Charlie Haughey stride the world stage with some style. As President of the European Council for the first six months of that year, Haughey was unstoppable. He spent lavishly on the Irish EC Presidency, spending £12m (€15m) alone on two summits at Dublin Castle, which were deemed successful. The first summit in March 1990 copperfastened EC support for German reunification and Haughey's deft chairmanship won the gratitude of Chancellor Helmut Kohl.

Haughey brushed aside all critics, safe in the knowledge that the EC was a major benefactor delivering a five-fold return in grants for Irish contributions remitted to Brussels. Chancellor Kohl's gratitude took a more tangible form as Germany backed major EC regional and social grants for Ireland right through the 1990s worth £1bn (€1.3bn) per year. Bertie Ahern was to play a prominent role in all this, as will be seen in more detail later. It was around this time too, as Minister for Labour, that he was to get his first experiences of EC affairs.

~ ~ ~ ~ ~

Bertie Ahern was canvassing in Ballyhaunis, Co Mayo, on a fateful Saturday in early November 1990, when a young woman grabbed him by the lapels.

'It's bastards like Pádraig Flynn ...' she literally spat at him.

Ahern was extremely puzzled. It was the fifth or sixth time he had been subjected to a barracking from women that afternoon. On each occasion, Pádraig Flynn's name was mentioned in this, his home county. A placatory Ahern had answered on a few occasions, 'Ah, sure Pádraig Flynn is a nice fellow.'

Still puzzled, Ahern phoned back to Dublin and found out the details. What he heard put the tin hat on one of his most miserable political experiences as director of elections for Brian Lenihan in the 1990 contest for the Irish Presidency.

The campaign had struggled even before it began. For a start Charlie Haughey was lukewarm about the candidacy of Lenihan, his old friend and confederate. Other Fianna Fáil grandees were in the frame, notably John Wilson of Cavan. Haughey was, among other things, fretful of the chances of Fianna Fáil winning the resultant by-election in Lenihan's constituency of Dublin West. Lenihan himself was trying to recover from a liver transplant at the Mayo Clinic in the US just 18 months earlier. He had endured a long illness and was on extremely heavy medication. Many Fianna Fáil veterans, including Bertie Ahern, still argue that the effects of illness and medication were a major cause of the extraordinary events in this campaign.

The Lenihan family, especially his wife Ann, was fretful about the strain of the election and also nervous about his chances. This put extra pressure on Ahern, who had let it be known years earlier that he had special affection and admiration for Lenihan more than for most of his other political colleagues. Indeed, Lenihan held a similar view of Ahern.

'In fact, it was Brian Lenihan and not Fianna Fáil who wanted Bertie Ahern to be director of elections on that occasion,' a confidante of Ahern's recalls today. The same source also indicates the Ahern caution by noting that it took him quite some time afterwards to ease the strain in relation to veteran, John Wilson, who had had his own presidential ambitions.

Brian Lenihan was almost universally popular for his affable manner and easy-going charm. Though he was a die-hard

Haughey loyalist, he had friends on the other side of the divide in Fianna Fáil and among the other parties at Leinster House. Ahern especially admired Lenihan for the way he could shrug off a bad experience. 'Ah well, you can't be right every day,' Ahern liked to recall Lenihan saying, when the latter recounted how he had slipped up and named suspects in a criminal case.

'Any other TD would have been shitting himself for a week,' Ahern admiringly said.

Once Lenihan's candidature was confirmed, a number of obstacles, most notably Fianna Fáil's apathy towards the contest, presented themselves. Lenihan was doing well in the opinion polls but nothing could be taken for granted. The stakes were higher than they appeared at first glance for Fianna Fáil and Bertie Ahern as director of elections. A candidate backed by Fianna Fáil had held the post of President continuously since 1945; defeat now would be a blow to morale and would likely have a knock-on effect in the next general election.

Fine Gael were also having a nightmare experience with this contest. Fine Gael leader Alan Dukes prevailed upon former SDLP politician, Austin Currie, to stand. Currie had successfully switched from Northern Ireland to the Republic to take a seat for Fine Gael in Dublin West in the June 1989 election. It was a considerable feat for Currie. Even so, everyone agreed he would struggle as a presidential candidate.

In Labour's case, they had chosen eminent human rights lawyer and former senator, Mary Robinson, who also had the support of the Workers' Party. Robinson proved an inspired choice and was able to broaden her appeal far beyond Ireland's small group of traditional left-wing voters. Ultimately, her victorious campaign was to prove both a symptom of, and a catalyst for, social and political change in Ireland.

The last election for the presidency had been back in June 1973 when Fianna Fáil's Erskine Childers surprised many by soundly defeating Fine Gael's fancied candidate, TF O'Higgins. The office was subsequently held by two nominated candidates with a definite Fianna Fáil pedigree: the jurist Cearbhall Ó Dálaigh, and for 14 years by Dr Patrick Hillery, the former Fianna Fáil government minister and a European Commissioner.

Emily O'Reilly, in her account of the extraordinary campaign in 1990, entitled *The Candidate: The Truth Behind the Presidential Campaign*, notes that Ahern faced several practical difficulties. One was that Ann Lenihan wanted her husband to return home each night, thus limiting canvassing and election rally appearances. Another was the insistence of older Fianna Fáil campaign workers on appearing in most photographs with Lenihan. This did not enthuse the national newspaper picture desks. O'Reilly notes that Haughey was opening his papers each day to see numerous photos of Currie and Robinson but none of Lenihan. This raised serious questions for Ahern as director of elections. Ahern also found it difficult to shake up the lethargy of the Fianna Fáil activists, many of whom often failed to turn out to meet Lenihan when he went on tour.

To add to all this, the events of 27 January 1982 were about to resurface in a bizarre series of circumstances. This was the incident where Haughey and several others phoned Áras an Uachtaráin in vain attempts to talk to President Hillery about delaying a general election.

Earlier in May 1990, an MA politics student, Jim Duffy, interviewed Brian Lenihan about a thesis he was researching on the Irish Presidency. Lenihan had told Duffy that he and others, including Haughey and Clare TD Sylvester Barrett, had phoned the presidential residence unsuccessfully trying to speak to President Hillery. The action was constitutionally improper as it sought to erode the President's independence and drag him into party political matters. But in all circumstances, it was unlikely to have the public up in arms for too long. As noted earlier, Haughey's hope in January 1982 was that he could form a new government, replacing the fallen Fine Gael–Labour Coalition, without an election. This would surely be short-lived, but he would be fighting a subsequent election with the advantage of being outgoing Taoiseach.

Duffy went on to write about his interview with Lenihan in *The Irish Times* in a series of scholarly articles he successfully sold to the newspaper in the run-up to the 1990 presidential election. Fine Gael seized on the issue, as research indicated public doubts about Lenihan's ability to keep Haughey out of presidential affairs. This was the only ace Fine Gael appeared to hold and they were to play it for all it was worth. Lenihan too was to play into their hands by publicly denying the phone calls at a meeting in UCD and later in an interview with the *Irish Press*. On Monday, 22 October 1990, Brian Lenihan denied on the RTÉ programme *Questions & Answers* that he had ever been involved in phoning Áras an Uachtaráin over eight years earlier.

'No. I didn't at all. That never happened, I want to assure you that it never happened,' Lenihan said in response to a question from a member of the Fine Gael election team, who was in the studio audience. This was Brian Murphy who was a friend of the MA student, Jim Duffy.

The problem for Lenihan, Ahern and the Fianna Fáil team was that Duffy had taped the research interview he had had with Lenihan the previous May. Soon the tape was to be made public and something which could have remained hidden for years became a major issue at a crucial time.

Two days later, *Irish Times* political correspondent, Denis Coghlan, published a story saying that his paper had clear proof that Lenihan did in fact phone the Áras. When Ahern saw Denis Coghlan's by-line, he knew they were in deep trouble, as he was an excellent journalist and totally reliable. However, Lenihan at first flatly denied that he had taken part in any interview about these phone calls.

Radio and television journalists were taking a keen interest and Ahern was due to speak on the lunchtime RTÉ news on a link from their Dáil studio. Other than that, Ahern had to find and brief other party representatives to go and bat for Lenihan in the media. Before going to the Dáil studio, he chanced upon Lenihan in a corridor, who told him he had now been reminded by his private secretary that he had done an interview on tape for Duffy. But again Lenihan insisted that there was no recording of an admission of his making those phone calls to Áras an Uachtaráin. Up to that point, the events of 27 January 1982 had left Ahern rather indifferent. Suddenly, he knew he was going to have to focus very closely indeed.

~ ~ ~ ~ ~

Live on radio it became increasingly clear to Bertie Ahern that they had huge problems. Listening to journalist Denis Coghlan, he suspected that there was a taped admission by Lenihan about the calls to Áras an Uachtaráin. Outside the studio, Garret FitzGerald warned Ahern 'man to man' to be careful. But FitzGerald, who had been present at the Áras on the night in question and talked of up to eight calls by people whose identities he did not know, would not go any further.

Ahern went straight to the office of government press secretary, PJ Mara, where he again met Lenihan. This time Ahern pressed Lenihan hard.

'You'd be better off just coming clean,' he told his candidate.

But Lenihan stuck to his story. Canvassing resumed but Ahern and key Fianna Fáil people were busy trying to find out all they could, as they feared the worst.

On Thursday afternoon, 25 October 1990, *The Irish Times* took the unusual step for a newspaper of calling a press conference. There a tape of the Duffy–Lenihan interview was played with Lenihan's admission that he had called Áras an Uachtaráin that fateful evening eight years previously. Pandemonium ensued but amidst it all, RTÉ's prime news anchorman and veteran political commentator, Seán Duignan, persuaded Lenihan to appear on the 6 pm television news and tell his story in full.

Ahern and Lenihan met in a room provided by RTÉ's head of news, Joe Mulholland. There, Ahern was gobsmacked to learn about Lenihan's plans. Lenihan was going to say that whatever he had previously said on tape was not factual. Instead, he would say that he did not try to ring President Hillery – at least not personally. Finally, he conceded that he and Sylvester Barrett went together to phone the President. But Barrett, being a close friend of President Hillery and with whom he shared a Clare home base, was the one who did the phoning and left a message. This account was borne out by Barrett. Journalist James Downey, in his engaging and sympathetic biography, *Lenihan: His Life and Loyalties*, lends great credence to this version of events, saying that Brian Lenihan always disliked using telephones.

That evening Lenihan went on air to be interviewed by Seán Duignan. From the start, he looked straight into the camera and addressed the Irish nation throughout. That stark image added to the astonishing nature of the broadcast. Staring into the camera was, apparently, in line with advice given to him by PJ Mara. However, Ahern firmly believes it was Lenihan's own decision.

Duffy's tape was played for the television viewers, with Lenihan's unmistakable voice admitting that he had phoned the Áras. Lenihan again faced the nation and said his 'mature recollection' was that his admission on the tapes was untrue. The unfortunate and inappropriate term 'mature recollection' was to enter popular folklore.

To Bertie Ahern's horror, Lenihan went on to say that he would be seeking the outgoing President Hillery's corroboration in all these matters. Effectively this meant that, having failed to drag the President into party politics in January 1982, he was hell bent on having another go now. Bertie Ahern was in despair. However, Fine Gael were getting ready to press home their advantage and they tabled a motion of no confidence in Tánaiste Brian Lenihan for the following week's Dáil session.

Late that night Ahern went home but slept very little. He arose early and walked into the centre of Dublin to buy the first editions of the morning papers. It was every bit as grim as he feared. Later, he was to tell *Candidate* author, Emily O'Reilly, that he had nobody to turn to for counsel. That isolated situation continued for three more days. But he determinedly persisted with successful efforts to dissuade Lenihan from pursuing President Hillery. For a time, Ahern's relations with the Lenihan family were under serious strain, at the very least.

The presidential campaign continued but the Progressive Democrats made it very clear that they could not vote confidence in Brian Lenihan. The type of behaviour being cited was precisely the reason why they had left Fianna Fáil. According to O'Malley, Lenihan had given two separate versions of events within days of one another.

Charlie Haughey saw that a general election loomed, if Lenihan could not be prevailed upon to quietly resign. The issue was discussed at Haughey's mansion in Kinsealy, Co Dublin, by the two old friends with Ahern present. The word resignation was not specified but everyone was clear what was at issue. Lenihan said he would consider things and went to Leinster House. There, some senior Fianna Fáil politicians asked Lenihan to resign. Albert Reynolds today insists that he was not one of those and had in fact warned Haughey that Lenihan, with 30 years' Fianna Fáil service, was entitled to better treatment.

Lenihan decided he could not resign; his family insisted that he should not. Haughey got a clear ultimatum from his junior coalition partner: if he did not sack his Tánaiste, the PDs would walk out. Without further ado, Charlie Haughey sacked his old friend of 30 years. At the last Fianna Fáil Parliamentary Party meeting before the presidential election, Kildare TD Seán Power asked Haughey a prophetic question about the whole episode:

what would Haughey do when the PDs came looking for the head
of the Fianna Fáil leader?

~ ~ ~ ~ ~

Bertie Ahern, beleaguered director of elections, was left with one
week to rescue Fianna Fáil's hold on the presidency. Despite the
body blow to his morale and his flagging health, Lenihan
campaigned with remarkable persistence and dignity.

At the height of the phone calls and tapes controversy, Mary
Robinson was 20 points ahead, according to one opinion poll. But
now Fianna Fáil could play the sympathy card – traditionally a
valuable stratagem in Irish politics. Lenihan's sacking and
humiliation finally delivered Ahern an enthused Fianna Fáil
organisation, which he had thus far sadly lacked. The party decided
to attack Mary Robinson as a dangerous leftist who had eight years
previously advocated the nationalisation of the banks. Fine Gael
had also sought to bracket her as a leftist. But with a week to go,
they relented and proposed a transfer pact which ultimately saw
her elected.

It was Pádraig Flynn's intervention however which put paid to
Ahern and Lenihan's hopes. It came on RTÉ's *Saturday View* radio
programme in the final days before the election. Pádraig Flynn was
keen to follow Fianna Fáil's attack on Mrs Robinson's would-be
trendy radical credentials. But he went further. Flynn also had the
disadvantage of contributing to the programme from the studio in
his hometown of Castlebar, while the others were in the Dublin
studio. Without eye contact and prior social contact with the other
contributors, it can often be difficult to gauge the mood and pitch
the tone of a contribution.

The programme was the first public appearance between
Fianna Fáil and the PD representatives since the bruising demand
for Lenihan's resignation or sacking. The PD representative was
party chairman, Michael McDowell. From the outset, Flynn could

not resist being snide and personal. He noted that Robinson's Labour/Workers' Party handlers had reconstructed her image, emphasising her role as wife and mother.

'But none of us, you know, none of us who knew Mary Robinson in a previous incarnation ever heard her claiming to be a great wife and mother,' Flynn announced.

McDowell intervened and castigated Flynn. The insulting remarks were repeated in the newspapers all weekend long. Another body blow had been delivered to Lenihan's chances of winning the presidency.

On 9 November 1990, Mary Robinson was declared Ireland's first woman President and became the first non-Fianna Fáil person to hold that office for 45 years. Some of her campaign staff believe that it was Flynn who won it for them. To this day, Ahern insists it was essentially due to the tape of Lenihan's admission of involvement in calling President Hillery in January 1982. He points to the vote result itself. In the first count, Lenihan had 44 per cent, Robinson 39 per cent and Currie 17 per cent. It was Currie's Fine Gael transfers which carried Robinson home, Ahern argues.

'Imagine getting 44 per cent and not winning. Lenihan was liked by many Fine Gael people. But the tapes scared them off and made them give number two to Robinson, even though they disagreed with many of her views,' he was to tell friends many years later. The Ahern view is buoyed up by another fact beloved of trivia collectors: Brian Lenihan's tally of almost 695,000 votes was the biggest total in the history of presidential elections thus far.

Whatever the causes, it was a catastrophe on Ahern's watch and he was resolved not to repeat it next time – whatever that took. The entire affair was to deliver another loss to Ahern, however. Charlie Haughey intended to use the replacement of Lenihan as Minister for Defence as an opportunity for a mini-reshuffle. The Taoiseach planned to move Bertie Ahern to Flynn's job in the Department of the Environment. Flynn was to move to Education and Mary O'Rourke, who had good union contacts, was to move to the

Department of Labour. But Flynn, battered and bruised after the Robinson remarks, flatly refused to move anywhere. Charlie Haughey backed off and Bertie Ahern missed an opportunity to get a big spending portfolio.

~ ~ ~ ~ ~

Soon the game would be up for Charlie Haughey as Fianna Fáil leader. Both Fianna Fáil and the PDs had showed considerable pragmatism and for over two years the Government worked. But by the middle of 1991 Charlie Haughey's public problems were mounting up. Privately, there was a mound of debt and lavish donations from 'friends' to save the day. But this would remain secret for several more years.

The great scandals and rows afflicting Haughey at this period have been half-forgotten now, given the enormity of revelations which have followed. But in the summer and autumn of 1991 they dominated the news. These included a row over the ownership of a subsidiary company at Greencore, better known as the Irish Sugar Company. Another concerned the sale of the former Carysfort teacher training college to University College Dublin, which involved a middleman who was a friend of Charlie Haughey's.

Fine Gael leader, John Bruton, and more especially Labour leader, Dick Spring, excoriated Haughey in the Dáil. There were allegations that 'a golden circle' of well-connected business people were benefiting from State assets. Questions were being asked about pipe laying at Haughey lands in Kinsealy which would enhance its value. Another controversy concerned the ESB testing wind power on Haughey's island of Inishvickillane off the Kerry coast.

Bertie Ahern had already helped Haughey fend off three leadership heaves in the years 1982/83. By autumn 1991 there was another such heave pending. The scandals led to mutterings that the PDs should cut and run from Haughey's first coalition.

Difficulties were compounded by a view among some within Fianna Fáil, including Albert Reynolds, that it was time to stand up to the PDs. But again Ahern came to the rescue. He mollified the Fianna Fáil hardliners and helped negotiate a mid-term renewal of the Coalition deal with the PDs, announced on 18 October.

That afternoon government press secretary, PJ Mara, organised a special briefing for three Sunday newspaper political correspondents, outlining how the deal was done. Bertie Ahern was in the Cabinet room at Government Buildings explaining the details to Sam Smyth of the *Sunday Independent*, Stephen Collins of the *Sunday Press* and Gerald Barry of the *Sunday Tribune*. Then the door opened quietly and the beaming face of Charlie Haughey appeared.

'He's the man. He's the best, the most skilful, the most devious, and the most cunning of them all,' an exuberant Haughey proclaimed, pointing at Ahern. Sam Smyth recalls that when Charlie Haughey left the room, Bertie Ahern looked at the three journalists resignedly and muttered, 'God, that's all I need.'

For that brief period Haughey felt he was unassailable. But the feeling proved false and fleeting. Some days later, Ahern advised Haughey it was time to indicate that he would retire soon and seek the time and space for a dignified withdrawal. Haughey heeded the advice after a fashion by telling a meeting of Fianna Fáil TDs and senators that he wanted to complete certain projects.

However, Kildare TD Seán Power, who had asked what would happen if the PDs sought his head, put down a motion seeking Haughey's removal as leader. Once more the nation was to be treated to Fianna Fáil internal strife being made public. All eyes were on Albert Reynolds, who had made a number of contentious public statements. Haughey demanded that Reynolds resign.

'I'm taking my example from you,' Albert Reynolds recalls telling Haughey as he refused. Haughey then promptly sacked him.

In Reynolds' view, Charlie Haughey had played up the description of Reynolds and his supporters as the 'Country &

Western' wing. It harked back to Reynolds' former career as a dance promoter and the regional origins of himself and his close associates.

'But I also believe it was an attempt to deprive me of Dublin TDs' support. However, in the longer run Haughey also underestimated how much Dublin support I had,' Reynolds recalls.

In the days before the vote was taken, Limerick West Fianna Fáil veteran, Gerard Collins, almost in tears, made a televised appeal to Reynolds 'not to burst up the party'. Despite speculation, and earlier involvement by Ahern in advising Haughey to step down, he remained loyal to Haughey.

The vote came on Saturday, 9 November 1991, and the meeting ran from 11.30 am until well after 2 am the following morning. Haughey successfully fought for an open vote and then won the main vote by 55 votes to 11. Charlie Haughey had survived his fourth leadership heave again with Ahern's help. Reynolds was joined on the backbenches by his supporters Pádraig Flynn and Máire Geoghegan-Quinn. There was a very keen sense among many at Leinster House that they were merely biding their time.

The episode brought a very good outcome for Bertie Ahern, however, as Charlie Haughey named him Minister for Finance in his revamped government. Ahern had finally got the job everybody agrees is necessary on the CV of someone with ambitions to become Taoiseach. But clever tactician to the last, he quietly approached Albert Reynolds and told him of the job offer and nominally asked his advice.

'I told him he'd be mad not to take it,' Reynolds recalls. Clearly, Ahern was preparing for a future in a world without Haughey.

Controversies old and new were to continue to bedevil Haughey. By the following January, the final blow was to be delivered by another figure from the past, Seán Doherty, the former Minister for Justice who had caused Haughey such heartache when in government from February to November 1982.

Doherty announced that Haughey knew all the time about the tapping of journalists' phones back in the early 1980s. Haughey's prior knowledge of these matters had often been alluded to over the years, but the formal position always remained that Haughey did not know what Doherty was doing. In the ensuing years, Doherty had remained a marginal political figure and there was and has been considerable speculation about the timing of this revelation all of 10 years later. Haughey denied Doherty's assertion and in other circumstances he might have been able to ride out yet another storm. But he was weakened by non-stop allegations of scandal and under attack from a rampant Opposition. Yet again, the Progressive Democrats said they would have to withdraw from government if Haughey did not step down. Seán Power's prophecy had come true.

On 30 January 1992, Charlie Haughey announced that he would resign as Fianna Fáil leader on 7 February. There were tributes and farewells – but the reasonable expectation that an era had come to an end proved totally wrong. More immediately, those who had remained loyal to Haughey through the previous fraught decade and a half looked to Bertie Ahern to see whether he would contest the Fianna Fáil leadership.

7

Dream Team

Just as St Augustine regarded virtue, Bertie Ahern really wanted to lead Fianna Fáil, but perhaps not just yet. Shortly after Haughey announced his imminent departure, Ahern told reporters following an EC meeting in Brussels in February 1992, 'Don't start speculating about me. I don't want it – though I might consider it in future.'

Looking back now, Albert Reynolds believes that Ahern had, as usual, done his homework and reckoned he had not the numbers to win a leadership battle. Ahern's friend, Tony Kett, is even more adamant.

'It was a very timid effort at seeking the leadership. His heart wasn't really in it. Apart from anything else, he had only been Minister for Finance for little more than six weeks and he was preparing his first Budget,' Kett remarks.

Seasoned politician Seamus Brennan takes a more detached view. He suggests that Ahern effectively put his hat in the ring and removed it almost before anyone could see it. In other words, he knew the value of putting down some kind of marker for future reference.

Others ensured that Ahern's leadership prospects did not pass unnoticed in February 1992, however. Former Haughey supporters looked to Ahern as the man who should follow 'the Boss'. Reynolds's supporters were keen that nothing be left to chance as they took steps to try to ensure Ahern's candidature would not take off. Having spent the previous two years observing the political game from the Fianna Fáil backbenches, Brian Lenihan made a strident call for his former presidential director of elections to enter the fray. Ray Burke was another who wanted Ahern to seek the Fianna Fáil leadership. Reynolds' supporters however could see Haughey's hand in both these instances. Never the less, Ahern had made a pact with Reynolds that he would stay at Finance.

The age gap between the two, Ahern aged 40 and Reynolds aged 59, suggested that time was on Ahern's side. Some Fianna Fáil sources say that Reynolds had intimated that he 'did not want to go on forever' and would back Ahern to succeed him five or six years later. In fact, the Reynolds–Ahern duo was being talked of as a 'dream team'.

But on a belt and braces principle there were dark innuendoes also being floated – some at least by the Reynolds camp – about Ahern's private life. Both sides these days try to play down that aspect. Yet the newspapers of January/February 1992 tell a rather different story. *The Irish Times* of Saturday, 25 January, noted that Ahern had taken the initiative some weeks earlier by going on an RTÉ television show presented by Pat Kenny called *Kenny Live*. There he tested public opinion about his marital status, when he admitted to domestic difficulties and living apart from his wife.

The Sunday newspapers of that last weekend in January 1992 also adverted to Ahern's personal life. Again *The Irish Times* of Monday, 27 January noted that Mr Ahern was considering his options after damaging rumours about his private life. The paper reported as follows:

> The Minister for Finance, Mr Ahern, is expected to spend the coming days assessing whether or not he should contest the leadership of Fianna Fáil in light of the publicity which now surrounds his private life.
>
> Referring to media comment on his private life, he confirmed that he had not been living at the family home with his wife Miriam for some time. He now has a place in

Drumcondra and he sometimes stays with a family who are good friends.

Mr Ahern said that "rumours" about his personal life were both damaging and exaggerated and left him in a position where it was difficult to go out with friends. Ms Celia Larkin, a friend for many years, attends functions with him and he had other women friends – "and they are only friends", he added.

"I have a social group that I go around with and Celia Larkin is one of that group. I do not live a wild life and rumours that are circulating are damaging to me. They have been overplayed by far," Ahern said.

Some Fianna Fáil TDs said that controversy over Mr Ahern's private life may have "some bearing" on the outcome of a leadership contest. But the majority of TDs would be concerned with political, not personal matters.

Commentators also noted that Bertie Ahern had no obvious kitchen cabinet with whom to discuss tactics. The theme continued through the week with *The Irish Times* reporting on Tuesday, 28 January 1992:

Mr Ahern said that people "went out to do me" over the weekend. "We all have to live with each other afterwards and I am not going to become involved in that type of campaign."

Ahern also said he was not going to make his mind up about a leadership challenge until after Budget day, January 29.

Looking back now, the drama makes Bertie Ahern's first Budget seem almost like a sideshow. But in fact he went much further than expected in the changes he introduced in a Budget designed to equip Ireland for the EC Single Market, due to start on 1 January 1993, and preparations for a single currency.

Ahern dropped the lower rate of income tax from 29 per cent to 27 per cent, while the top rate went from 52 per cent to 48 per cent. He also surprised many by cutting duty on petrol by 9 pence per gallon but raised the pack of 20 cigarettes by 16 pence to £2.31 (€2.93).

The Minister for Finance insisted that it was not a giveaway of largesse but a Budget to stimulate job creation. The main income tax cuts were offset by a 20 per cent hike in road tax, a new tax on fringe benefits and the closure of a number of tax loopholes. All in all, commentators believed the Budget enhanced Ahern's political status, yet the Reynolds' camp remained bullish about their man's leadership prospects.

Pressure however continued for Ahern to run. Those urging him to have a go also included Dr Rory O'Hanlon of Cavan-Monaghan and Gerard Collins of Limerick West, who knew well he would be sacked if Reynolds won out. *The Irish Times* of Thursday, 30 January 1992, reflected this pressure and ongoing speculation about the impact of personal matters.

> Those backing Mr Ahern continued to insist last night that he would be a candidate, although they conceded that frank references he made last weekend in relation to his private life had "done him no good". However, it did not appear that he was seriously damaged by the publicity.

These reports bear out the strong view held by Ahern's friend Tony Kett that Ahern was determined to face down this kind of innuendo about his personal life and let it be seen for what it was. But the issue did not go away. Reynolds was quoted around this time as saying,

'People do like to know where the Taoiseach of the day is living.'

Subsequently, on 1 February 1992, the *Tipperary Star* reported that Nenagh-based veteran Michael O'Kennedy would not be contesting the Fianna Fáil leadership. But it added that O'Kennedy's North Tipperary constituency colleague, Michael Smith, would support Albert Reynolds in any leadership race once

Charlie Haughey resigned. The *Tipperary Star* noted that Smith backed Reynolds for several reasons, not least the many problems the country faced. However, Smith then added that Reynolds was 'the envy of politicians in terms of his family life'.

To this day Michael Smith trenchantly insists that this was not a reflection on Bertie Ahern's personal life. He says that he himself came from a big united family and could see shades of that in the Reynolds family. It was merely a positive comment about Albert Reynolds, which was wrongly twisted and styled a snide innuendo against Ahern.

As it turned out, Michael Smith was a major and successful campaigner for Albert Reynolds. Others included Charlie McCreevy and Brian Cowen, whose late father Ber Cowen was a great friend of Reynolds. Pádraig Flynn, who had resigned from Government in support of Reynolds, hung back fearing he would alienate as many as he would persuade to vote for Reynolds.

In the event, Ahern did not stand for the leadership. None the less, he had set down a very strong marker for the next occasion. He had also successfully tested the political waters on the likely impact of his personal situation in any future leadership bid. In reality, he had defused any potential fall-out on this issue next time. Yet Brian Lenihan was dismayed enough to issue a statement because he felt Ahern had the skills to end the intermittent and bitter internal Fianna Fáil strife.

'I am disappointed by the decision of Bertie Ahern TD not to contest the leadership of Fianna Fáil. In my view, he was in a position to unite the different strands of the party and meet the challenges of today's Ireland,' Lenihan said. He added that he would vote for his sister, Mary O'Rourke, in the leadership contest.

~ ~ ~ ~ ~

On 6 February 1992, Albert Reynolds was elected the new leader of Fianna Fáil and Taoiseach-designate with a handsome majority.

Remarkably, the man who could only muster limited support three months earlier got 61 votes to Dr Michael Woods' 10 votes and six for Mary O'Rourke. It is clear that, had Ahern contested, the result would have been much closer.

At a news conference following his election, Albert Reynolds astonished many by mapping out a mission to work with everyone in Ireland and Britain to try to end the conflict in Northern Ireland. Up to that moment, few people associated the hard-headed pragmatic businessman with strong feelings on the North. Yet talking against the background of a spate of killings in the previous few days, he also appeared to speak from the heart. He said his election should have been a day of exhilaration and hope – but instead he felt diminished by so much death and destruction.

'So often we have condemned these murderous acts that we have impoverished the vocabulary of outrage. We must prove that we have not bankrupted our determination to find a solution to this problem,' Reynolds said, speaking in an uncharacteristic register from a prepared script. It was to be the start of something truly momentous in Irish life.

By promising to restore openness and honesty to public life, Reynolds also sought to distance himself from Haughey's more authoritarian style of leadership. He said he would pick a Cabinet team on merit and stressed the word 'team', as if to contrast with Haughey's more peremptory stance.

On 11 February 1992, Albert Reynolds took office as Taoiseach. There was a mellow mood in the Dáil as Charlie Haughey took his leave and proposed his successor, elected by 84 votes to 78. Reynolds then moved to make a decisive break with the past when he announced his new Cabinet.

He sacked two thirds of the Fianna Fáil Ministers and followed on a few days later by dumping a dozen junior ministers. Of the Fianna Fáil Ministers, Bertie Ahern was the only one to retain his previous post as Minister for Finance. The two Progressive Democrats stayed in their posts also, with Des O'Malley and

Bobby Molloy retaining the industry and energy portfolios, respectively. Others to keep their jobs but move to different posts were: John Wilson, Tánaiste and both Minister for Defence and Minister for the Gaeltacht; Dr Michael Woods, Minister for the Marine; and Seamus Brennan, Minister for Education.

Among those promoted were maverick Kildare TD Charlie McCreevy, who became Minister for Social Welfare; former Labour TD and Haughey confidant, Dr John O'Connell became Minister for Health; long-time anti-Haughey dissident, David Andrews became Minister for Foreign Affairs; Pádraig Flynn became Minister for Justice and Máire Geoghegan-Quinn was appointed Minister for Tourism, Transport and Communications.

Those dropped included Ray Burke and Gerard Collins, who had publicly urged Reynolds 'not to burst up the party'. Others omitted were Michael O'Kennedy, Brendan Daly, Rory O'Hanlon, Vincent Brady and Noel Davern. Defeated leadership contender Mary O'Rourke was also dropped, but this caused such a furore that Reynolds later gave her the pick of the junior ministries, where she was to play a high-profile role.

The Reynolds clear-out left a bitter after-taste, which was to come against him when he ran into trouble later. But 12 years on he is largely unrepentant.

'Maybe in hindsight it might have been a little overdone. But I'm like that – I take risks. Anyway, I went out to pick the best available team for the job. Most of my appointments were to stand the test of time. And at all events, I thought all of those I sacked were against me anyway,' he reflects.

Reynolds concedes that leaving out so many household Fianna Fáil political names was 'high-risk stuff'. But he also argues that it was time to reinvigorate Fianna Fáil and make space for a new generation. His comments on his decision to exclude Ray Burke from government are interesting and have resonance for a disastrous subsequent decision by Bertie Ahern in June 1997 to appoint Burke to government. Reynolds is adamant that there is no hindsight added to his recollection of this matter.

'I had my mind made up about Ray Burke,' he says simply.

By 1992, tales of planning corruption surrounding Ray Burke were making their way back to Leinster House by various routes, according to Reynolds, and the situation was impacting on Fianna Fáil's vote in the Dublin area.

'It was widely discussed but no – not necessarily by the dogs in the street. I have every respect for the dogs in the street, who were my best customers,' the former dog food manufacturer jokes.

~ ~ ~ ~ ~

Everyone within Fianna Fáil around this time agrees that Ahern easily transferred his loyalty from Haughey to Reynolds. But things were somewhat different; Ahern was 15 years in politics and now held the second most important job in the Government.

At first he struggled to make his mark at the Department of Finance and the word in Dublin was that he was a prisoner of his senior officials. From the autumn of 1992 he faced a very serious and complex problem as the EC's currency grid, the Exchange Rate Mechanism (ERM), underwent a series of upheavals as international money markets bet against the prospect of Economic and Monetary Union (EMU).

Ireland had joined the ERM from its inception in 1979 breaking a link with the British currency, which had persisted since the foundation of the State. The ERM had been an effective means of controlling currency fluctuations and facilitating trade. It proved remarkably effective for long periods and before the feverish activity of autumn 1992, there had been no major changes for 15 years.

However, on 'Black Wednesday', 16 September 1992, unprecedented currency market speculation drove sterling and the Italian lire out of the ERM. The speculation was part of a whole syndrome driven by a view that the EC leaders' decision at Maastricht in December 1991 to create a single currency would not happen. The immediate catalyst was an expectation that French voters would follow the example of their Danish counterparts the previous June and vote against the Maastricht Treaty, which had created the EMU.

The departure of sterling from the ERM made more problems for Ahern as Minister for Finance, since Britain still accounted for one-third of Ireland's trade. It was increasingly unlikely that Britain would join an EC single currency – if it happened at all – and there was considerable debate about what Ireland should do.

Ahern kept arguing that, whatever the future would bring, it was beneficial in itself to continue to aim for the single currency membership targets of low debt, curbed inflation and minimal deficits. But there were three months of speculation that the punt would have to considerably devalued. Strongly rejecting these claims, Ahern insisted that Ireland would maintain a strong currency.

Predictions about the Irish currency's devaluation continued in Brussels and other capitals with the growing view that Ahern's stance was unsustainable. The only real issue was *when* he would devalue. But by November, Ahern had even fewer options as Reynolds led Fianna Fáil into an election with 'a strong currency within the ERM' among its political slogans.

Fianna Fáil's first-ever venture into coalition with its hated, breakaway Progressive Democrat rivals had endured enormous stresses and strains over three years. Many within Fianna Fáil, including Albert Reynolds, felt the price may have been too high. In fact, Reynolds paved his way to Fianna Fáil leadership victory by capitalising on this antagonism towards the PDs.

A commonly held view was that Fianna Fáil had sacrificed a Tánaiste and presidential victory in 1990, and a Taoiseach 18 months later, all just to keep the PDs on side. But it was the accession to PD demands in May 1991 to set up a tribunal to investigate the beef industry that ultimately proved the Coalition's undoing. The internal PD pressure for a tribunal was driven and augmented by a huge push from the Opposition Labour benches with party leader Dick Spring and veteran Barry Desmond to the fore. The big issue was the provision of taxpayer-backed export credit insurance to the Goodman organisation, facilitating the export of beef to volatile countries in the Middle East and Africa. There were reports that much of the beef was sourced outside the jurisdiction.

During five days of evidence to the Beef Tribunal in July 1992, Des O'Malley accused Reynolds of malpractice in the operation of the insurance scheme between 1987 and 1989 when he was Minister for Industry and Commerce. Reynolds used his appearance at the tribunal in late September to effectively accuse O'Malley of perjury. He described O'Malley's evidence as 'reckless, irresponsible and dishonest'. In response, O'Malley's lawyer, the current Supreme Court Judge, Adrian Hardiman, spent a long time unsuccessfully trying to get Reynolds to modify his accusations against his Government partner.

The only thing which delayed a total Government collapse was the need for other officials concerned to give their evidence to the Beef Tribunal. Things came to a head on 5 November with a Government no-confidence motion in the Dáil. Bertie Ahern was prominent among those who spoke on the Government side and did not spare the PDs. He said he never had any fear of fighting elections, but on this occasion he could not see the point.

'I have to interrupt work which could not be more important, to fight an election brought about by a small group who present themselves as the conscience of the nation,' he said.

Ahern went on to point out that all parties were united in the need to defend the punt on international money markets. Other important work included convincing Brussels that Ireland merited major EC grant aid and preparations for the Single Market. In addition, he said that all politicians had at some time in their careers to choose between sitting and whinging or trying to move on from problems and learn from them. For Ahern the PDs had chosen to sit and whinge.

'They are addicted to outrage, to annoyance and are hooked on a high moral tone. Consequently, at a time of international economic instability they are prepared to halt progress and stability to pay homage to the outraged feelings of their leader,' he said.

But this and other strong statements did not change anything. The PDs joined the Opposition in voting no confidence in the Reynolds-led Government and polling day was fixed for 25 November 1992.

The election was a disaster for Fianna Fáil and Albert Reynolds, who the voters decided was the aggressor in the Government collapse. The pre-election state of the parties was Fianna Fáil 77 seats, Fine Gael 55, Labour 16, Progressive Democrats 6, Democratic Left 6, Others 4, the Workers' Party 1, and the Green Party 1. In early 1992, the Workers' Party had split with the bulk of its TDs opting to form Democratic Left.

Seán Duignan in *One Spin on the Merry-Go-Round* – his uproarious account of working as Albert Reynolds' press secretary – recounts how quickly a sense of desperation and loss set in. He recalls being summoned early in the campaign to a strategy meeting. One of the ministers present was Bertie Ahern, whose reply to Duignan's query about the state of things was simply to roll his eyes to heaven.

Still, Ahern put his shoulder to the wheel and batted for Reynolds and the party, especially on radio and television. They published a six-point programme which included a £750m (€950m) job creation fund. But it failed to catch the public imagination, as did a pledge by Bertie Ahern to increase mortgage interest relief, partly to help borrowers suffering from the ERM turbulence and increased interest charges.

Little more than 10 days before polling, Reynolds conceded privately to Duignan that the jig was up as the voters had made up their minds. Surveys showed Fianna Fáil were stuck on 40 per cent, while Albert Reynolds' personal rating was down at an abysmal 28 per cent.

All the surveys showed Labour and Dick Spring would be the big winners. Spring had made huge headway by repeatedly and effectively heaping scathing criticism on Charlie Haughey and his party, and later on Albert Reynolds. As polling day approached, surveys put Labour on 22 per cent nationally, 32 per cent in Dublin, with Spring's personal rating on an unprecedented 71 per cent.

Duignan recalls that while flying back from campaigning in Waterford on the evening of 19 November, six days from polling day, he heard Albert Reynolds half mutter to himself, 'Labour will drive a hard bargain'. From then on Duignan began to see references to a potential Fianna Fáil–Labour Coalition all around him.

Around this time, Pádraig Flynn buttonholed Reynolds and warned him against the idea of coalescing with Labour. EC Commissioner and former Minister for Finance, Ray MacSharry, made a business call on Reynolds and urged him to publicly disown the idea of any coalition. According to MacSharry, such a declaration would be worth 2–3 per cent extra on polling day.

Meanwhile, Brian Lenihan had published an article in *In Dublin* magazine advocating a Fianna Fáil–Labour Coalition. In fact, Ahern was later to recall that the word across the party was 'avoid personalised attacks on Labour'.

When the votes were counted on Thursday and Friday, 26/27 November the scale of Fianna Fáil's woes and Labour's delight became clear. The result was Fianna Fáil 68 seats, Fine Gael 45, Labour 33, Progressive Democrats 10, Democratic Left 4, and Others 6. The interesting thing was that Fianna Fáil got 39.11 per cent of the vote and just 68 Dáil seats – five years later Ahern was to get 77 seats with just 39.33 per cent.

Reduced from five to four seats, Dublin Central reflected the anti-Fianna Fáil swing, leaving Ahern as the sole party representative. Again he polled hugely, taking over a quota and a half or 11,374 votes. The other two Fianna Fáil candidates did badly with outgoing TD, Dr Dermot Fitzpatrick taking just 1,800 votes; and the third candidate, Olga Bennett, getting just over 1,000 votes. The other TDs returned were Labour's Joe Costello, who had almost deprived Fianna Fáil of a seat in June 1989; Independent Tony Gregory; and Fine Gael's Jim Mitchell. Ahern was at his most open to allegations of not being a team player in this election because there were enough votes for two seats.

The November 1992 election also saw the arrival of a second Ahern at Leinster House. Bertie's older brother, Noel, who had helped launch Bertie's political career in 1977, was elected on the 11th count to the second of four seats in Dublin North-West. It was the elimination and distribution of votes from veteran Fianna Fáil TD Jim Tunney, a colleague of Bertie Ahern's in his first constituency and fellow defender of Charlie Haughey, that carried Noel Ahern home.

In Brussels on the evening of the count, Bertie Ahern was attending an important EC Finance Ministers' meeting in preparation for a major leaders' summit on regional and social grant aid. Afterwards, he told RTÉ's Europe correspondent, Tommie Gorman, that Fianna Fáil should abandon all ideas of coalition and head for opposition and the rebuilding of its run-down organisation. But within days, Ahern was in the thick of trying to fix a new Fianna Fáil–Labour Coalition.

~ ~ ~ ~ ~

In fact, Bertie Ahern was at the heart of several weeks of very feverish political activity, which took in EC as well as domestic issues. As Albert Reynolds' Government continued in a caretaker capacity, Ahern remained with one nervous eye on the ERM crisis. On polling day itself the crisis drew more political speculation about the fate of the punt. The Spanish peseta and the Portuguese escudo were devalued that same evening. In a lighter aside to it all, Reynolds' constituency manager, Mickey Doherty, explained his boss's late arrival at the Longford count centre by saying there was a crisis Cabinet meeting about the currency. Indeed Duignan notes that this added to the currency turmoil, knocking two pfennigs off the deutschmark on international markets.

Ahern was later to confess that his original comments against coalition with Labour were based on the assumption, current in political circles, that the new government would be a Rainbow Coalition drawn from the 'ABFF' – Anybody But Fianna Fáil – configuration. Things went badly wrong however in talks between Fine Gael leader, John Bruton, and Labour's Dick Spring. The chemistry between Bruton and Spring appears to have been quite poor with problems hanging over from the previous Fine Gael–Labour Coalition of 1982–86. Essentially, the Rainbow's prospects foundered because Bruton would not agree to Spring's demand that the Democratic Left, previously known as the Workers' Party, be included to protect Labour's far-left flank.

Fine Gael were also smarting after the loss of 10 seats and Bruton himself had a difficult time in Meath where his Fine Gael running mate, John Farrelly, lost his seat. Matters were definitely not helped by Spring talking about 'a rotating Taoiseach' with himself and Bruton taking turns at two years each.

When Ahern heard about Bruton's obduracy and the Fine Gael–Labour problems generally, he knew that a Fianna Fáil–Labour line-up was looking increasingly possible. Inside Fianna Fáil, positive signals were being sent out and Labour-friendly policy documents were being prepared. Ahern's presence was invaluable because of his pro-union image and his good personal relations with several people in Labour such as Ruairí Quinn.

But in Dublin political circles the assumption strongly persisted that a Rainbow Government would emerge. This was largely driven by the view that Labour, which had made unprecedented gains on the basis of anti-Fianna Fáil sentiment, could not coalesce with Fianna Fáil. Spring's contribution to the Dáil debate on 5 November 1992, which saw Reynolds' Government ousted, was

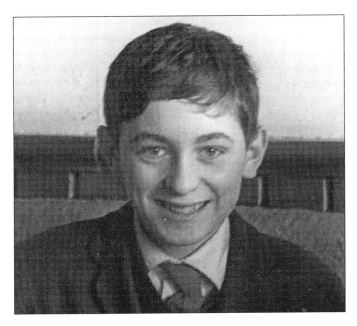

A youthful Bertie Ahern at St Aidan's CBS.

Seventies Man – Bertie Ahern attending
Rathmines College of Commerce, 1970.

One Step Behind – Government Chief Whip Bertie Ahern and Taoiseach Charles J Haughey outside Leinster House, 1982.

The newly elected Lord Mayor of Dublin with parents, Con and Julia Ahern, in 1986.

Comrades All 1989 – Minister for Labour, Bertie Ahern and
Minister for Justice Ray Burke in Charles Haughey's Cabinet.

Budget Day Specials – Minister for Finance, Bertie Ahern with
daughters, Georgina and Cecilia, 1992.

GAA Man – a lifelong supporter of the Dublin football team.

Milestone in the Life of a Taoiseach – Bertie Ahern signing the
Good Friday Agreement in 1998 with
British Prime Minister, Tony Blair.

Celebrating St Patrick's Day in the White House – US President
Bill Clinton and Taoiseach Bertie Ahern.

Taoiseach Bertie Ahern at the Great Wall of China
on a State visit to China, 1999.

The Great and the Good – Bertie Ahern meets
President Nelson Mandela.

All the World's a Stage – Bertie Ahern on a visit
to East Timor in 2000.

Celebrating their daughter Georgina's graduation – Bertie Ahern and wife Miriam.

Knee-deep, Bertie Ahern surveys damage done to his constituents' homes during the winter flooding in 2002.

Bertie Ahern and Celia Larkin.

Leaders of the Free World – US President George Bush meets
Bertie Ahern, President of the EU Council,
at Dromoland Castle in 2004.

one of the most devastating anti-Fianna Fáil speeches in modern Oireachtas history. After castigating Albert Reynolds, Spring turned specifically and at length to Fianna Fáil.

> We believe one political party in this House have gone so far down the road of blindness to standards, and of blindness to the people they are supposed to represent, that it is impossible to see how anyone could support them in the future without seeing them first undergo the most radical transformation. We will not support any Government with the track record of this one.

Those words, and others which accompanied them, made a Fianna Fáil–Labour line-up appear most unlikely. But that assumption was hopelessly wrong. Things moved quickly enough towards a government where Spring would be Tánaiste to Reynolds as Taoiseach.

In the meantime there were rumours of an anti-Reynolds heave within Fianna Fáil. David Andrews' name was mentioned as a potential replacement. However, Andrews quickly scotched both ideas and it became clear that a Fianna Fáil–Labour Coalition would not involve deposing Albert Reynolds or sharing the job of Taoiseach.

~ ~ ~ ~ ~

Albert Reynolds got his first piece of good news in a long time on 12 December 1992 in Edinburgh. He had been attending an EC leaders' summit, whose task it was to agree an overall aid budget with special emphasis on the so-called 'poor four nations' of Spain, Portugal, Greece and Ireland.

The negotiations with the leaders of the so-called 'paymaster states' – less than enthused about the prospect of paying a major level of aid – were long and fractious. The would-be recipients had pitched it as their price for participating in the Single Market and the single currency. Spanish Premier Felipe González at one stage made to walk out but was persuaded to return to the table by German Chancellor Helmut Kohl.

It was getting on for midnight when Reynolds met the press and announced that he had secured £8bn (€10.16bn) for Ireland over the coming seven years. Earlier that year, he had dismayed many Irish Europhiles by urging people to endorse the Maastricht Treaty and help themselves to £6bn (€7.6bn) in EC free money over five years. Now the grant-aid timescale was extended to seven years and the amount increased proportionately.

Reynolds' announcement was based on a number of sweeping and generous assumptions about what Ireland's share would be of the overall fund. Soon it was to prove to be an unrealistically high estimate. But despite this, Ireland was on target to take in the biggest ever infusion of overseas cash in the State's history. Unsurprisingly, Albert Reynolds was focused totally on the domestic impact.

'Eight billion, Diggy, eight billion – tell that to the begrudgers. Now watch me put a Government together,' he is recorded by Seán Duignan as saying as he emerged from the conference room.

None the less, Reynolds faced some hostile questioning from Brussels-based journalists about the basis for his assumptions – when all the summit amounted to was an aid fund being created. But he brushed them aside. Seated alongside Reynolds, Bertie Ahern kept nodding his head and at one stage interjected, 'I think in fact that is a conservative estimate.'

Meanwhile, the pace of negotiations on a new Fianna Fáil–Labour Government were about to move into top gear. Labour had been talking to Democratic Left (DL) and the two parties framed a joint document. John Bruton and Des O'Malley were holding out the prospect of a Fine Gael–PD link-up with Labour. However, Spring's hopes of a centre-left coalition evaporated when Democratic Left's Eric Byrne lost a marathon recount in Dublin South-Central to Fianna Fáil's Ben Briscoe. Now Labour–DL–Fine Gael would be one TD short of their requirement.

When Labour sent their joint document with Democratic Left to Fianna Fáil they could not believe the response. Thanks to prior preparation and the drafting skills of backroom guru, Dr Martin Mansergh, they had a reply within hours, which was deemed very 'Labour friendly'. Most interestingly to Spring and his colleagues, it posited a partnership government of equals.

On Reynolds' return from Edinburgh, direct Fianna Fáil–Labour Coalition talks began. These continued over the Christmas holidays and there was anxiety as Dick Spring gave evidence to the Beef Tribunal, a forum which he had successfully agitated to have set up. Clearly, given the PD experience, this had the potential to derail a new Fianna Fáil–Labour Government before it ever got out of the station. But Labour adviser Fergus Finlay noted that none of Spring's allegations directly affected Reynolds. Seán Duignan had the distinct impression that Spring was definitely pulling his punches. It heaped irony upon irony and all less than two months since Spring excoriated Fianna Fáil and Reynolds in epic terms.

Bertie Ahern was back in the role he found himself in June/July 1989. Along with Noel Dempsey and Brian Cowen he negotiated the new coalition programme with Brendan Howlin, Ruairí Quinn and Mervyn Taylor on the Labour side. The key negotiators, however, were Ahern and Quinn and soon their deliberations produced the 'Programme for a Partnership Government', which was laid before the Fianna Fáil and Labour parliamentary parties on Thursday, 7 January 1993. Reynolds was able to brief Spring on exciting and ambitious plans to move things forward in Northern Ireland.

The document contained an amalgam of both parties' policies, including a jobs fund, a commitment to law reform including a divorce referendum, abortion legislation and decriminalisation of homosexuality. There was to be more support for mortgage payers, but both parties made a strong commitment to the EC single currency rules.

Labour held a special conference in the National Concert Hall on Sunday, 10 January, where the programme was overwhelmingly endorsed. Only a handful of the 1,200 delegates opposed it. Labour had got their biggest share of power in their history with six Cabinet posts and Dick Spring installed as Tánaiste with a more clearly defined role and civil servant back-up. Fianna Fáil took a much clearer step towards banishing its 'core value' of shunning power sharing.

The six Labour Ministers and their portfolios were: Dick Spring, Tánaiste and Minister for Foreign Affairs; Ruairí Quinn, Minister for Enterprise and Employment; Mervyn Taylor, Minister for Equality and Law Reform; Michael D Higgins, Minister for Arts, Culture and the Gaeltacht; Niamh Bhreathnach, Minister for Education; and Brendan Howlin, Minister for Health. They very definitely had driven a hard bargain.

Reynolds' personnel problems were eased by the departure of Pádraig Flynn to an EC Commissioner's post in Brussels, the retirement of John Wilson from politics, and John O'Connell ruling himself out due to ill-health. It was felt Flynn's departure would enhance the Government's survival chances; his antipathy towards Labour was more than reciprocated. Fianna Fáil survivors included: Michael Woods (Social Welfare); Máire Geoghegan-Quinn (Justice); Michael Smith (Environment); Joe Walsh (Agriculture); Charlie McCreevy (Tourism and Trade); and Brian Cowen (Transport, Energy and Communications).

In the Government, formally appointed on 12 January 1993, Bertie Ahern was once more ensconced in the Department of Finance. He was also once again grappling with the horrors of ERM turmoil and the imminent threat of devaluation.

On an appallingly wet and cold Saturday night, 31 January 1993, the EC's powerful and secretive Monetary Committee, comprising Department of Finance and Central Bank officials from each of the capitals, hastily convened in Brussels at Bertie Ahern's request. The meeting was brief and the outcome was announced on a one-page communiqué. The Irish punt was devalued by 10 per cent. It was the biggest single devaluation of any currency since the money grid was established in 1979. Observers said the size of the devaluation was at least partly caused by the refusal to devalue during the November election campaign and subsequent coalition talks. Speculation immediately moved on to whether Ireland could continue to remain part of the system if sterling continued to fall in value.

Bertie Ahern was left to explain a policy u-turn, which was always inevitable. He went on RTÉ radio that Sunday to defend his handling of the crisis and blamed Germany and, to a lesser extent, France for not showing more solidarity in defending the smaller currencies from money market sharks. The Finance Minister sounded a little feeble urging traders to try to increase business with mainland Europe, especially France and Germany, in order to lessen dependence on trade with Britain. But he redoubled his determination that Ireland would be in the first group to join the single currency in the European Union (EU), which would officially come into existence later that year.

8

So Near – Yet So Far

As he presented his second Budget on 24 February 1993, Bertie Ahern wore ashes on his forehead. It was also Ash Wednesday, the day he always wears the trademark ashes. But that day, however, it seemed in keeping with the austere package he was delivering. He avoided whacking the 'old reliables' of petrol, tobacco and alcohol too hard. Instead, 20 cigarettes went up by 10 pence (13 cent); heavy fuel oil by 1p per gallon. The only alcohol to be hit was cider, which was levied with 4p per pint. A cider spokesman told reporters he was 'appalled'.

However, it was nothing to the reaction of the unions, as workers were stung by a 1 per cent income levy to go into a special job creation fund. In fact, Ahern told the Dáil that the Budget generally, and the levy specifically, were about creating jobs.

'The Budget is framed on the principle that the overriding national priority is jobs. The better off in our society will have to make some sacrifices to help the unemployed and the less well off,' he told the Dáil.

There were more than 300,000 people out of work – or 17 per cent of the workforce. Only Spain had a worse jobless rate in the EC. The levy applied to everyone earning over £9,000 (€11,500) per year and was expected to net £300m (€380m) in a full year. It arrested a trend of small tax reductions begun when Albert Reynolds became Minister for Finance in 1988 and continued by Ahern the previous year. Ahern insisted the levy was only temporary but Irish people had heard that story too often in the past in relation to other austerity measures. The bitter row over it enmeshed with efforts to renew social partnership and he dropped it in the following Budget. Yet other rows were to prove less easily resolved.

The new Reynolds–Spring Coalition had 101 of the Dáil's 166 seats, the biggest majority in the State's history. It began on a note of considerable goodwill between Fianna Fáil and Labour. There were some encouraging signs that the economy was slowly going in the right direction and the promise of great largesse from Brussels to further boost things. In addition, there were strong but latent hopes of a breakthrough in the Northern Ireland conflict, which could end over 20 years of violence. Fianna Fáil's eternal optimist, Brian Lenihan, predicted that this 'Fianna Fáil–Labour production would run and run'. But he was wrong, the Government appointed on 12 January 1993 was out of business by 17 November 1994.

A decade on, neither the Fianna Fáil nor the Labour side can agree on the rights and wrongs of the bust-up. There was a rolling series of rows that were for the most part managed and defused. Fergus Finlay, a key adviser to Dick Spring, remembers that Bertie Ahern was among the conciliators in several of these rows.

'Bertie Ahern was a conciliator and showed himself capable of sustaining coalition. In fact, if Ahern had replaced Reynolds as leader after the 1992 election it is probable that the Government would have run its full term. It would in fact have had a very good chance of being re-elected,' Finlay says.

The circumstances of the final row are bizarre in the extreme, involving a tangled tale of the extradition of two paedophile clerics, the appointment of the High Court President and unresolved disputes over which politician knew what and when. One senior Fianna Fáil figure at the time absolves many readers of guilt over failing to grasp too many of the Byzantine details involved.

'I followed everything; I was there for most of it. I still don't understand it,' he concedes with admirable candour.

~ ~ ~ ~ ~

Both Fianna Fáil and Labour people active in the period can agree that the handling of the publication of the final report of the Beef Tribunal in July 1994 was a big factor in the collapse of the Government. None the less, there had been good collaboration on many fronts between Fianna Fáil and Labour.

Over a year earlier in February 1993, when Dick Spring attended his first meeting of EC Foreign Ministers in Brussels, he showed clear solidarity with Ahern's difficulties in handling the ERM crisis and the enforced devaluation of the punt. Spring argued that there were serious doubts about the EC's ability to present a united front against currency speculators. He spoke of 'piecemeal measures, bilateral arrangements and selective reactions' in a clear reference to France and Germany's exclusive stratagem to cope with their own problems by ignoring the minnows like Ireland.

In early August that year Ahern had what for him was a more pleasant experience regarding the ERM. On Sunday, 1 August, he was back in Brussels for another crisis meeting. This time the French and German currencies were in the sights of the money market sharks and both these governments were at loggerheads. The situation again demonstrated that Ahern had done what he could in Ireland's devaluation difficulties earlier that year. The meeting was delayed, however, due to the sudden death of Baudouin, King of the Belgians. But the final remedy was to expand the currency grid's fluctuation bands to such an extent that critics questioned the system's very existence. Leaving the meeting, Ahern dismissed the critics and insisted those attending the meeting were determined that the EC single currency could not be stopped. He stressed also that Ireland would be in the front rank of members.

The collaboration between Fianna Fáil and Labour continued. The following year, in March 1994, when Labour's Minister of State for the Environment, Emmet Stagg, was questioned by

Gardaí at a place in the Phoenix Park where gay men meet, Albert Reynolds put the word out that Fianna Fáil politicians were not to make any adverse comment. Mr Stagg remained as a junior minister.

One of the early misfortunes to befall Ahern in that Government was a second controversy surrounding the sugar company, Greencore. He decided to hire the firm of Davy Stockbrokers to help sell the taxpayers' remaining 51 per cent stake in the company. There were serious questions about their handling of the affair, however, seeing that they were selling some of the shares to clients of their own. Fine Gael's finance spokesman Ivan Yates called for Ahern's resignation amid heavy criticism of the Minister for Finance in the newspapers. But eventually the matter was resolved with the raising of £70m (€88m) for the Exchequer and an Attorney General's investigation deciding there was no wrongdoing.

During the early months of the Government, the major flashpoints between Reynolds and Spring concerned taxation. The first involved a tax amnesty which offered cheats a chance to pay just 15 per cent tax to bring undisclosed money back into the system. Given that most workers were paying 48 per cent and more on social charges, this was wildly unpopular. The media dubbed it 'a fiddler's freebie' and Labour's credentials were quickly called into question.

Vehemently opposed to the idea, Bertie Ahern could not see the need for the amnesty. Labour say they were relying on Ahern to drive the Opposition as they did not want to undermine relations with Reynolds. But on decision day at Cabinet, Ahern sang dumb and the amnesty was carried without demur from anyone. Labour's Fergus Finlay insists that Ahern in this instance was the dog who did not bark. On the contrary, sources on Ahern's side of the argument say he did not oppose it because he had been told by Labour that they would accept the amnesty.

'The irony was that Ahern had to go and defend the measure in the Dáil after he had been against the idea,' the source says.

Finlay is adamant however that he cannot accept the Ahern arguments on this issue.

'We always understood that Bertie Ahern was strongly opposed to the tax amnesty. In fact, the night before the issue was taken at Cabinet, he rang a colleague of mine to ensure that he could count on Labour support,' Finlay insists.

The second taxation row involved a move to ease the regulations on Irish super-rich tax exiles in the enabling legislation which followed the 1993 Budget. Whatever happened on the previous occasion, it is clear that Labour went to war on this one.

Albert Reynolds was on holidays in Limassol, Cyprus when Dick Spring discovered what was going on. He faxed a very angry letter to Reynolds, who replied by fax with a letter handwritten in block capitals. Seán Duignan records that Reynolds had earlier phoned from Cyprus warning that this matter could break the Government. The Labour side was equally adamant. Fergus Finlay recalls Ahern arriving to see Dick Spring at the Hotel Europe in Killarney. The ever-appeasing Ahern was trying to defuse the issue but was told by Spring that there was no possible compromise. A day later, however, Duignan was able to write in his diary that the row was over. Labour had faced down Reynolds, though the matter did not become public until much later. In fact, Finlay's assessment of Ahern on this and other Fianna Fáil–Labour flashpoints is very interesting.

'He was doing his damnest to be the glue which kept things together and was a constant conciliator. The problem was that he appeared to have little influence over Albert. Other people who had more influence, such as Brian Cowen or Charlie McCreevy, were busy managing things in their own departments,' Finlay recalls.

Another controversy concerned revelations that a wealthy Saudi Arabian family called Masri – who invested in Ireland – had been granted Irish passports under a special scheme. The difficulty was that their £1m (€1.3m) investment was a low-interest loan to

C&D Foods Ltd operated by the Taoiseach's son, Philip Reynolds. Albert Reynolds insisted that he had ceased any role in running the business in 1987 on appointment to government. Labour were alarmed but agreed to an investigation by Minister for Justice Máire Geoghegan-Quinn, who concluded that all was in order. When Labour accepted the outcome, Michael McDowell of the PDs accused Spring of being 'brain dead'.

Things trundled on. In July 1993, Spring represented Ireland at lengthy and acrimonious negotiations to sign off on the mammoth EC aid plan, otherwise known as structural funds. Spring was left to insist that Ireland had to get £8bn – even though he had utterly nothing to do with the original claim made by Albert Reynolds in Edinburgh the previous December.

A month earlier, after EC Finance Ministers' talks in Luxembourg on 7 June, Ahern had insisted that Ireland would get the £8bn pledged by Albert Reynolds. Moreover, he said he had recently held discussions with EC Commission President, Jacques Delors. Speaking of his talks with Delors, Ahern declared, 'He certainly said nothing to ring any alarm bells.' Indeed that claim was to come back on Ahern. Eventually, Ireland was the only dissatisfied party holding up a package worth some £63bn in total, which had big benefits for all 12 member states. The EC Commissioners and senior officials were furious and there was zero sympathy among the national delegations for a country which was already the biggest per capita beneficiary with a total of £6.5bn. Spring and Ireland's EC Commissioner, Pádraig Flynn, put aside their mutual antipathy and did a major job of combined negotiation. In the early morning of 21 July 1993, Spring announced that he had got £7.85bn in EC aid.

It was near enough to Reynolds' £8bn original claim to save face all around. But this tangle was not quite finished. The following October, when the EC Commission were signing off on their implementation programmes, it emerged that Ireland had in fact got just £7.2bn. Spring rushed back to Brussels and met

Commission President, Jacques Delors, who soon afterwards emerged angrily from the talks only to be met by Irish reporters.

Speaking in English – a language he learnt late in life and rarely used – Delors said, 'I never promised seven point eight billion punts. This is a liar [sic]. I said Ireland would get seven point two billion punts.'

Delors added that he had made all this clear to Bertie Ahern, who had in fact asked him to hold off any announcement of the bad news until the Irish Government published its £20bn National Development Plan a week prior to all this drama. It was remarkable that Delors spoke in terms of 'Irish punts', as he was obviously very keen to make his point in citing Ahern's request.

Later Ahern said that he had no recollection of making any request about delayed announcements to Delors in the margins of a meeting in early October. Yet he conceded that Delors' claims could be the genuine product of a 'misunderstanding'. For his part, Albert Reynolds denounced Delors and said he went back on his word. Flynn too risked getting into hot water by also publicly criticising his Brussels boss. Some Brussels officials said Ireland had in fact been foxed by being presented with a so-called 'fourchette', or a range of funding. The maximum in the range was £7.8bn and the minimum, which was what materialised, was £7.2bn.

Whatever the reality, EC officials just shrugged and got on with their day. Delors' spokesman told reporters that Flynn's criticism was 'just inside the red line' and understandable in all the circumstances.

Life resumed and Ireland had got proportionately the biggest slice of the EC aid cake and the largest ever infusion of overseas cash in the State's history. Thanks at least in part to Reynolds' shenanigans, it was £700m more than what was originally on offer. Spring had played his part without protest. Ireland's approach to EC issues did not always look very pretty but it was often effective.

~ ~ ~ ~ ~

There were other Fianna Fáil–Labour rows. The then Minister for Health, Brendan Howlin, clashed with Bertie Ahern in September 1993 over a nationwide dispute by dental health assistants. Howlin was keen to settle but Ahern, as Minister for Finance, warned that it would break the national pay deal. When the dispute escalated, Ahern – to Howlin's fury – offered to intervene.

This was somehow symptomatic of Ahern at this time as he occasionally showed nostalgia for his Department of Labour and strike-fixing days. Sometimes, chatting socially to reporters, he gloried in reverting to talk about 'retrospection', 'arbitration', 'relativities' and other terms known only unto the industrial relations world.

But such rows and territorial squabbles are the stuff of all governments – even single-party administrations. The Cabinet was backed by a system of programme managers and officials who kept policy matters and legislative details co-ordinated. The system attracted a lot of adverse media comment about 'jobs for the boys' and Labour got more than its share with some commentators arguing that the term 'brother and sister' had taken on a new meaning.

None the less, the Government could also point to some solid achievements. Contrary to business fears about the strong Labour presence, the economy was continuing to strengthen and there was rigorous compliance with the Maastricht Treaty economic guidelines. The Government's peace initiatives were slow and there were reverses. But, as we will see in a later chapter, Albert Reynolds' efforts on Northern Ireland were bearing fruit. This was clearly a government with major potential.

However, the biggest Fianna Fáil–Labour row of all emerged in August 1994. With so many people on holidays, and the news pages largely filled by weak stories, this can be a treacherous time in politics if there is an issue on the boil. Not surprisingly, this major row concerned the Beef Tribunal.

Some weeks earlier, Labour had let it be known that if Albert Reynolds were cited as culpable in the final conclusions of this investigation – which took three years and cost £30m (€38m) – then they would abandon government. Reynolds was enraged and took the public message as an advance slur. The story was printed in the *Sunday Business Post* newspaper and Fergus Finlay identified as the source. Looking back now, Finlay says that what he stated was a simple fact and that he made no secret of being the source of the comments.

'But I was not on a wrecking mission. It was a simple reality that if Albert Reynolds was deemed culpable in the report, Labour could not stay in government with him.'

Tribunal chairman, Mr Justice Liam Hamilton, had finally finished the report and doorstop volumes of it – running to 900 pages apiece – were returned from the printers on Friday, 29 July. Dick Spring was on holiday in Kerry while his adviser, Fergus Finlay, was holidaying with his family in the UK.

Meanwhile, Reynolds was ready and waiting in Government Buildings and had the help of barristers and advisers to make sense of a mammoth report which had neither summary conclusions nor index. Seán Duignan recalls how they had divided it into sections and after a time one of those present told the Taoiseach that he was in the clear.

Reynolds promptly told Duignan to go and tell the political correspondents. However, Duignan was loath to do this because it seemed to him to breach a deal with Labour that there would be no comment or revelation on the report contents until the two parties consulted each other. But Reynolds was insistent that he had lived with blame by innuendo for too long. As a reluctant Duignan went about his job, Fergus Finlay and John Foley, who was Dick Spring's government press officer, suddenly arrived on the scene. Finlay had interrupted his holiday. Rows and recriminations ensued, but Duignan had no option but to follow the Taoiseach's instructions.

What emerged was a blur because Labour managed to convey to the media their rage about the manner in which the Beef Tribunal findings were being revealed. There was no evidence found that Reynolds, or Fianna Fáil, had extended preferential treatment to beef baron, Larry Goodman. In fact, the report did not contradict Reynolds' contention that he acted in the best national interest.

But equally, Mr Justice Hamilton did find that there should have been more investigation and analysis by Government before export credit insurance was extended. The Judge noted that in all probability this would have revealed that some of the beef concerned was 'sourced outside the jurisdiction', offering no real benefit to the Irish economy by insuring it.

Predictably, Des O'Malley, by now retired from the PD leadership, poured cold water on the idea of 'vindication' for Reynolds.

'To characterise the very serious criticisms implicit in the tribunal's report concerning the Taoiseach's actions as "vindication" perverts the ordinary meaning of the words,' O'Malley commented.

Subsequently, Fine Gael made a teasing offer that a rainbow coalition was still an option for Labour. Seán Duignan however suspected that Labour already had made a decision in principle to quit coalition with Fianna Fáil and Albert Reynolds. Privately, Ahern believed that they had probably reached breaking point. He was later to tell friends that 'the Beef Tribunal report was the one'.

~ ~ ~ ~ ~

But as with all politics, events intervened to take the edge off this row for a time. On 31 August 1994, the IRA announced a ceasefire. It was a major achievement for all concerned but particular credit was due to Albert Reynolds for his vision.

Next day, the Dáil debated the Beef Tribunal report and Spring said some harsh things but did not exactly lambaste his

Government colleagues. The Labour leader confined himself to an expression of disappointment at broken trust between his party and Fianna Fáil on the issue, adding a warning that it would take effort on both sides to rebuild trust.

Problems did gather pace in the middle of that month when Albert Reynolds sought to appoint Mr Justice Liam Hamilton, then President of the High Court and author of the Beef Tribunal report, to the post of Chief Justice or head of the Supreme Court. Fine Gael maverick Jim Mitchell, by then a constituency colleague of Ahern's, had to apologise to the Dáil for remarks about Hamilton and promotion for services rendered.

It was also clear that Reynolds wanted to put his Attorney General, Harry Whelehan, in to replace Hamilton as President of the High Court. Yet Spring and his Labour colleagues saw this as another breach of trust. None the less, Albert Reynolds believed there was precedent for appointing the Attorney General to the judiciary in this way, though Fianna Fáil sources believe Labour might have lived with him becoming an ordinary judge of the Court. But Labour were also suspicious of Harry Whelehan because they saw him as a reactionary Catholic who would likely oppose their plans. In particular, they wanted their term in government to change the orientation of the judiciary and make it more liberal.

Labour's views on Whelehan were not helped by the strange events in the spring of 1992 when he was also Attorney General to Albert Reynolds, then in coalition with the PDs. Whelehan had stepped in to stop a 14-year-old pregnant rape victim procuring an abortion in Britain. His action dislodged an enormous politico-legal tangle for Reynolds – known as the X case – which enmeshed with EC policy, as Ireland had secured an anti-abortion protocol be added to the Maastricht Treaty. Whelehan insisted that in this matter he was acting as guardian of the Constitution rather than as the Government's lawyer. The issue, which long pre-dated Whelehan, has since led to several court cases and two multi-part referendums, yet remains unresolved. It was in time to preoccupy Bertie Ahern who has to this day not succeeded in finding a resolution.

Moreover, Labour's reservations about Whelehan were heightened by his role in the summer of 1992 in preventing the Beef Tribunal from questioning ministers or former ministers about Cabinet deliberations. Whelehan successfully argued in the Supreme Court that this breached the sacrosanct tenet of Cabinet confidentiality. But Labour feared in this instance that it hampered efforts to get at the truth.

In the event, Spring proposed Mr Justice Donal Barrington rather than Hamilton for the Supreme Court, but this proved legally impossible because Barrington could not at that stage transfer directly from his post at the EC Court of Justice in Luxembourg. Labour subsequently proposed Ms Justice Susan Denham for High Court President. Soon Labour were making it clear that they would quit government if Reynolds insisted on forcing the Whelehan appointment.

However, Labour were showing abysmally in the opinion polls and Labour backbenchers, fearing a wipe-out, warned Spring that this was no issue on which to pull down a government. In mid-October, in a late-night meeting at Baldonnel military aerodrome, Reynolds and Spring did a deal: Whelehan could become High Court President in return for a new system of appointing judges in future.

The deal, however, was undisclosed and then, a few days later, mayhem ensued. It turned out that an inveterate paedophile priest, Fr Brendan Smyth, had been living in Cavan while wanted in Northern Ireland for child sex offences. In April 1993, the RUC had forwarded nine extradition warrants to the Attorney General's office in Dublin concerning Fr Smyth, where they lay unattended for seven months. Subsequently, Smyth had gone North to face trial voluntarily, where he received four years in prison for offences variously dating back to up to 24 years. Once this became public, Labour revoked the 'Baldonnel deal'.

Afterwards, Bertie Ahern strongly insisted that he did not believe anybody in the Government or the Attorney General's office was covering up for, or trying to protect, a paedophile priest. The reality was that Albert Reynolds was not entirely sure what the word 'paedophile' actually meant. But there were, at all events, lamentable inefficiencies and archaic procedures in the service and those at the top were accountable.

Never the less, Albert Reynolds persisted with Harry Whelehan's appointment as High Court President. Labour withdrew from Government, but it was unclear for a time whether they were resigning or simply on a temporary protest boycott.

Part of the explanation for the delay on the Smyth warrants was caused by legal doubt arising from a long time lapse since Smyth committed the offences. But then it emerged that a similar case had been treated two years earlier involving a cleric named Duggan. He had been extradited to the North without any quibbles over the time lapse between the offences and the court process.

The drama dragged on with an ironic by-product of the Whelehan appointment being that Reynolds now had a totally new Attorney General, Eoghan Fitzsimons, who had to read himself into the tangled affair and provide new legal advice. Fianna Fáil held a melodramatic, ramshackle rolling meeting of their Cabinet ministers on Monday, 14 November, which gave them little direction. It is now known that in the course of that Monday the new Attorney General told the Fianna Fáil Cabinet members all about the Duggan case. Whether anyone grasped the significance of it all at that confused time is still disputed. Yet the Attorney General, Eoghan Fitzsimons, was sent to Harry Whelehan's home to ask him to agree to delay his swearing into office as High Court President for a few days. Whelehan declined, saying it would be inappropriate.

On Tuesday, 15 November, Reynolds went into the Dáil apparently with his preparations unfinished. He made a very conciliatory speech expressing 'regret' at what had happened. He promised major reforms and increased resources for the Attorney General's office, which he admitted was operating a system designed for another era. An intriguing detail of Reynolds' Dáil appearance still remains to be resolved. Attorney General Eoghan Fitzsimons arrived with his considered advice just after the Taoiseach had gone into the Dáil chamber. The document containing the advice was passed through various officials and politicians to Bertie Ahern, sitting in the chamber beside Reynolds. But Ahern never passed it on to Reynolds. He later insisted that this omission was based on lack of thought in the midst of the massive confusion. It is also questionable whether it would have made any difference to Reynolds' contribution. But there are grounds for arguing that it could ultimately have changed things.

Overall, Ahern frankly concedes that their handling of the entire affair was 'a total mess'. Apart from anything else, there were too many people involved, giving each other conflicting advice. Looking back now, a decade later, Ahern told this author of one big lesson he had learnt.

'I've been through an awful lot since. I've been through all of the inquiry stuff and all of the stuff that bounced back about Haughey. But I have to say, I never went back to that "kitchen cabinet thing",' he admits.

Eventually, Labour declared they would definitively quit government if Albert Reynolds did not resign as Taoiseach. Reynolds duly went to Áras an Uachtaráin on 17 November 1994 and presented his resignation to President Robinson. In a further irony, soon afterwards, Harry Whelehan resigned as High Court President, apologising for overlooking the Duggan case and its significance when he explained the Smyth case facts to the Taoiseach.

In his defence, he said he was never made aware of the Smyth extradition warrants before the entire controversy erupted. But he resigned because he did not wish to taint the High Court office with political controversy.

Many in Fianna Fáil felt Reynolds might have survived if the timing had been different. There was a very confused meeting of Fianna Fáil TDs and senators where Duignan records several of them – including Bertie Ahern – as suggesting things might not be over for Reynolds. But Reynolds was in fact finished as Taoiseach and Fianna Fáil leader and somebody wanted to make sure. Indeed Duignan recalls Reynolds' surprise at an RTÉ announcement that a meeting had been fixed for two days later to pick a new leader of Fianna Fáil.

Publicly and unequivocally, Reynolds then announced that he wanted to avoid forcing an election which might destabilise the fledgling Northern Ireland peace process. In a show of support, Ahern later said Reynolds might have been able 'to toughen it out' but deserved credit for not wanting to cause an election.

In summary, two extremely stubborn men – Reynolds and Spring – had between them brought down what was a good functioning government in many respects. Over a decade later, the game has moved on but both sides will haggle over the details for the years to come. Reynolds felt Spring and Labour had tried to reduce him to the role of half-Taoiseach. Spring felt the two parties cut a documented coalition deal and any flashpoints which arose were outside the terms and spirit of that deal.

A new Fianna Fáil leader was to be chosen on Saturday, 19 November 1994. There were mutterings about a Rainbow Government and Labour were non-commital. But every expectation was that Labour would do a new deal with Fianna Fáil led by Bertie Ahern.

~ ~ ~ ~ ~

Bertie Ahern was watching television in the flat overhead the offices at St Luke's late on Sunday night, 4 December 1994. The political discussion programme was focused on the survival chances of John Bruton as Fine Gael leader and did not rate those chances too highly. Ahern happily noted that there was scarcely a mention of himself and the assumption that he would soon be Taoiseach in a renewed deal with Labour. The Dáil vote was just two days away on Tuesday afternoon, 6 December. He switched off the television and went to sleep as he had an early start for an EU finance ministers' meeting in Brussels next morning.

Ahern had been the Fianna Fáil Parliamentary Party's unanimous choice as leader. At 43 years old, he was Fianna Fáil's youngest ever leader and the youngest of the current bunch of party leaders. It was over 17 years since he had started his political career as Fianna Fáil candidate in Dublin-Finglas. His rise was steady, workmanlike and not terribly flash. In days, his political journey would apparently be complete as he acceded to the highest office in the land.

Undoubtedly, Ahern had been greatly helped in the run-up to the leadership election by the support of veteran Brian Lenihan. Though hospitalised for a check-up, Lenihan became a clearing house for political intelligence and never failed to canvass his Fianna Fáil visitors on Ahern's behalf.

Ahern's expected rival was Máire Geoghegan-Quinn who had been a popular Minister for Justice in the Fianna Fáil–Labour Government and a Reynolds' supporter. Other names mentioned in passing were Michael Smith and Dr Michael Woods. Journalists assessed Geoghegan-Quinn's support at about a dozen TDs – one put it at 14. On the day, she withdrew in the interests of unity, however.

Ahern was not just the youngest Fianna Fáil leader – he was also the first to be separated from his wife and in a new relationship. This was in a climate where the Fianna Fáil legacy of its founder, Éamon de Valera, still prevailed. De Valera had written the 1937 Constitution, which still expressly prohibited divorce legislation.

Early in Ahern's first press conference as leader, veteran tabloid journalist, Paddy Clancy, asked him about his marital status. The new Fianna Fáil leader hushed his supporters' angry jeers and prevented parliamentary party chairman, Deputy Joe Jacob, from disallowing the question. Ahern said it was public knowledge that for several years he had been amicably separated from his wife, Miriam. Even so, he said he was glad of the understanding shown him by colleagues. To loud cheers from supporters, Bertie Ahern added that Irish society now took a more enlightened view of people in his situation. Furthermore, he was committed to holding a referendum on divorce, which he believed should be an option in Ireland. But the old Ahern caution kicked in when asked about prospects of renewing coalition with Labour and Dick Spring.

'Whether we're in opposition, or whether we're in government, that's something we're going to take some days to reflect upon,' he said.

Ahern added that he was asking TDs to take soundings in their constituencies. That was an easy one – the public were mystified by the Government break-up and loath to face an election. A *Sunday Independent* opinion poll that weekend showed 43 per cent of people wanted the return of Fianna Fáil–Labour against 19 per cent backing a Rainbow Government. The approval ratings of both Spring and Labour had also dramatically rallied.

Bertie Ahern promised to be a consensus leader and appealed for an end to the sporadic factionalism and heaves, which had characterised the terms of his three predecessors, Jack Lynch, Charlie Haughey and Albert Reynolds. Later he was to be told by Brian Lenihan that the underlying and ongoing fault line in the party dated right back to the resignation of Ahern's hero, Seán Lemass, in December 1966.

Negotiations for a re-fix with Labour were established quickly and doing well. The one real bugbear was establishing an investigation into the entire circumstances surrounding the previous collapse.

So, all the signs were good as Ahern headed for Dublin Airport and Brussels that Monday morning. In the car, he read a page one story in *The Irish Times* by political correspondent Geraldine

Kennedy. It appeared to pick back over the events surrounding the collapse of the Reynolds' Government, but he later insisted that at the time he made light of it.

At the EU Council of Ministers' Building in Brussels Ahern was met by a journalist from the *Evening Herald*, brandishing a faxed copy of the Kennedy article. Yet still he appeared unconcerned. In the course of the day he spoke on the phone with Dick Spring and Brendan Howlin of Labour. Ahern again later recalled that he did not believe much was wrong. Labour had told him they wanted an Attorney General's report arising from the issues in the newspaper article. Still technically Taoiseach, Albert Reynolds was in Budapest and saw a faxed copy of the Attorney General's report but refused authorisation to release it. It was late in the evening before Ahern finally managed to have the report handed over to Labour.

In his book, *The Power Game*, Stephen Collins recalls that gossip had it that Reynolds was enraged on his return and decided to sack Ahern from his government job as acting caretaker Tánaiste. But if that happened, it was quickly rescinded and not discussed later because much larger issues loomed into view.

It was past 2 am on what was now technically, Tuesday 6 December, when Ahern's phone rang at the flat overhead St Luke's constituency offices. He had as usual shunned the prospect of an overnight in Brussels and returned to Dublin. There were little over 12 hours to go to the Dáil vote expected to make him Taoiseach. The caller was Dick Spring to tell him Labour could not renew coalition with Fianna Fáil. He said *The Irish Times* story of the previous morning essentially spelt out that all members of the Fianna Fáil Cabinet knew as much about the paedophile cases as Albert Reynolds had on Monday, 14 November.

The final break with Reynolds came when Labour discovered he had been less than candid about what he knew. They were all – including Ahern – equally culpable, as they all knew of the existence of the Duggan case. There were strong arguments put about in political circles that this was not especially new information. Many in Fianna Fáil believed that Labour simply used it as an excuse to wriggle out of a new link-up with Fianna Fáil, which they thought would not benefit them in the longer run. Besides, Fine Gael were attacking Labour vigorously and with some effect.

To this day, Labour insist that what then and later may have seemed an arcane fact had all the danger of a ticking time bomb. Had they gone back into government, they would soon be publicly told that they did a new deal with Ahern, who was as tainted as Reynolds.

All the while the public struggled to understand with very little success. But Bertie Ahern had no such difficulty comprehending the situation. He had been within 12 hours of becoming Taoiseach – now he was just leader of a rather battered opposition. He had come so near – and yet so far.

9

End of the Rainbow

Eight days later, on 15 December 1994, Bertie Ahern was sitting shell-shocked on the Opposition benches looking at John Bruton's election as Taoiseach. Bruton, the man everybody assumed was finished politically, had taken the top job. Without an election, the Fine Gael leader formed a three-party Rainbow Government along with Labour and Democratic Left, the party he had refused to have any truck with two years previously.

In his own Dáil contribution on that day, Ahern avoided acrimony or embittered personal attacks. The mask of calm and business-as-usual had slipped a few days earlier when Ahern rounded on combative Fine Gael TD Gay Mitchell, who had been barracking outgoing Taoiseach Albert Reynolds. Adopting the belligerent tones of a street fighter, Ahern had barked, 'You're a waffler, a waffler and you've always been a waffler!' It was most uncharacteristic. But now calm was restored and Ahern even reflected that Bruton had come through a tough time and was maybe due a little positive limelight. However, Ahern also reflected that Ireland had seen government configurations like this rainbow alliance in the past at some cost to the public. He especially drove home the point that during the term of the Fine Gael–Labour Coalition of 1982–87 the national debt doubled to £25bn (€32bn). Indeed this theme – that Fine Gael and Labour cannot handle the national economy – is one of Ahern's recurring political stratagems, and people can expect to hear it again and again ahead of the next general election due in 2007.

None the less, friends insist that Ahern bounced back very quickly. Senator Tony Kett recalls meeting him one night, when his appointment as Taoiseach seemed imminent, and having a lot of fun over a drink together, picking a make-believe Cabinet.

'The following night, after the whole thing fell flat on its face, I remember meeting him again. We were having a drink in one of our favourite haunts in Drumcondra and he was totally unfazed. In actual fact, I was more upset about the whole thing than he was. I have to say I saw a side of him that night that I hadn't seen before, but I have often seen since: he is not easily fazed,' Kett recalls.

In their biography of Ahern, journalists Ken Whelan and Eugene Masterson record his own memory of hearing he would not become Taoiseach thus:

> When Dick Spring called at 2 am on Tuesday, 6 December, to break it off I was left shaken. For about four minutes I dropped myself back down on the pillow and said "hell". Within about five minutes I was down in my office and back on the phone ringing around the ministers.

Both privately and publicly, however, this loss of power hurt like hell and it is far more likely that he avoided showing his emotions and threw himself into the job in hand. He had every reason to believe that he was Taoiseach and had even taken to shaping his Cabinet. Friends say that, for months afterwards, he used to take out the news cutting of the Geraldine Kennedy story, which had proved his undoing, and study it. He often wondered at its provenance and many conclude that it is more likely to have come from Fianna Fáil sources.

At a Dáil committee of inquiry into the events surrounding the Government collapse, chaired by Cork Fianna Fáil TD, Dan Wallace, Ahern made it clear who was to blame for the entire thing. Asked directly by constituency rival, Tony Gregory, if he was asserting that he had been undone by unelected backroom people in Labour, Ahern replied:

'I'm afraid that is my conclusion. When I left for Brussels at six o'clock in the morning of Monday, 5 December, I had no reason other than to be optimistic that I would be Taoiseach the following day. I am still a bit bewildered about what changed so much.

The new Fianna Fáil leader appeared on the RTÉ discussion programme, *Questions & Answers*, and again asserted that he had been done down by unelected Labour backroom personnel, including Fergus Finlay and others. Finlay, in his bestselling book, *Snakes & Ladders* recalls being both surprised and hurt by similar criticisms levelled by Reynolds' former adviser, Martin Mansergh, at the committee of inquiry. Unsurprisingly, given the tangle of events and the vagaries of human memory, that committee's findings were inconclusive.

Things took a while to settle down. Ahern delayed naming his front bench until January 1995. Then he unveiled it with great ceremony at the Royal Hospital in Kilmainham. Observers agreed that it was a very conciliatory line-up with room for former Hougheyites and anti-Hougheyites; Reynolds' supporters and opponents; and also some new faces.

From the Reynolds' side, Charlie McCreevy got responsibility for finance; Brian Cowen got agriculture; Noel Dempsey environment; while Michael Smith survived any offence that might have been taken at his real or imagined personal innuendo two years previously. The old Haughey wing was represented by Ray Burke, who was made foreign affairs spokesman. Younger TDs, also identified as Haughey supporters, were included with John O'Donoghue becoming justice spokesman and Dermot Ahern becoming social welfare spokesman.

Clare TD Síle de Valera was given her first front-bench responsibility in Arts, Culture and Heritage, providing a link with her grandfather and party founder, Éamon de Valera. David Andrews, who had been banished from all preferment under Haughey, was also on the team. Mary O'Rourke became deputy leader, enterprise and employment spokeswoman; and his would-be leadership challenger, Máire Geoghegan-Quinn was also included. Cork South-Central TD Micheál Martin, first elected to the Dáil in 1989, became education spokesman.

Relatively quickly, it was appreciated by many within the parliamentary party that Ahern was trying above all else to end the endemic factionalism that had waxed and waned for the previous 29 years and had raged through most of the Haughey years. Veteran Seamus Brennan recalls the state of play as Bertie Ahern took over the leadership.

'The party was riven. There was the residual Haughey gang, the Albert Reynolds gang, and other gangs. Worst of all, the party had only 69 TDs,' Brennan recalls. However, he believes that gradually under Bertie Ahern, Fianna Fáil became 'a genuinely nice place', where there 'wasn't a single cabal'. Additionally, Brennan argues that Ahern has somehow maintained that standard in the succeeding decade of leadership for all the discontents and disappointed egos.

'There are no 10 or 12 people on the inside track. He has managed to keep everybody on the inside track – or maybe there is no inside track,' Brennan says.

It seems more likely, as we will see later, that there is no 'inside track' in Bertie Ahern's Fianna Fáil.

In opposition, Fianna Fáil were deeply unhappy but still much happier than facing the prospect of an election. So the Rainbow Government was not a totally unwelcome development.

'Every Fianna Fáil TD – and I speak for myself as well – was very relieved to see John Bruton elected Taoiseach. The way things worked out, it suited Fianna Fáil to let somebody else in to take the flak for a time,' Limerick East TD Willie O'Dea recalls.

~ ~ ~ ~ ~

Inside the Dáil chamber, Bertie Ahern and his team were making slow headway in trying to dent Bruton's administration.

Progressive Democrat leader, Mary Harney, a formidable debater and public speaker, easily outshone him in the Dáil and his own front-bench team had some difficulty finding their feet.

Never the less, Ahern was very active elsewhere as he began the job of overhauling Fianna Fáil at grassroots level. On this front, almost everyone in the party is in awe of the energy and commitment he showed. Former Agriculture Minister Joe Walsh, active in national politics since 1977 and among those least likely to gush with praise, puts it like this:

'He has extraordinary stamina for grassroots and constituency matters. We all get bored listening to tedium from morning to night. But he literally cannot get enough of it. When it comes to tending the grassroots, he's in a class of his own. Any one of them – Jack Lynch, Des O'Malley, Charlie Haughey – couldn't hold his coat.'

Mary O'Rourke remembers a certain parallel with Charlie's Haughey's notorious 'rubber chicken' circuit in the 1970s, when Haughey ingratiated himself with local party cumainn by attending socials and dinners in the most far-flung parts of the country. But in Ahern's case it was far more programmed and pre-planned. During this period, Pat Farrell was Fianna Fáil general secretary and had had little direct dealing with Ahern prior to his election as Fianna Fáil leader on 19 November 1994. Having worked under the two previous leaders, Haughey and Reynolds, Farrell has no doubt that Ahern was the one most committed to organisational matters.

'He believed there were a huge number of people out there in Fianna Fáil, but they were being underutilised,' Farrell says.

For the first time an electronic database was created holding the name, address and contact details of all 50,000 Fianna Fáil members. Wryly, Farrell notes this fact led to the quip that Fianna Fáil had more members than Democratic Left – now part of government – had voters. According to Farrell, Ahern's first priority was to tour all 41 constituencies then in existence. He had a pretty stock speech about reorganisation, which he gave everywhere. One of his tricks was to ensure that his general secretary was in his line of sight where he invariably cited him by name and pointed to him, and then told the audience that Farrell was in total charge.

'That was very empowering for me. The bottom line for me was that I always felt 100 per cent secure in my decisions. I was never second-guessed,' Farrell recalls.

When it came to candidate selection, some of those decisions were extremely robust and led to a great deal of bitterness. Pat Farrell, as it turned out, was to prove a useful shield for his leader, who strove to avoid direct involvement in any unpleasantness.

Ahern appointed a special constituencies' committee, headed by former EC Commissioner, Ray MacSharry, and with inputs from veteran Tipperary North TD, Michael Smith; former Minister and MEP, Gene Fitzgerald; Ahern's former Dublin-Finglas constituency colleague, Jim Tunney; Michael Murphy, a veteran volunteer and figures expert; assistant general secretary Seán Sherwin; party accountant Seán Fleming; Meath TD and rising Fianna Fáil star Noel Dempsey; and PJ Mara. There were also sporadic inputs from other politicians, including Charlie McCreevy.

These political brains went to work on a constituency-by-constituency basis using all available data to choose candidates. Their approach was clinical and brooked no sentiment about past service to the party. The single premise was simple: who was most likely to win. The committee had an important secondary role however and Farrell's view of that speaks for itself.

'Their work was important in itself. But it also bought us a deal of political cover. In situations where disputes arose, we were able to point to the committee's work,' Farrell says. He also believes that it was the first time in the history of the organisation that decisions on candidates were made 'irrespective of hurt or personal sensibility'.

In 1995, PJ Mara, Haughey's long-time colleague and friend, was appointed Fianna Fáil director of elections. Mara himself insists he is not now and never has been a close friend of Bertie Ahern's. None the less, Mara has been a big political presence in Fianna Fáil since Ahern took over the leadership, after being largely absent during the Reynolds' years. Mara is good humoured, very approachable and much liked by journalists. But, as a heavy-hitter within the Fianna Fáil organisation, he is not universally popular, though he is highly rated by many as a first-class political strategist.

These days Mara works as a public affairs lobbyist and, as a former member of the Seanad, his perks include free parking at Leinster House and access to the Members' Bar, a sort of politicians' inner sanctum. He brushes aside any inferences of having an inside track as a result of these perks and/or his ready access to Government Buildings.

On his personal relationship with Ahern, Mara remarks, 'Nobody can justifiably claim to be close to him. He is very reserved and somewhat aloof. That is how he has been all his life.'

According to Mara, he got the voluntary and unpaid post of director of elections at least partly because he let it be known in Fianna Fáil circles that he would relish the challenge. He adds that Bertie Ahern shared his own view that it was time to break with the established practice of having a senior member of the parliamentary party take on the job. Both agreed that it was better for a more neutral figure who was not compromised by old friendships or rivalries.

At the time, special groups were set up to deal with policy and research. These groups met regularly for intensive preparations over a period of 18 months. Ahern kept in touch with the workings of all these groups by sitting in on meetings at least on a monthly basis.

Much has been made in recent times about the involvement of US political consultants with Fianna Fáil in the 2002 general election. But Pat Farrell says they were involved as far back as 1996, when Fianna Fáil took a radical new look at its research policy.

'I believed the world had moved on considerably, but we were stuck in a model opinion research which hadn't changed in two decades. With the old model you simply asked 1,000 people how they would vote. The result helped us fix where we were in comparison to the others. But what it told us was very limited. You simply confirmed the arithmetic, but not what you needed to do to get the right result. Focus groups were valuable in helping us crack this,' Farrell explains.

The three renowned US political consultants, Bob Schrum, Tad Devine and Mike Donilon, visited Ireland two or three times and advised on focus groups and the interpretation of qualitative research. The bulk of Fianna Fáil's research was done by the firm Behaviour & Attitudes headed by Des Byrne. Both Mara and Farrell agree that what emerged drove home the message that what often preoccupies politicians and political journalists is frequently of minimal interest to potential voters.

~ ~ ~ ~ ~

Bertie Ahern's declaration on his election as Fianna Fáil leader about the need for divorce in Ireland was quickly put to the test. The Rainbow Coalition fixed the 24 November 1995 as the date for a referendum proposing an end to the constitutional ban on divorce in Ireland, in place since 1937.

It was getting on for a decade since his own marriage to Miriam had run into trouble. Yet it is interesting to note the evolution of his thinking on social issues during those years. In his 'Bertie-the-lad' interview published in *Hot Press* magazine in June 1986, Ahern was asked about his views on divorce. The interview was published just three weeks ahead of a referendum, proposed by the Fine Gael–Labour Coalition headed by Garret FitzGerald, which was soundly defeated, at least in part due to the unofficial intervention of Fianna Fáil politicians. Officially, Fianna Fáil remained neutral throughout the 1986 campaign. But Charlie Haughey spoke strongly against the proposal and later conceded that the bulk of Fianna Fáil activists had campaigned in a private capacity against divorce. In fact, Haughey said he was not surprised the proposition was defeated, but was surprised by the 2:1 scale of the defeat.

During this period, Ahern was also the Fianna Fáil Chief Whip who ensured all party TDs opposed Fine Gael–Labour contraception legislation a year earlier and played a strong role in the expulsion of Des O'Malley for breaking ranks on the issue. The Coalition measure ended the requirement for non-medical contraceptives to be restricted to married couples and with a doctor's prescription. In the interview Ahern was asked about couples living together, and replied:

'Well, I would rather see marriages. But I know loads of people who are just 'shackin' up'. I'll tell you this, if the referendum is passed, it won't make much difference to them.'

Moreover, he said that for the future he would not like to see his two daughters, then aged six and four, living with a partner to whom they were not married. Even so, he showed a certain 'live-and-let-live' attitude on the issue.

'I have two experiences close to me, involving young people – people who are very close to me who are living together – and I'd have to say it hasn't done them any harm. I think they will end up married. They haven't done any of the mad things people say you are going to do.'

In the run-up to that June 1986 referendum, there were reports that pro-divorce campaigners were claiming Ahern's support. Though he strongly rejected this idea, he conceded that he had sympathy for the difficulties faced by separated people in new relationships. He told the *Hot Press* interviewer that the social fall-out from the acceptance of divorce might be exaggerated.

'People are saying if the yes's win, you are going to have a whole load of destabilised marriages, which I don't believe,' he said.

It is fair to assume that in June 1986 Ahern felt the time had not yet come to make divorce available and, at all events, in

Opposition, Charlie Haughey's Fianna Fáil opposed everything the Government proposed. Ahern's stance was also in keeping with Fianna Fáil's pragmatism, which involved divining and then following the public mood while avoiding alienating any significant section of the electorate.

Another interesting feature of that *Hot Press* interview was his view on homosexuality. Quite frankly, he said he had never met any homosexuals and had not followed the marathon legal case brought by gay rights campaigner, David Norris, for the decriminalisation of homosexuality.

'It's like a lot of Irish crimes – is it a crime? Does anyone go near them?' Ahern asked in a comment reminiscent of Haughey's 'Irish solution to an Irish problem' when speaking about contraception.

The Norris case culminated in a 1988 ruling by the European Court of Human Rights instructing Ireland to decriminalise homosexuality. It was Ahern's leadership rival, Máire Geoghegan-Quinn, who as Minister for Justice finally put through the enabling legislation in June 1993.

In preparation for the November 1995 divorce referendum, Minister for Law Reform, Mervyn Taylor of Labour, laid down a body of law dealing with marriage, separation, children and property rights. Shortcomings on these issues, especially succession law gaps, had proved a major factor in divorce being rejected in June 1986.

Clearly, the proposal was problematic for Ahern and Fianna Fáil. Ahern biographers, Whelan and Masterson, note that traditional party activists were in a majority against divorce. One survey showed that 49 per cent of Fianna Fáil voters were against to 38 per cent in favour of divorce. One of the strident divorce opponents inside the Fianna Fáil Parliamentary Party was his own brother, Noel Ahern, a TD for Dublin North-West since November 1992. Ultimately, Ahern was also obliged to expel Limerick West TD, Michael Noonan, from the parliamentary party for abstaining in the Dáil vote on a referendum.

Ahern came out strongly and unequivocally in favour of a 'Yes', though he tempered it by calling for the strongest possible restrictions to be specified in the Constitution. This meant there would have to be another referendum before any future liberalisation could take effect. 'The spirit of majoritarianism in Ireland has had unfortunate effects,' Ahern warned. He declared the vote would be a defining moment in showing how Irish people could respect minority rights.

On the day, the measure was carried by a hair's breadth. Six out of 10 voters went to the polls and 819,000 voted 'yes' to 810,000 saying 'No'. The margin in favour equated to little more than half of 1 per cent. On polling day, heavy rains in the rural west of the country contrasted with finer weather in the urban east, perhaps influencing the turnout and outcome. It is also clear that Ahern took a strong personal stance. One is left to reflect what the outcome might have been had his personal circumstances been different.

~ ~ ~ ~ ~

For more than a year in advance of the June 1997 general election, Fianna Fáil knew where they were going to get their posters and knew who was going put them up and where.

'The result was that we had all our posters up on major routes within 48 hours of the election being called – something which was outside our control. The Government parties, which called the election, had not their posters up until much later,' the Fianna Fáil general secretary boasts.

There was also a minute-by-minute plan devised a year ahead of the election for the Taoiseach's tours and other rallies. Former Army Commandant, Maurice O'Donoghue, had a major input here. The planning ensured that if 100 people were to be at a named crossroads to greet the Taoiseach at a specific time, they were there and not at another one some distance away. In addition, a constituency-by-constituency book of issues and problems was compiled on items such as a hospital or other services issue. A pre-prepared response was worked out and on hand for use.

The candidate choices were the source of some bitterness, which lingers in some areas to this day. What turned out to be one of the easier ones was three-seat Cork North-West, which had been dominated by Fine Gael who held two out of three seats for over 20 years. Farrell says that they were repeatedly told that there was only one suitable candidate; the sitting TD Donal Moynihan from Ballymakeera. Eventually, central office added Michael Moynihan (no relation) from Kiskeam in the northern end of the constituency. Both Moynihans succeeded and were re-elected in 2002.

The five-seat Wicklow constituency, where a badly divided Fianna Fáil party held just one seat, proved a bigger problem. Farrell used the rules to put in an interim executive to run the constituency and Dick Roche, promoted to Cabinet in September 2004, ultimately won a seat alongside veteran Joe Jacob.

But these were not all happy tales. In Kerry South, the Fianna Fáil selection convention – held on 27 October 1996 in the Gleneagle Hotel, Killarney – selected two candidates: outgoing TD, John O'Donoghue from Cahirciveen, and Brian O'Leary of Killarney, who was the son of veteran TD, John O'Leary, retiring after 30 years' service. A third contender, Jackie Healy-Rae of Kilgarvan, lost out and began a campaign to be added to the ticket. He was a veteran county councillor and Kerry backroom strategist who had worked for over 30 years for Fianna Fáil. Healy-Rae took his case directly to Bertie Ahern and travelled to Dublin to meet him on 14 February 1997. Donal Hickey's remarkable book, *The Mighty Healy-Rae: A Biography*, tells how Ahern warmly welcomed the Kilgarvan man and listened patiently as he explained his case. Healy-Rae concluded with an impassioned plea to Ahern not to force him to stand as an 'independent FF' candidate.

Then he said, "Jack that'll never happen. I'll be meeting Ray MacSharry on Monday morning and that'll be all sorted out." We shook hands and I left his office. The next contact I had with him was when one of his officials rang on his behalf after I was elected [as 'independent FF'] and they wanted me to support the Government.

The incident aptly sums up Ahern's use of headquarters and the constituency committee as a shield. He had no intention of interfering with Pat Farrell or the MacSharry Committee's work – but equally he had no intention of telling this to the people in the firing line. Another veteran Fianna Fáil TD tells of contacting Ahern about what he felt was a very unfair constituency canvass divide.

'He muttered something about "those guys in Mount Street" and promised to mediate. And that was the last I ever heard of it.'

However, the former Fianna Fáil general secretary is unrepentant about the hardline stance taken against Healy-Rae. On the contrary, he argues that without being rebuffed by the party, the Kilgarvan man would not have been elected. In fact, Fianna Fáil's rejection allowed Healy-Rae to harness dissident political activists across the constituency whose support he never would have got as a regular party candidate. Farrell describes this as the 'Seán Ó Neachtain' effects using the June 2004 case of the Connemara-based Fianna Fáil MEP who benefited from being profiled as 'the man Dublin were doing down'. As a native of Leitrim himself, Farrell finds it ironic that Fianna Fáil's headquarters was being portrayed as 'Dublin', when in reality there were only two Dubliners, Seán Sherwin and PJ Mara, involved in candidate selection.

Pat Farrell also sets great store by two morale-boosting Fianna Fáil by-election successes on 3 April 1996. The first saw Brian Lenihan Jnr elected to the seat held by his late father and former presidential candidate, Brian, who had died in late 1995. The second saw Cecilia Keaveney elected in Donegal North-East to a seat held since 1948 by maverick Neil Blaney, who had been sacked along with Haughey in the 1970 Arms Crisis and who died in November 1995.

Farrell's interest in these two contests is heightened by the fact that in each case it was Fine Gael transfers which carried the Fianna Fáil candidates home. It augured well for their hopes of vote management and optimising transfers in the upcoming general election.

On the subject of transfers, Seamus Brennan noted that under Ahern's leadership the party was more prone to getting transfers because he did not incite the antipathy in other party supporters that Haughey and even Reynolds had done. Indeed, Farrell believes that Ahern had brought a new dimension to the party's approach to campaigning.

'Bertie put as much emphasis on chasing number twos and threes and so on, as he did on getting number ones,' Farrell says.

~ ~ ~ ~ ~

Then, just when everything appeared to be falling into place for Bertie Ahern and Fianna Fáil, chaos descended. Charlie Haughey, Ahern's mentor and patron, who had sloped out of Irish public life with quiet dignity in February 1992, was suddenly back in the limelight for all the wrong reasons.

Haughey had stayed on in the Dáil until the November 1992 general election, when he quit politics altogether and his Dublin North-Central seat was taken by his son, Seán Haughey. The Fianna Fáil National Executive had hosted a dinner for him on 1 October 1992 and presented him with an array of gifts. Haughey, who had quoted Shakespeare's *Othello* in his Dáil valedictory address as Taoiseach, chose Yeats on this occasion.

Think where man's glory most begins and ends,
And say my glory was I had such friends.

Well, it turned out that Charlie Haughey had many 'friends' indeed. In fact, Haughey was barely a week out of office as

Taoiseach when one of those friends, supermarket tycoon Ben Dunne, was arrested in Miami under the influence of cocaine and in the company of a prostitute. The incident dislodged an internal Dunne family feud and investigations, which led others in the family to discover that Ben Dunne had given over £1m (€1.3m) to Charlie Haughey.

Haughey steadfastly rebuffed all attempts by the Dunnes to recover the money and forcefully denied ever receiving any donations from Ben Dunne. However, pressure mounted on Haughey, especially in December 1996 when the Rainbow Government requested Judge Gerard Buchanan to investigate irregular payments by Dunne to Tipperary North TD, Michael Lowry, who had been forced to quit as Minister for Transport and Energy in the Rainbow Government the previous month.

The Lowry affair was originally greeted with glee in Fianna Fáil but soon the party hierarchy realised that the Dunne case had very serious implications for them also. Ultimately, it set in train a series of events that had ramifications for many of the leaders of Irish business, especially in relation to their less than frank relations with the Revenue Commissioners.

Word began to circulate in political and journalistic circles that a very senior former Fianna Fáil politician had received over £1m from Dunne. But the speculation was mixed with a degree of disbelief. One senior civil servant summed up the mood by telling this writer at the time, 'Look, Haughey was far too cute to be caught in the past. Do you think he's going to be caught now that he's out of politics and retired?'

But that was exactly what happened. Shortly afterwards, Haughey was named by the satirical magazine the *Phoenix* as the recipient of the Dunne money. Judge Buchanan's report led to the establishment of a tribunal of inquiry chaired by Mr Justice Brian McCracken of the High Court to examine the cases of Dunne, Lowry and Haughey.

In dramatic circumstances, and under obvious pressure from his own lawyers whom he had misled, Haughey was to confess all about donations from Ben Dunne totalling some £1.3m (€1.7m) to the McCracken Tribunal in July 1997. But by then Bertie Ahern had been elected Taoiseach.

In hindsight, it was some feat by Bertie Ahern. The man who had led Fianna Fáil for over 12 years, and to some personified the party for that period, was suddenly at the centre of major scandal which called his integrity into question. Ahern was not just his successor as leader – he was Haughey's protégé and chief lieutenant for most of his years as leader. How could Ahern avoid being fatally tainted as he faced into an election in the summer of 1997?

Haughey's wealth had been the subject of widespread sporadic speculation down the years. One popular and widespread theory was that Haughey made money from land speculation in the 1950s and 1960s, possibly benefiting from his political connections to direct his investments. That was unethical, but probably somehow acceptable given the political mores of the time. Thereafter, it was assumed that he had invested shrewdly and was extremely well fixed financially.

Albert Reynolds recalls his utter astonishment at the revelations surrounding Haughey receiving cash gifts from a wide variety of business people totalling some £9m (€11.5m).

'I had no clue of anything like that at all. In the back of my mind I believed he had made money from land and property speculation. He was well off and I reckoned he would have been a shrewd investor. It just never entered my mind.'

The weekend of the Fianna Fáil Ard Fheis in April 1997 was a pretty troubled one for Bertie Ahern. The McCracken Tribunal was due to hear Dunne's evidence the following week and it was well known that he would say he gave huge sums to Charlie Haughey. By now Haughey was 'the ghost at the Fianna Fáil feast' and had ignored public requests by prominent former colleagues – including Ahern – to put his hand up and acknowledge his link to Dunne.

'Haughey could have made a public statement and the whole thing would have been something of a seven-day wonder. Instead we have months of it and tribunals and God knows what else,' one prominent Fianna Fáil TD told this writer at that time.

In his presidential address to Ard Fheis delegates on Saturday evening, 19 April 1997, Ahern sought to put as much distance between his old mentor and party leader as possible. He pledged a new set of ethical guidelines for all party members and everyone in public life.

> We will not tolerate any deviation from the benchmarks of honour, at local level or in Leinster House, be it in the past, present or future. No one is welcome in this party if they betray public trust. I say this and mean this with every fibre of my being. We will write new ethics standards and independent enforcement into the law of this land.

As we will see later, Ahern now says he found it hard to say such harsh things at the Fianna Fáil Ard Fheis. He says he regrets having to 'dump' his old patron and mentor, but says he had no choice.

The surprising thing now at this distance is that Ahern and Fianna Fáil were insistent that the McCracken Tribunal's work should not be interrupted during the imminent election. They wanted all details of Fine Gael man Michael Lowry's case put into the public domain. In fact, the governing parties were somewhat inhibited in using the Haughey revelations as a stick to beat Ahern and Fianna Fáil. Along with the Lowry factor there was also a danger of being accused of prejudging the judicial inquiry which they set up.

Bruton's Government would have liked to postpone the election until after Haughey had given his evidence. But the furore caused by Fianna Fáil seemed to disabuse them of that idea. In the end, John Bruton dissolved the Dáil on 15 May 1997 and polling day was fixed for 6 June. The McCracken Tribunal delayed taking evidence until after the election.

~ ~ ~ ~ ~

Pat Farrell freely admits that the Haughey revelations were a devastating blow to Fianna Fáil at all levels as they prepared for a general election in 1997.

'It was on a scale that was difficult to comprehend. And just when you thought that was it – out came something else. There was disbelief across the organisation.'

Despite these criticisms, Farrell retains some loyalty to Haughey and insists that any negative remarks be leavened with the view that his former boss was a man of some vision and ability. He is also keen to stress that Haughey was not, in his experience, the ogre as has been depicted elsewhere, though he did not suffer fools gladly.

'In dealings with Haughey I found him at all times totally professional. In meetings I learnt it was best to be brief, be focused – be gone,' Farrell sums up.

In many instances, decent veteran Fianna Fáil campaign workers suffered the indignity of being abused on doorsteps and reproached as representing 'a shower of gangsters'. None the less, the party effort soldiered on.

Both Pat Farrell and PJ Mara warn that in hindsight the scale of the Fianna Fáil challenge in 1997 risks being largely forgotten. The Rainbow Government had done a good job and the three parties hung together well, perhaps for the very good reason that they had nowhere else to go. John Bruton's Fine Gael were appreciative of a very lucky break against the run of play; Labour were careful not be seen as serial government wreckers; Democratic Left were keen to show that a small far-left party could behave responsibly and do real politics.

At the first sign of difficulty there was swift action. Popular Minister of State for Finance Phil Hogan was promptly sacked for being held ultimately responsible for the leaking of the 1995 Budget and three months later another Fine Gael Minister, Hugh Coveney, was sacked for lobbying on behalf of his family firm. Even the heavy blow of the Lowry affair was swiftly dealt with by his prompt sacking. This Coalition cohesion was to carry through to the end of the administration and beyond to the general election, where they presented a united front.

The economy was coming on in leaps and bounds and Ireland's first-ever Labour Minister for Finance, Ruairí Quinn, remained committed to the Maastricht public finance rules. The Rainbow Government ran an effective EU Presidency in the second half of 1996 and Quinn distinguished himself in leading difficult single currency negotiations.

Again Farrell and Mara agree that there was a strong view that Fianna Fáil were headed for an unprecedented second election defeat. Northern Ireland and the economy were posited as the two election issues, but neither was capturing the public imagination hugely. The reality was that the election was something of a popularity contest and Ahern, buoyed up by superior logistics and planning and in spite of the 'Haughey factor', was quickly in the lead. Indeed, Farrell insists that Ahern's pleasant personality and popularity was the decisive factor. 'The trump card was Bertie Ahern's personal approach with people on the campaign trail,' he says.

Fine Gael leader John Bruton went about mainly by train with the result that for long periods he was closeted in a railway carriage with a group of aides and journalists. Meanwhile, Ahern took to the road by a combination of aeroplane, helicopter and car. This maximised his visibility and the key feature of the whole campaign: photo opportunities.

In this respect, Farrell says the job was to ensure that Ahern soaked up as many of these as possible. More importantly, the handlers set out to ensure that no negative photos were taken. These included wearing hard hats or hairnets on factory visits or being presented with a glass of champagne by well-wishers – the more so since Ahern only drinks beer. On one occasion, Farrell and Ahern abandoned the car and ran through a traffic-clogged Dublin to be photographed with movie star Sylvester Stallone at a promotion for his Planet Hollywood Restaurant on Stephen's Green, which opened later in the year.

There was also a bitter row with RTÉ over the assignment of journalists to the two main leaders. Ahern had Charlie Bird, one of RTÉ's highest profile reporters, while Bruton was assigned Joe O'Brien – a true professional to his fingertips – but with only a fraction of Bird's oomph and ego. Fine Gael complained bitterly as Bird's notoriety was such that on occasion he generated more buzz around the country than Ahern did. Indeed, Farrell argues that the 'Bird bonus' only came into play because things were going well.

'I have a very clear view on this. Charlie Bird creates excitement and hype where he goes. That was a help. But if we had a bad campaign, Charlie Bird's presence would have heightened that and compounded our problems. The simple reality was that we had a good campaign and Charlie Bird's presence did give that a further lift,' Farrell argues.

Fianna Fáil strategists also decided that the Democratic Left card was the one to play when it came to chasing the farmers' vote, much of which traditionally went to Fine Gael. They took up billboard slots in the vicinity of marts, and in some cases inside marts, and highlighted some glib comments about farmers by Democratic Left leader Proinsias De Rossa. This generated a row within a row, giving the poster campaign a level of publicity money could not buy.

Yet if Fianna Fáil were going from strength to strength, the same could not be said for their potential coalition partners, the Progressive Democrats. In effect, the PDs handed a gift to the Rainbow by pledging to cut 25,000 public service jobs. The *Star* newspaper caught the public mood by remarking that they were talking about cutting 100 jobs per week for the next five years. This was compounded by another gaffe by PD leader Mary Harney who made disparaging comments about unmarried mothers and their dependence on State support. Eventually, Ahern fixed a meeting with Harney for the Green Isle Hotel on Dublin's Naas Road for

25 May. The word was spread to journalists that Harney had agreed the job cuts idea was a mistake and pledged to work more closely with Fianna Fáil.

By the end of May, it was clear that Fianna Fáil might just about shade it; the doubt focused on the strength of the PDs. Then Fianna Fáil had a small setback when Ahern was deemed to have lost a televised debate with Bruton. There was also controversy when the *Irish Independent* carried an eve-of-polling page-one comment piece urging voters to choose Fianna Fáil.

Even so, when the votes were counted, Fianna Fáil had 77 TDs and the PDs had four. The Rainbow bloc of Fine Gael/Labour/Democratic Left had a total of 75 seats. Crucially, the balance of power rested with some of the 10 Independent deputies. Ahern had added nine extra TDs to the tally achieved by Reynolds in November 1992. The really remarkable thing was that Fianna Fáil had just 39.33 per cent of the poll compared with 39.11 per cent achieved by the party in 1992. Equally, Fianna Fáil had 44 per cent of the poll in 1989 and only returned the same number of TDs as Ahern in 1997. Under Ahern, Fianna Fáil's era of successful vote management had arrived.

In Ahern's own four-seat Dublin Central constituency, the news was also good, as newcomer Marian McGennis took a second seat for Fianna Fáil. In volume terms, Ahern had the third-highest vote in the country with 12,175 in total. But in multiple of quota terms, it was equivalent to 1.7 quotas and the best performance in the country.

Others elected in Dublin Central were Independent Tony Gregory, now a veteran of six general elections, and Fine Gael stalwart Jim Mitchell. Nationally, Fine Gael fared well with 54 TDs, and like Fianna Fáil an increase of nine on their 1992 performance. But Labour got a drubbing, dropping from 33 TDs to 17 and evidently paying a heavy price for coalescing with Fianna Fáil and later with the Rainbow. Equally, the PDs had a terrible election, dropping from 10 to just four deputies. None the less, it was fortunate for them that Fianna Fáil needed them to make up the numbers. The Green Party had just two TDs but in shades of things to come, Sinn Féin returned their first TD for many years.

Bertie Ahern needed just three more votes to secure his election as Taoiseach. Very soon it became clear that he would get them. On 26 June 1997, he was elected Taoiseach. It was 20 years and nine days since he had begun his political journey by being first elected a Fianna Fáil TD and he was approaching his 46th birthday.

10

Not His Best Decision

Sipping tea at Dublin Castle, Bertie Ahern agonised over whether Ray Burke should be in or out of his new Cabinet. It was mid-morning on 26 June 1997, and he and colleagues had just attended the religious service which marked the start of a new Dáil and Seanad term. That afternoon he was due in the Dáil to be elected Taoiseach and shortly afterwards he would have to name his government. Though warned to shun Ray Burke, who was the subject of a persistent whispering campaign about planning corruption, Ahern felt it was not that simple. He was absolutely sure who the other ministers would be; he just couldn't decide what to do about Burke.

Ahern crossed the room and approached Burke to ask him for perhaps the tenth, and now definitely, the last time, 'Ray, are you sure there's absolutely nothing in this?'

Having eyeballed his party leader, Burke then said, 'No, everything is fine.' It was the same message Burke had repeatedly given to Ahern and to Fianna Fáil emissaries, such as PJ Mara and Chris Wall, Ahern's constituency fixer, when they questioned him about the planning corruption rumours. Finally, the Taoiseach-designate relented – Ray Burke would be named the new Minister for Foreign Affairs. That decision would soon bring great trouble down on the Fianna Fáil–Progressive Democrat Coalition.

The days between polling day, 6 June, and the Taoiseach's election had been filled with frantic negotiations. Long before the election, Labour had rebuffed Fianna Fáil overtures on the prospects of another coalition. Though Ahern, the eternal pragmatist, was prepared to forget the recriminations of December 1994, if it meant a passage to power. On 12 April, Dick Spring had informed Labour Party conference delegates that they could not coalesce with Fianna Fáil–PDs after the upcoming election. Instead, the election would be a battle between the Rainbow Government and the two main opposition parties.

'Centre-left against centre-right – let it be,' the Labour leader had announced.

In all circumstances, Fianna Fáil had done as well as anyone could have expected, going from 68 to 77 TDs. The problem however was that the PDs' vote had imploded and they now had just four TDs compared to the 10 after the previous election. Ahern quickly deployed all his conciliatory skills to open negotiations with some of the so-called 'FF gene pool' of Independent TDs, and indeed most observers believed he would succeed.

Bertie Ahern's creaky three-legged stool government began to have solid support from the three Fianna Fáil-friendly Independents who voted for him as Taoiseach on 26 June. In Kerry South, Jackie Healy-Rae's post-election told-you-so rhetoric quickly switched to hard-headed bargaining. Rejecting the idea of joining a grouping of Independent TDs, he quickly calculated that Ahern had the numbers to put together the most stable government.

Healy-Rae, Mildred Fox of Wicklow and Harry Blaney of Donegal North-East had held a quiet meeting together at the Lucan Spa Hotel, outside Dublin, on 16 June and found common cause. They negotiated separately with Fianna Fáil and each had several successful meetings with Bertie Ahern. There were no deals running into hundreds of millions but all were satisfied that they could show results to their constituents in terms of roads, schools, bridges and other projects.

All three Independent TDs were also guaranteed access to ministers in case of problems, extra secretarial back-up and a senior civil servant was appointed to liaise with them. It was all very reasonable and essentially meant their support was secured. Special treatment accorded the PDs and the three Independents caused considerable jealousy among some Fianna Fáil backbench TDs who felt at once taken for granted and excluded. In the medium to longer term this led to public dissent and a loosening of Fianna Fáil's previously rigorous discipline. But it all gave Ahern the stability he needed to carry on.

Ahern had squared away one opposition vote by getting the necessary agreement to have the 'Father of the House', Séamus Pattison, a Labour TD for Carlow-Kilkenny since 1961, elected as Ceann Comhairle.

On the day, Ahern was elected Taoiseach defeating Fine Gael leader, John Bruton, by 85 votes to 78. The 85 Ahern voters included the 77 Fianna Fáil TDs, the four PDs, three Independents seen to have Fianna Fáil links – Harry Blaney, Mildred Fox and Jackie Healy-Rae – and Sinn Féin's new Cavan-Monaghan TD, Caoimhghín Ó Caoláin.

The level of change in Irish politics can be gauged from the fact that it was the first time in 10 years that a Taoiseach and Government were elected cleanly on the first day of a new Dáil session. Proceedings after the previous two elections in 1992 and 1989 involved prolonged periods of negotiations with caretaker administrations remaining in place.

There were few surprises as six Fianna Fáil frontbenchers were brought into Cabinet and seven former ministers returned. Mary Harney was appointed Ireland's first woman Tánaiste and also given responsibility for the Department of Enterprise, Trade and Employment. She was joined in the Government by PD colleague and Galway-West veteran, Bobby Molloy, officially described as Minister of State to the Government working in the Department of the Environment. In practice, he was a 'super-junior minister' systematically attending Cabinet but not voting, though he did enjoy the privilege of having a State car and driver.

The PDs did very well given their depleted numbers, as Dublin South TD Liz O'Donnell became Minister of State at the Department of Foreign Affairs with responsibility for Overseas Development. They also received four of the Taoiseach's 11 Seanad nominees.

As the new Fianna Fáil deputy leader, Mary O'Rourke, lined up for a photograph with her nephews and fellow party TDs, Brian Lenihan Jnr and Conor Lenihan, she joked that if the Lenihan family had achieved just one more TD they could also have had ministers, junior ministers and senators.

The largesse extended to the junior coalition partner seemed excessive to some within Fianna Fáil. However, it was to prove a good investment as, combined with a bad election fright, it ensured the PDs were to remain locked into coalition despite the problems to come. Ahern prided himself on keeping good relations with the PDs; he had negotiated well with them in 1989 and 1991 and believed in including them as best he could. For her part, Mary Harney showed signs of wanting to atone for her election gaffe about cutting public service jobs by telling the Dáil that nurses, teachers and Gardaí had nothing to fear and that she wanted a dynamic public service.

In a spirit of reform, Ahern undertook a substantial reorganisation of departments. He merged the Department of Equality and Law Reform into the Department of Justice and appointed newcomer, John O'Donoghue of Kerry South as Minister there.

O'Donoghue had done well as opposition justice spokesman by successfully proposing a new Criminal Assets Bureau to seize the crime barons' assets. This arose in the aftermath of the gangland killing of campaigning journalist, Veronica Guerin, in June 1996. In a mark of respect, Ahern pointed out that the Dáil had reconvened on the anniversary of her death. Outgoing Minister for Justice, Nora Owen of Fine Gael had had a miserable time in office as O'Donoghue excoriated her for every difficulty she faced. Yet he had done less well in proposing that Ireland adopt the New York 'zero tolerance' approach to combating crime.

More old faces were back in the Cabinet. Mary O'Rourke took over a new Department of Public Enterprise, which merged the Departments of Transport, Energy and Communications. Reynolds loyalists were included with Kildare veteran, Charlie McCreevy becoming Minister for Finance, and Laois-Offaly TD Brian Cowen becoming Minister for Health. Long-time Haughey-supporter, Dr Michael Woods, became Minister for the Marine.

The Cork area, having delivered big seat gains, was rewarded with two ministers. Cork South-Central TD Micheál Martin became Minister for Education, and Joe Walsh of Cork South-West once again became Minister for Agriculture. Veteran Reynolds' backer, Michael Smith of Tipperary North, was not on the first team, but was appointed Minister of State at the Department of Enterprise and Employment with responsibility for science and technology. According to Smith, there was no rancour about controversies past as Ahern assured him of an early call up to Cabinet if a vacancy occurred.

Having argued his way beyond the job of a 'senior junior ministry', Seamus Brennan got as far as the Cabinet room. As Government Chief Whip, he could not vote on decisions but at least was close to the action. His painstaking conciliatory work over the coming five years was to prove invaluable to Ahern's minority coalition, especially in maintaining the support of the Independent TDs.

All in all, it appeared a cautious enough choice with almost all the ministers getting posts they had shadowed in opposition. Observers wondered if Ahern had not given hostages to fortune with past promises and criticisms coming back to haunt those now in power.

The announcement of his new team, however, hit a snag straight away. Ahern had told the Dáil that the new Minister for Defence, David Andrews, would also have responsibility for EU affairs under the aegis of the Minister for Foreign Affairs, Ray Burke. The Taoiseach added that Andrews would also 'assist' Burke at the Northern Ireland talks. Immediately, the idea was challenged from the Opposition benches by Fine Gael leader, John Bruton, and Labour leader, Dick Spring. Together they argued that it was not possible or lawful for one minister to be under the direction of another. Heeding their concerns, Ahern relented and abandoned the idea of linking departments.

It was a lucky let-off for Ahern. Apart at all from the legal and constitutional difficulties involving the Department of Defence in EU affairs, it would have given the entirely wrong signal to those who warned about threats to Irish military neutrality. Soon Ahern would also do an about-face on a promise in opposition to hold a referendum on Ireland joining the NATO-linked 'Partnership for Peace' (PFP).

Clearly, it was not the most sure-footed start to Ahern's new role as Taoiseach and was grist to the mill for those who continued to insist that he was not up to the top political job in the land. But worse was to follow.

~ ~ ~ ~ ~

There is a Dáil bar story about Ray Burke's father, Paddy Burke, apparently missing the funeral Mass of an important constituent back in the 1950s, much to the glee of his local rivals already smugly ensconced in the church pews. But the story goes that the rivals' glee was short-lived as the priest arrived on the altar only to be followed by a solemn-faced Paddy Burke carrying the holy water container. Thus the man they called 'the Bishop' had upstaged his opponents yet again. That piece of political folklore may or may not be true. However, it is mirrored by another story about Ray Burke – also concerning a funeral – which a veteran rural Fianna Fáil TD swears is true.

> Soon after Bertie Ahern was elected leader of Fianna Fáil, we were all at a big Fianna Fáil funeral at some big church on the northside of Dublin. All the boys were there but there was no sign of Burke showing. Then Bertie's car arrived and who steps out first only Burke. We all knew then the lie of the land.

In 1973, Raphael P Burke, known as Ray, succeeded his father, 'the Bishop,' to a Dáil seat held by Burke Snr for almost 30 years. As early as 1974 there were reports of planning irregularities in North Dublin and there followed a Garda investigation into Ray Burke. However, nothing came of the inquiries, Burke survived and his political career prospered.

Burke was not, as is now commonly thought, originally a Charlie Haughey loyalist. In the 1979 leadership election which followed Lynch's departure, Burke voted for George Colley and against Haughey. Later he sided against Haughey in one of the heaves but was retained as a member of government and held several senior posts under Haughey after 1987.

Though engaging company and capable of great charm, Burke was always one of the Fianna Fáil tough guys respected more than liked. One memorable story relates to a by-election in Dublin West in 1982. As Minister for Environment, he ordered the planting of young trees and shrubs in one estate, and then after Fianna Fáil lost the election he promptly ordered their removal in reprisal for the voters' ingratitude.

Among the eight dropped by Albert Reynolds in February 1992, Burke was strongly defended by PJ Mara soon after his sacking. The former Haughey press secretary, and future Ahern director of elections, described Burke as one of the few among those sacked to have a political future. The friendship between Mara and Burke was frequently commented upon and indeed

Burke was the only politician present at a farewell function for Mara in 1992.

Seasoned Fianna Fáil politicians believe that Burke was returned to the centre of things by Ahern – after winning the leadership in November 1994 – for a number of reasons. Burke provided some old guard credibility for such a young leader and was a link to the Haughey era. Moreover, he had backed Ahern's leadership ambitions and encouraged him to stand against Albert Reynolds in February 1992. Above all, Burke was an able politician who had a great way of making himself useful and working his passage.

As opposition spokesman on foreign affairs, Burke struck a strident tone of not caving in to Northern Unionists' demands. He also adopted a somewhat sceptical voice about EU defence ambitions and was behind Ahern's pledge to hold a referendum on Ireland's PFP membership. In addition, Burke was among the first of the Fianna Fáil politicians in opposition to visit Brussels to meet senior policy-makers and European Parliament members.

Various members of the parliamentary party at the time watched with interest Ahern's deliberations about whether or not to appoint Burke to Government in June 1997. These deliberations included contacts with senior Gardaí and repeated questioning of Burke as outlined above. Notoriously, the Fianna Fáil leader delegated his then Chief Whip, Dermot Ahern, to go to London and meet a builder reputed to have given a large donation to Burke. The builder, Joseph Murphy Jnr, however told the Fianna Fáil emissary that no money was paid to Burke in return for favours. Dermot Ahern (no relation of the Taoiseach) returned and reported his belief that nothing untoward had happened. Even so, the Taoiseach also took the precaution of taking his future Tánaiste Mary Harney into his confidence before taking the plunge and disastrously appointing Burke.

~ ~ ~ ~ ~

August 1997 should have brought Ahern some time to rest, draw breath and plan ahead for his new government term. But it brought no such thing. Earlier, on 19 July, he received a very welcome fillip when the IRA announced they were restoring their ceasefire, broken 17 months previously. The news was warmly welcomed by Ahern and his new British counterpart, Tony Blair of Labour, who had just been elected in May, bringing an end to 18 years of uninterrupted Conservative Party rule. Ahern had high hopes for all-party talks fixed for 15 September and to be chaired by US envoy, Senator George Mitchell. In the meantime, however, he had more immediate concerns.

On 25 August, Mr Justice Brian McCracken published his findings on the cases of supermarket boss, Ben Dunne, and politicians Michael Lowry and Charlie Haughey. Following 18 days of hearings, the Judge had done his work in just five months and his findings were robust, restoring some confidence in the tribunal process after disappointments surrounding the 1994 Beef Tribunal Report.

The McCracken Report found that former Fine Gael Minister Michael Lowry had evaded taxes by not reporting almost £400,000 (€500,000) received from Ben Dunne for work done at his supermarkets by Lowry's refrigeration firm. The payment had come in the form of building work done at Lowry's home in Thurles.

The tribunal also found that Haughey received £1.3m (€1.7m) from Dunne. Furthermore, it found that Haughey had obstructed the tribunal and lied to its investigators on 11 separate occasions. The Judge asked the Director of Public Prosecutions to assess whether there was enough evidence to charge Haughey. If found guilty, Ahern's old mentor could have faced up to two years in jail.

The only crumb of comfort for Ahern was that Mr Justice McCracken found no evidence of political favours given to Ben Dunne in return for his money. In fact, Lowry, who had been handsomely re-elected as a TD, insisted that he had been cleared of any political corruption allegations.

The Revenue Commissioners, however, took a keen interest in the proceedings, not just as they related to Dunne, Lowry, Haughey, but also to many others. The tribunal lawyers had followed a money trail leading to the Cayman Islands where they found US$50m of deposits by Irish citizens, many of whom were trying to dodge paying tax.

More generally, the Judge delivered a scathing commentary on Irish politics where there were no sanctions against the peddling of influence. He said it was appalling that politicians could accept money from business people without having to report it. Furthermore, he noted that the potential for bribery was considerable and recommended new laws on donation declaration and tax compliance, and tough sanctions against anyone who lied.

Bertie Ahern fixed a special Cabinet meeting for three days after the report's publication. He would also face a special Dáil session a fortnight later to debate the findings. As Taoiseach, he reiterated his pledges to legislate for a new code of ethics in public life.

The acute embarrassment arising from the misdeeds of a former Fianna Fáil grandee so close to himself was one problem for the new Taoiseach. However, there was a far more urgent issue coming down the tracks in the form of recurring allegations against his current Foreign Affairs Minister, Ray Burke. Indeed, the summer had brought wave after wave of reports about planning corruption which clearly concerned Burke – but without specifically naming him. On 7 August, Burke was forced to issue a statement saying he had received an unsolicited election donation of £30,000 (€38,000) from builders Joseph Murphy Structural Engineers (JMSE) back in June 1989. Even so, Burke insisted 'no favours were asked or given' and he had done nothing wrong or unethical.

'I find myself the victim of a campaign of calumny and abuse,' the Foreign Affairs Minister said.

Later Ahern went on radio and defended his Foreign Affairs Minister. He said considerable efforts had been made to ensure there was nothing untoward done by Burke.

'We were up every tree in North Dublin,' he said in a remark to haunt him for years to come.

A month later, the Dáil returned to discuss the McCracken Tribunal findings and both Lowry and Burke made special statements to the house. The process was dominated by Burke's case with a lengthy question and answer session. Burke repeated his statement of the previous month and acknowledged receiving the £30,000. He said he remitted £10,000 to Fianna Fáil headquarters, gave a further £7,000 to the local organisation and spent the rest on his own election campaign. The seasoned TD said elections were expensive and all politicians received donations, though he acknowledged that this was the biggest contribution he had ever received. In an epic piece of metaphor mixing, Burke declared:

'Whatever comes out of the woodwork now is a line in the sand. From this on, D-Day, I am going on to the peace process.'

Ahern proceeded to establish a new tribunal to investigate the broader issue of political donations in the wake of the McCracken findings. This would be chaired by another High Court Judge, Mr Justice Michael Moriarty. Soon Ahern would also have to bow to internal PD and external opposition pressure and establish another tribunal to examine Dublin planning allegations in connection with Ray Burke and others, this time chaired by Mr Justice Feargus Flood. However, there was an outcry when Ahern failed to set up a special investigation into the so-called Ansbacher Deposits, or overseas accounts, unearthed by the McCracken Tribunal. Ultimately, a High Court inspector's investigation was conducted into these under the aegis of Mary Harney's Department of Enterprise, Trade and Employment..

In the course of his contribution in the Dáil that day Ahern sought to mitigate his criticisms of Charlie Haughey. The former disciple said Haughey had done much good, and after Seán Lemass, had been a major influence in Ireland throughout the second half of the 20th century. None the less, Ahern added that it was sad that Haughey had demeaned himself by accepting such huge sums from Ben Dunne.

Yet Ahern also gave a hostage to fortune as he responded to questions from Labour leader, Dick Spring, about the Leaders' Account. This was a grant set up by Éamon de Valera in the late 1940s to help political parties fund their running costs. It had been widely rumoured that Haughey was helping himself to this money. In response, Ahern told Spring that he had looked as best he could, given limited records, and believed things were in order with the leaders' funding, especially with cheques signed by Charlie Haughey and countersigned 'by another senior party member'. What Ahern did not say was that *he* was that 'senior party member' doing the countersigning over a lengthy period.

Pressure mounted on Burke, especially as questions were raised about his role in issuing 11 passports to a wealthy Arab banking family called Mahfouz in 1990 under the controversial investment scheme. It later transpired that Burke had in fact received two payments of £30,000. One was from JMSE builders and the second from a subsidiary of Tony O'Reilly's firm, Fitzwilton.

On 7 October 1997, Burke announced that he was quitting not just Cabinet, but also the Dáil and politics generally. In explanation, he said he did so because he could not devote his full energies to the Northern Ireland talks and important developments in Europe. Still he protested his innocence of any wrongdoing. 'I want to make it clear that I did nothing wrong,' he said. On the day, Burke's resignation coincided with the funeral of his brother Seán, who had died tragically.

There were angry exchanges in the Dáil that day. Minister for Defence, David Andrews, walked out when Fine Gael leader John Bruton rose to express his regret at the circumstances of the resignation on a sad day for the Burke family. Bertie Ahern blamed Burke's departure on 'the persistent hounding of an honourable man ... on the basis of innuendo and unproven allegations'.

Burke's departure left Bertie Ahern battered and at a very low ebb. However, Ahern used the resultant vacancies to promote further conciliation with the old Reynolds wing of Fianna Fáil. Minister for Defence, David Andrews, moved to Foreign Affairs and Minister of State for Science and Technology, Michael Smith, moved to Defence, while Noel Treacy from Galway East took Smith's old job. The Smith promotion honoured to the letter a pledge made the previous June.

None the less, the bitter taste lingered on even as Ahern built bridges inside Fianna Fáil. In the Dáil, Ahern declared that Burke's career was ended by 'Mr Bruton and his likes' rather than by any fault within Fianna Fáil.

'I hope he is proud of his handiwork and that he never comes to an untimely end,' Ahern said. It was a far cry from accepting that he had erred in choosing and confiding in a now disgraced minister.

All this high drama occurred against the background of a forthcoming presidential election. President Mary Robinson had left the post a few months early to take up the prestigious international post of United Nations High Commissioner for Human Rights. Labour were trying to emulate their 1990 success and about to chose children's welfare campaigner, Adi Roche. Fine Gael were to chose another woman, veteran Dublin MEP, Mary Banotti. A number of Independents, including former Garda union leader, Derek Nally, and former Eurovision Song Contest winner, Dana Rosemary Scallon, expressed an interest. The big question was: who would stand for Fianna Fáil?

~ ~ ~ ~ ~

In October 1997, the newspapers were awash with stories about how former Taoiseach Albert Reynolds was 'horribly shafted' in his unsuccessful quest for the Fianna Fáil nomination in that year's presidential election. Those stories left little doubt about who delivered the 'shafting': Bertie Ahern.

Precisely seven years after the events, Albert Reynolds says that he has moved on. But he retains a very clear belief about what happened.

'There is no earthly doubt in anyone's mind that I was well and truly shafted for the nomination. I felt betrayed by Bertie Ahern and by the party. Seven years on, I've put it out of my mind. But I was led to believe that I had this nomination and that it was only a matter of form,' Albert Reynolds told this writer.

Then Reynolds added half-wistfully, half-mockingly, 'It was the only election I ever lost in my entire lifetime.'

Unsurprisingly, Bertie Ahern has a completely different take on the events running up to the presidential nomination. But, at all events, by October 1997 Ahern was definitely feeling that things should have been far better for him and his fledgling first government.

The Irish economy was moving rapidly towards an era of unparalleled prosperity. Bertie Ahern and his ministers knew they would soon have a pile of money to give away – if they could defy the 'naysayers' and stay in office. North of the Border, the guns were silent and Sinn Féin were locked in talks with all the main parties with the exception of Ian Paisley's Democratic Unionist Party.

However, once Burke had quit the Dáil in such ignominious circumstances, there was zero prospect of Fianna Fáil winning the resultant by-election in Dublin North. The untimely death of Jim Kemmy, the stalwart Labour politician from Limerick, raised the prospect of two morale boosting by-election wins for the Opposition, while the Government had lost its second most senior minister overboard.

Ahern was around long enough and could read the runes – he needed a political boost very badly. This urgency added to his own personal interest in Fianna Fáil regaining the presidency, which was lost after 45 years on his watch as Brian Lenihan's director of elections in November 1990. Within Fianna Fáil, the prospective candidate, Albert Reynolds, raised some fears, however.

The hope by Ahern and others that Robinson would stay in the job had been dashed months before the general election on 12 March 1997, when she announced that she was not interested in seeking another term. Ahern freely conceded that Mary Robinson had made a great job of what was previously a moribund sinecure for retired politicians. Given her consistently high popularity ratings, Fianna Fáil would not have dared run against her.

The next hope of an honourable Fianna Fáil exit was an all-party agreed candidature for SDLP leader and veteran Northern Ireland peace and civil rights campaigner, John Hume. All opinion research showed that he would have been elected with an enormous vote. However, the fear existed that his departure would jeopardise the peace process and that he was temperamentally unsuited to the job. Either way, Hume announced in September 1997 that he was definitely not interested. But a month earlier, Albert Reynolds had announced during a visit to Belfast for the McGrory Memorial Lecture that he wanted to stand for the presidency.

'My name was there, maybe unconfirmed for the last two months. It was there for a long time back. It is not news to anybody,' he said.

According to Reynolds, he was pushed forward because his understanding was that he would get a clear run with Fianna Fáil backing. He insists that at first he had not been that keen and indeed his family strongly warned him against it. As the architect of a peace breakthrough, he was in demand on the lecture circuit and also had many business opportunities.

Senior Fianna Fáil sources say their understanding was that Albert Reynolds was coaxed into standing again for the Dáil in Longford-Roscommon in June 1997 when he was contemplating retirement. Moreover, he was twice seen lunching and in earnest conversation with Bertie Ahern in Dublin restaurants in 1996 and 1997. By all appearances, the return for ensuring another seat for Ahern's government ambitions was a clear run at Áras an

Uachtaráin. As the man who took risks for peace in the North and won, Reynolds appeared a good bet for the presidency. By late August 1997, he had his own private poll results, commissioned at a cost of £10,000 (€12,700), which showed him on 45 per cent – and in his terms 'unbeatable'.

However, what Albert Reynolds did not understand was that there was a growing 'ABBA' – Anybody But Bloody Albert – movement within Fianna Fáil because of the fear that he could not win.

'Let's face it – Albert screwed up royally and had brought down two governments inside two years. Peace in Northern Ireland or not – there was some doubt about his statesman appeal,' one TD recalls.

Then Mary McAleese arrived on the scene. McAleese was a 46-year-old Belfast-born academic lawyer with a brilliant career at Queen's University Belfast. She had worked in Dublin as an academic and as a journalist/television presenter at RTÉ and had later unsuccessfully stood for Fianna Fáil in a Dáil election. The RTÉ experience she recalled for her official biographer, Ray Mac Mánais, as the worst experience of her life, a rating which included the horrors of sectarian attacks in the Troubles.

The idea for her candidature gathered pace very quickly and she began picking up support from people like Mary O'Rourke and Dermot Ahern, Minister for Social, Community and Family Affairs – both sacked by Reynolds in January 1993 – and others like Wicklow TD Dick Roche.

Justine McCarthy in her unauthorised biography, *Mary McAleese: The Outsider*, notes that PD leader Mary Harney warned that she could not support Reynolds' candidature. The rancorous manner in which his Fianna Fáil–PD Coalition fell asunder in the autumn of 1992 still left political scars. The eight senior ministers and 12 junior ministers sacked by Albert Reynolds were also likely members of the nascent 'ABBA' grouping.

'You could say that when Mary McAleese came looking for the nomination from the Fianna Fáil Parliamentary Party, she was starting with 20 votes in the bag,' one veteran Fianna Fáil politician of that era comments.

Yet Bertie Ahern remained aloof and neutral.

'Bertie told me twice he was staying out of it. I remember saying to him, "Christ, we're going to lose this unless you make a decision",' McCarthy cites Dick Roche as saying.

On 9 September 1997, Mary McAleese and her husband Martin met the Taoiseach at Government Buildings. He listened with interest but was non-committal. Afterwards, Chief Whip Seamus Brennan gave her a list of the Fianna Fáil Parliamentary Party and their contact details. Her dedicated canvass team stepped up their already advanced networking and canvassing, especially targeting the 38 newcomers to the Fianna Fáil Parliamentary Party.

On 17 September, some 100 Fianna Fáil TDs, senators and MEPs gathered to pick their presidential candidate at the party rooms in Leinster House. It was a confused situation. The three candidates, McAleese, Reynolds and Tipperary North veteran, Michael O'Kennedy, were invited to put their case to the meeting. There would be no proposers and seconders.

Albert Reynolds recollects that he had received a phone call earlier that morning from Bertie Ahern asking whom he wanted as his director of elections. Seeing that he was not especially concerned, he agreed to Ahern's suggestion of Martin Mackin, who would soon afterwards succeed Pat Farrell as Fianna Fáil general secretary. Reynolds says Ahern told him there was no need for speeches and only the candidates' proposers and seconders would speak.

Stephen Collins in *The Power Game* cites various TDs as saying the procedures were changed at the last moment largely due to confusion. However, Albert Reynolds only heard about the changed procedures when he arrived and neither he nor O'Kennedy had prepared a speech. In contrast, McAleese had worked long and hard on her script the previous evening and delivered it with fluency and commitment. O'Kennedy had sensed that there was a set-up in the offing the previous evening, but reversed his initial thoughts of withdrawing in protest. His speech was peppered with references to declining standards in Fianna Fáil, however. Those present found Reynolds made a poor speech and his lack of preparation told.

When the ballot papers were distributed, Ahern walked across and showed his paper to Reynolds to confirm that he was voting for the former Taoiseach. Munster MEP Brian Crowley was sitting close by and famously told Reynolds, 'You're finished now.'

The first vote had Reynolds ahead on 49 votes, to McAleese's remarkable score of 42, with O'Kennedy on 21 votes. Reynolds, a veteran of many campaigns, knew what was coming in the next round. It was his turn to cross to where Ahern was sitting.

'I walked over and said, "Whether I win or lose the next count – I won't be taking the nomination anyway." It was very clear to me what was afoot.'

In the event, McAleese beat Reynolds by 62 votes to 48. It was a defining moment for Ahern who had showed some steel many might not have credited him with having. To this day, opinion divides on the treatment of Albert Reynolds.

Ahern's critics within the party say the episode was central to his inability to face people and deliver hard truths. The same deputy who scathingly cited Reynolds' role in pulling down two governments in as many years offered this assessment seven years on:

'The point was Albert should not have been allowed to believe right to the end that he had a clear run at the nomination. That was dishonest and unfair.'

But another Fianna Fáil politician of that era, who insists he had no dislike of Reynolds, offers a polar opposite view.

'Albert Reynolds was a very experienced operator, a senior minister and former Taoiseach. He should have known the score.'

Even today, Ahern still remains sensitive about the accusation that he 'shafted' Albert Reynolds. Recently he told friends that he wanted to stay out of the thing entirely, recalling that his support for Brian Lenihan's Fianna Fáil nomination in 1990 had alienated him from another pretender, John Wilson, for a number of years.

'He didn't feel that he was responsible for winning the nomination for Albert or anyone else and he didn't campaign for anyone. Remember a lot of people didn't like Albert – but he did vote for him,' a friend recalls.

Ahern's assessment was that the parliamentary party had to decide whether they stayed with the past, in the form of Reynolds, or opted for a new era in the form of Mary McAleese.

After a tough and sometimes bitter campaign, Mary McAleese went on to win the presidential election. Ultimately, Bertie Ahern had laid the ghosts of the disastrous 1990 campaign which he had supervised and his government gained a very valuable boost.

~ ~ ~ ~ ~

Whichever way you look at it, Bertie Ahern etched himself into political folk memory with his handling of the 1997 presidential nominations. It was not pretty, but he proved that he did possess the steel required for the nasty times in politics.

In the autumn of 1997, he also laid another unhelpful stereotype that had dogged him for many years. It was the time 'Bertie the anorakman' was formally laid to rest. On 30 September 1997, he was voted BEST GROOMED MAN AT LEINSTER HOUSE by the 20 women TDs and 10 women senators.

At the time the annual award was sponsored by Gillette. Presenting the award, his deputy leader Mary O'Rourke confessed she had voted for her boss but insisted there was no vote-rigging, pointing to other winners such as Labour's Dick Spring and Fine Gael's Michael Creed in previous years. Ahern, sporting a sharp Magee suit, a crisp white shirt and spotted tie, set off by black Irish-made leather shoes, said he was surprised to win. In a short light-hearted speech, he conceded that he had not always been at the cutting edge of fashion. He also confessed that 'the famous fashion accessory of mine' was sold at a charity auction to raise funds for his old school. The £2,500 (€3,200) prize money would also go to charity.

Ahern acknowledged the counsel of his then partner, Celia Larkin, and his office administrator, Denise Kavanagh, as well as help from his old school pal and tailor, Louis Copeland, and finally Alan Markey, the proprietor of a menswear shop across the road from St Luke's. Thus, the slaying of 'anorakman' was not a solo effort and had been gradually happening for some years. Now the media were acknowledging it and the stereotype created by colour writers in the 1980s was finally finished.

The turnaround is also a commentary on changing values in Irish society with image, public relations and the increasing influence of television coming into play more and more. In June 1998, the *Sunday Times* newspaper revealed that the Taoiseach's make-up bill for the three months March to May was £3,608.85 (€4,582.29). In the years since then, the cost has escalated and at last count totalled €140,000 since he became Taoiseach. News of the make-up generates mild titters and some light-hearted media coverage. But the boy from Drumcondra is not fazed by any of it – nor indeed is the great mass of the general public.

11

Peace Works

As 2004 draws to a close Bertie Ahern is on the cusp of brokering a deal to end generations of sectarian strife in Northern Ireland. After seven years of tirelessly nursing the fragile peace process, a definitive agreement, this time involving that implacable foe of Dublin, the Rev Ian Paisley, is now tantalisingly close to completion.

Just 17 years old when the Northern Ireland Troubles erupted in the summer of 1969, Bertie Ahern vividly remembers the prevailing anger of the time south of the Border. He had just joined the local O'Donovan Rossa Cumann in the Dublin Central constituency, which had encapsulated the tensions within the party about how to approach the issue. Both Minister for Industry and Commerce, George Colley, and Minister for Finance, Charlie Haughey, were the sitting Fianna Fáil TDs. Haughey was seen to favour a more interventionist approach to help beleaguered Northern Catholics defend themselves from loyalist extremists and a deeply suspect police force. In a controversy, to this day not entirely explained, Haughey was sacked from Government, charged with conspiracy to import IRA arms, but later acquitted. At the time at least, Colley appeared far more circumspect and sided with Fianna Fáil leader Jack Lynch, who sacked Haughey.

Ahern recalls that he had no difficulty picking his side.

'I supported Haughey regardless of whether he was right or wrong,' he recalled in the 1986 interview with *Hot Press*. However, he added that he never understood the full details of the notorious 1970s Arms Trial.

'Haughey was accused of assisting the Northern groups in some way or another. We were the Catholic people. We claimed jurisdiction over the North – he wouldn't have been doing his job if he didn't do something. Now I am not talking about putting up money for arms: he was acquitted of that,' Ahern went on to say in the interview.

Indeed, we should not marvel at his choice of 'side' in Dublin Central, as both his father and mother were staunch Republicans. Con Ahern was too young for a major role in the 1919–21 War of Independence, but chose the anti-Treaty side in the subsequent Civil War and was imprisoned in his native Cork and later interned in Tintown Camp on the Curragh of Kildare.

Over the years, Bertie Ahern heard stories of his father's experiences, including two hunger strikes, but insists these were told in a very factual way by Con Ahern, not one to boast about his exploits. At home nobody pushed their views on him, Ahern recalls, yet he absorbed a nationalist code of political values none the less. In a radio interview on RTÉ Lyric FM in September 2004, he told interviewer Theo Dorgan that his father both shaped and tempered his own views on the North at that time. The older and wiser Con Ahern, then in his mid-60s, counselled against any rush to support violence and abhorred the Provisional IRA's bombing campaigns which exposed innocent civilians to death and destruction.

'My father had been an active Republican and had been a Volunteer. But he was very much against the activity against ordinary citizens. He could never understand that and I must say that view formed my mind from an early date,' he told Theo Dorgan.

In fact, Bertie Ahern was to see the effects of 'activity against ordinary citizens' close to home during the Troubles. He recalls that he was the administrator on call at the Mater Hospital when three loyalist bombs exploded in Parnell Street, Talbot Street and South Leinster Street in Dublin on Saturday evening, 17 May 1974. These, combined with another bomb in Monaghan, claimed the lives of 34 people, and are still the biggest atrocity of the Troubles. They also remain one of the great travesties of the period for which nobody has been brought to justice, while a deep suspicion of some form of collusion by elements of the British security forces still lingers.

'It was enormously troublesome and sad. I can remember that night so well, watching people coming in and the injuries, which were horrendous. Now 30 years later I'm involved in the inquiries,' he told the radio interviewer.

From the 1970s onwards, Ahern says that he was 'immersed' in following the Northern Ireland issue and attended all protest marches and rallies in Dublin. At times he felt quite angry about what was going on, but says his father's influence, coupled with his own Fianna Fáil membership, helped to rule out any involvement in the IRA.

He recalls that there were other tensions within his local Fianna Fáil cumann and remembers an emotional evening when 10 local activists resigned to join Aontacht Éireann. This was a party set up by Kevin Boland, a minister who had resigned from government in 1970 in support of Charlie Haughey. But equally, he reflects that, as time went on, more and more of his friends were largely indifferent to politics and the North.

'Most of my friends at that stage didn't take a blind bit of interest in politics or what was going on – You could say it disappoints you – but there's always only a small proportion of people in life that will actively engage in anything,' he remarked.

As noted in Chapter 4, Ahern expressed orthodox Fianna Fáil Republican views in September 1983 at the commemoration for Old IRA leader Liam Lynch in Fermoy. There he asserted that Republicanism for him was primarily about removing the British presence from every part of Ireland, though he also condemned violence as a way of achieving anything.

'It is the political weakness of Northern Ireland, not the military strength of its defenders, that must be challenged. Let it be clearly recognised that violence cannot achieve the political objectives which we all desire,' he said.

In the 1986 *Hot Press* interview, Ahern rejected the emerging Sinn Féin doctrine of mixing political and paramilitary action. This view had been summed up by Sinn Féin publicity director, Danny Morrison, as the infamous 'armalite in one hand and the ballot box in the other'. But in that same interview Ahern also showed traces of ambivalence towards some forms of IRA violence, prevalent in the Republic at the time. Asked how he viewed the IRA shooting a British soldier, he replied:

'Well, I think violence is totally wrong. But if that is the only action they were involved in, in a war position, they would have an argument. It's an argument certain people will vote for. It's not an argument I agree with.'

~ ~ ~ ~ ~

By November 1994, when Bertie Ahern took over the leadership of Fianna Fáil, several things had happened in relation to Northern Ireland that gave rise to hope. A number of efforts to resolve the centuries-old impasse in the previous decades had been initiated, but largely failed.

A deal initiated by Taoiseach Jack Lynch and completed by his successor Liam Cosgrave at Sunningdale in 1974 led to the North's first-ever power-sharing government. However, this was wrecked by a loyalist workers' strike in 1974. Later, in 1985, Dr Garret FitzGerald signed the Anglo-Irish Agreement but this also foundered on the rock of Unionist opposition. In fact, Ahern was Fianna Fáil Chief Whip when Charlie Haughey opposed the deal, a stance he later reversed.

In 1988, Charlie Haughey started making tentative contact with the IRA leadership through his adviser, Dr Martin Mansergh, and a Belfast Redemptorist priest, Fr Alec Reid. Son of a distinguished Anglo-Irish historian, Mansergh was to prove a key figure through two decades, working in turn for Haughey, Reynolds and Ahern. As previously noted, when Albert Reynolds took over as Taoiseach in February 1992, he identified delivery of a settlement in the North as his key objective.

Meanwhile, Social Democratic and Labour Party (SDLP) leader John Hume had already courageously begun a controversial dialogue with the Sinn Féin and IRA leadership for which he was vilified over a long period. Towards the end of the summer of 1993 both Adams and Hume went public on the content of their discussions. Essentially, they had been trying to outline a nationalist consensus on the way forward with a strong hint of a possible IRA ceasefire.

Contacts had also continued between Albert Reynolds and his British counterpart, John Major, who had struck up a rapport at EU level when both served as Ministers for Finance in their respective governments. On 15 December 1993, the two leaders signed the so-called 'Downing Street Declaration', which set the parameters for a future settlement. The Dublin Government recognised that a United Ireland would require the consent of a majority in the North; London declared that they had 'no selfish, strategic or economic interest in Northern Ireland'. A potential deal would have three dimensions: an internal Northern Ireland element, a cross-border element and a British–Irish dimension.

Reynolds and his Labour Tánaiste, Dick Spring, won warm praise in the South. Reaction in the North was more cautious; but the then mainstream Ulster Unionist Party (UUP) did not reject it out of hand, unlike Ian Paisley's Democratic Unionist Party (DUP). Sinn Féin said they needed 'clarification'; a process that took months and wearied people of all hope that an IRA ceasefire would materialise.

Finally, on 31 August 1994, the IRA declared a 'complete cessation of hostilities'. Albert Reynolds' finest hour had come and he welcomed Sinn Féin president, Gerry Adams, to Government Buildings in Dublin. However, in London, John Major had a very precarious situation in parliament and was largely held hostage by the Ulster Unionists whose votes he needed to stay in power. On 13 October 1994, the Combined Loyalist Military Command also announced a cessation of hostilities.

Domestic political events saw Albert Reynolds lose power, and Ahern almost gain power, only to be supplanted by Fine Gael leader John Bruton taking over as head of a Rainbow Coalition. For their part, Bruton and Spring tried to maintain the momentum but were stuck with Major's problems and a certain Sinn Féin suspicion of Bruton. In early 1996, warnings about Republicans' impatience were ignored and on 9 February the ceasefire ended with a major IRA bombing at Canary Wharf in London, where two innocent people were murdered.

The IRA blamed Major's poor response to a 16-month ceasefire and his failure to start all-party talks that included Sinn Féin. Furthermore, they said they had delivered their side of the bargain – a ceasefire – but the Dublin and London governments had not kept their end. During this time John Bruton also came in for heavy criticism for accepting Major's view that IRA weapons decommissioning had to happen before Sinn Féin were allowed into talks.

Subsequently, Major caved in to Unionist demands that elections be held in the North, which saw Sinn Féin build on their support to almost 16 per cent of the vote. Meanwhile, there was no major renewal of IRA violence and by the summer of 1997 fresh hope had emerged. In London, a new British Prime Minister, Tony Blair, had taken over as head of the first Labour government since 1979. In Dublin his counterpart, Bertie Ahern, was head of a Fianna Fáil-dominated minority coalition. When a new IRA ceasefire was called on 21 July 1997, hope again soared that a breakthrough was possible.

In the course of new talks, Bertie Ahern found it relatively easy to win the trust of Sinn Féin's leadership; apart from anything else, during his period as Fianna Fáil leader in opposition he had frequently criticised Sinn Féin's exclusion from talks. Furthermore, he accused Northern Ireland secretary, Patrick Mayhew, of 'putting the cart before the horse' by insisting on IRA weapons decommissioning before settlement talks.

In yet another historic move, Ahern had in 1995 sought a British apology for their negligence in allowing millions to die in the 1845–47 Irish Famine – something that was delivered two years later by Prime Minister Tony Blair. In addition, the Fianna Fáil leader asserted a readiness to consider changing Articles 2 and 3 of the 1937 Constitution, which claimed jurisdiction over the North. But he also insisted that the right to an Irish identity and nationality by all the people on the island who wanted it could not be denied.

In a relatively short period Ahern had built an excellent relationship with Tony Blair. The two new leaders had several things in common: each was viewed with a certain scepticism within the political organisations they led; Ahern was prepared to conciliate and share power with virtually any other group; and Blair was busy modernising the British Labour Party and moving it towards the political centre.

In July 1997, there were several phone contacts between the two leaders and Blair appreciated the pragmatic and moderate stance adopted by Ahern over flashpoint Orange Order parades going through nationalist areas. Establishing a relationship with the Northern Unionists, however, appeared to be a more tricky matter. But here again Ahern had done his homework.

~ ~ ~ ~ ~

Bertie Ahern rated Ulster Unionist Party leader David Trimble as a pragmatic leader with whom he could do business and who could bring the bulk of his people with him. Indeed Trimble's instincts about Ahern were similar. In his biography entitled *Trimble*, writer Henry McDonald notes that contacts between the two men had been set up in the months before Ahern was elected Taoiseach on 26 June 1997. In fact, the pair had met secretly on three occasions in Armagh city.

McDonald cites Trimble as saying in the summer of 1997, 'I can definitely do a deal with Bertie.' But with the marching season at its height Trimble stalled on any public meeting with Ahern, lest he alarm his nervous and suspicious party members. Moreover, the UUP leader recognised that with Blair in power in London it was time the Unionists cut a deal with Dublin.

Meanwhile, the lull in Ahern's domestic political difficulties, largely delivered by the victory of Belfast-born Mary McAleese in the October 1997 presidential election, freed up the Taoiseach to devote virtually all his energies to the cause of peace in the North. It was a slow and difficult process facing an uphill struggle, but soon Ahern and Blair had fixed an ambitious timetable.

In late June, Blair suggested weapons decommissioning could happen in parallel with settlement talks. The renewal of the IRA ceasefire in July led to agreement that full-scale talks could begin on 15 September, chaired by US Senator George Mitchell. The ceasefire also ended a ban on ministers in the Dublin Government meeting with Sinn Féin.

However, when the all-party talks got under way, the Unionist parties would not attend because of the IRA weapons issue. But on 17 September 1997, David Trimble led the UUP into the talks. Six days later the first meeting between Sinn Féin and the Ulster Unionists in 75 years took place. Contacts continued to be built up in the succeeding weeks despite repeated reverses and mini-crises and a continuing threat of violence.

On 12 January 1998, Blair and Ahern published their new settlement plans based on the 1993 Downing Street Declaration. Then the two leaders in late February announced a concerted push to achieve all-party agreement by the ambitious target of Easter 1998. Senator Mitchell fixed the deadline as 9 April, which was Holy Thursday, for completion of negotiations. 'It is a race against time and the window of opportunity is small,' read an analysis on 5 March in the British newspaper, the *Guardian*.

The scene was set for one of the most dramatic weeks in modern Irish history, with talks, including participation by Ahern and Blair, at Hillsborough Castle, Co Down, fixed for Holy Week. Nothing like it had been seen since the Treaty negotiations in 1922. Memorably, Blair said he could 'feel the hand of history on his shoulder'.

For Ahern it proved a bittersweet week as intensive and marathon talks coincided with the death and funeral of his mother, Julia, aged 87 years, and always his most loyal political supporter. Though Julia Ahern was 40 years old when her youngest son Bertie was born, they retained a close bond. Recently, Ahern confided that he genuinely liked his father, but like many fathers of his generation, he was an aloof man rarely demonstrating affection. By contrast he and his mother were always close.

Julia Ahern died on the Monday morning of Holy Week while her son was in Belfast waiting for real negotiations to begin and conducting preparatory meetings. He later recalled how he got the news.

'I had my first meeting at 9 am and I met the SDLP at 11 am. Just as I was leaving the SDLP people, I got the call. It stunned me. I [had] spent all day hoping that she would not die while I was in a meeting because I wanted to be there. It meant a lot to me to be there.'

Still, friends of Ahern say that, while naturally he was deeply saddened, he was also somehow at peace because he had managed to steal much time at her bedside even while intensive preparations for the negotiations were going ahead.

On the following day, Tuesday, the remains of Julia Ahern were removed to the Church of St Vincent de Paul in Marino, Dublin. Writer Deaglán de Bréadún in his book, *The Far Side of Revenge: Making Peace in Northern Ireland*, notes that while attending the removal that Tuesday evening, Ahern was approached by aides with the latest on the talks at Hillsborough. A crisis over Unionist demands on reducing the number of cross-border bodies had emerged. The advice of Ahern's officials was to hold firm. However, on reflection the Taoiseach relented and gave what chairman, Senator Mitchell, later described as a concession which kept the UUP in the talks. Early next morning, Ahern flew to Belfast for a breakfast meeting with Blair, returning later for the Requiem Mass and burial of his mother. All week long, negotiations seesawed and teetered on the brink of collapse. But on Good Friday, a day after the deadline, an agreement emerged.

The deal, which quickly became known as the Good Friday Agreement, provided for a power-sharing government in Belfast including the SDLP and Sinn Féin along with the Unionists; paramilitary prisoners on both sides would be released under a form of amnesty; and there would be a North-South Ministerial Council. The proposal was to go to a referendum on both sides of the Border.

Subsequently, Ahern made a big commitment to the referendum campaign with Fianna Fáil spending £500,000 (€634,000) promoting a 'yes' vote in this and the accompanying vote on the EU Treaty of Amsterdam. On 22 May 1998, almost 95 per cent of those voting in the Republic endorsed the deal. Skilfully, Ahern had helped to sell the replacement of Articles 2 and 3 of the Constitution – which claimed Dublin's jurisdiction over the North – with a provision that expressed the hope of future unity by consent. The outcome was less certain north of the Border but 71 per cent of those voting endorsed it – a figure which indicated that it also had a majority of Unionist voters' support. The outcome was groundbreaking and a new era of hope flourished. Yet there were also strong indications that an entire raft of problems had been shelved rather than resolved.

The IRA still held their weapons and a major internal war of nerves went on between the 'hawks' and the 'doves'; those who wanted to maintain the armed struggle and those who felt it was time to commit definitively to constitutional politics. Standing disapprovingly and raucously on the sideline, Ian Paisley and his DUP colleagues – who had shunned the negotiations and excoriated the deal – predicted that it would not work.

A major feature of Ahern's involvement in the process was his growing relationship with Tony Blair. Interviewed in the week following the deal, *Sunday Times* journalist John McManus asked the Taoiseach about his working relationship with Blair.

'We genuinely have a friendship. We took over the leadership of our parties when we were both in opposition. We had lengthy discussions on things such as the European Union. I think we like each other. But I would not like to spend every week stuck in a room with him for over 40 hours,' Ahern said.

Some six years later there is ample evidence that the relationship between the two leaders has grown and deepened. Their meetings are characterised by talk of family, football and their mutual Manchester United support and, of course, politics. They often compare notes on how to deal with adversaries within and outside their respective governments and both men hold strong personal religious convictions.

Evidence of the warmth between the two emerged in September 2003 when Ahern and Blair were jointly awarded the prestigious Thomas J Dodd Prize for International Justice and Human Rights by the University of Connecticut in the US. Ahern was there to receive his prize but Britian's Deputy Prime Minister, John Prescott, stood in for Blair who was unable to travel.

Accepting the award, which carried a prize fund of US$75,000, Ahern departed from his prepared script to deliver an extraordinary personal tribute to Blair.

'I was brought up in a house quite frankly that was not particularly fond of British Prime Ministers. We probably went to bed at night not just cursing the dark but other things as well,' Ahern said.

He added that over the years working together in efforts to definitively end the Northern Ireland conflict, Blair's home and offices at Downing Street and Chequers had become an extension of his own office and home. Magnanimously, he said Blair was a wonderful person to whom he hoped history would be kind.

'As Irish leader, as Irish Taoiseach I say that Tony Blair is a great person whom we deeply appreciate,' Ahern concluded.

The overall result of the 1998 Good Friday Agreement and referendum was an unreserved triumph for Bertie Ahern in the Republic and opinion polls soon afterwards showed him to be the most popular Taoiseach ever. The entire process enhanced his image as a potential statesman of some skill and standing. In addition, the outcome showed his pragmatism and ability to adapt his political thinking to a new reality in which he showed real leadership and not a little political ability.

~ ~ ~ ~ ~

Such political highs rarely last, however, and soon the tangled allegations of sleaze associated with key Fianna Fáil figures were back in play. One veteran Fianna Fáil TD recalls the dread which every day was beginning to bring to the party in late 1998 and early 1999.

'It got to the point where any revelation of scandal in any corner of the country just filled us with a terror that it would involve another one of our fellows,' he said.

Magill magazine reported that Rennicks, a subsidiary of Tony O'Reilly's company Fitzwilton, had also donated £30,000 (€38,000) to Ray Burke prior to the 1989 general election. It turned out that the £10,000 remitted to Fianna Fáil was from this money – not the JMSE donation as Burke had implied in his explanations to the Dáil the previous October. Subsequently, former Fianna Fáil accountant and by then a TD for Laois-Offaly, Seán Fleming, explained this to the Dáil. In the course of his explanation, Fleming made it clear that the party general secretary, Pat Farrell, had known this fact in the summer of 1997, just after the party had won the general election.

More embarrassing for Ahern was Fleming's statement that the issue had been discussed in the presence of Des Richardson, who not only was a Fianna Fáil fundraiser but also a long-time friend of Ahern's. In fact, Richardson is one of the trustees of St Luke's, Ahern's constituency headquarters.

This put the first of a number of strains on relations with Mary Harney and the Progressive Democrats, who had not been kept informed of these facts. Yet again Ahern's conciliatory skills were called into play to keep the Government on an even keel. As a consequence, the Government expanded the Planning Tribunal's remit to deal with a range of other allegations of irregular donations to politicians.

Some weeks later it emerged that a £2m (€2.5m) tax assessment against Charlie Haughey had been reduced by the revenue appeals commissioner to zero. The difficulty here was that the appeals commissioner was Ronan Kelly, Ahern's brother-in-law. Worse again, he was appointed during Ahern's term as Minister for Finance in 1994 – though it appeared that Ahern had merely rubber-stamped a personnel decision.

In January 1999, another Fianna Fáil skeleton came tumbling out of the closet when EU Commissioner Pádraig Flynn appeared on RTÉ's *Late Late Show*. On the programme, Flynn was extremely dismissive of allegations made by a Sligo-born builder, Tom Gilmartin, that he gave £50,000 (€63,000) to the then Environment Minister in 1989. Bluntly, the Commissioner said Gilmartin had not been well and that his wife was also ill. Enraged by Flynn's television performance, Gilmartin – living in Luton at the time – reversed an earlier decision and announced that he would testify to the Planning Tribunal. In the Dáil, Ahern had a difficult time answering detailed questions about Gilmartin, who had been seeking approval and support for developments in Dublin. Indeed, Ahern had earlier revised his view that he had only met the builder once and said he had in fact met him on a few occasions.

The issue also had a knock-on effect in the Fianna Fáil Parliamentary Party when Flynn's daughter, Beverly Cooper-Flynn, refused to support a Dáil motion of censure against her father and lost the party whip for a time. Ms Cooper-Flynn was already in a little difficulty given that she had previously worked selling investment products for National Irish Bank, one of the financial institutions implicated in alleged tax fraud. More problems were to follow on that score.

The Fianna Fáil–PD Coalition tensions on these matters were sharpened when former leader Des O'Malley – in fact the only one of the quartet of PD TDs without some kind of government office – decided to cut loose and publicly reflect on the Haughey days when he had been drummed out of Fianna Fáil in the mid-1980s. O'Malley recalled that Pádraig Flynn was very comfortable in Charlie Haughey's Fianna Fáil – and so was Bertie Ahern.

The Haughey revelations were only beginning to surface at this time also. First, the Moriarty Tribunal revealed the full extent of Haughey's debts through the 1970s, culminating in Allied Irish Banks writing off a huge portion of the liability soon after Haughey was elected Taoiseach in 1979, as detailed earlier. Then came revelations of cash gifts to Haughey totalling some £9m (€11.5m) from a 'Who's Who' of Irish business. It was all very embarrassing for Ahern, his long-time protégé and associate. Time and again Ahern would have to publicly insist that he had no clue of the state of Haughey's personal finances and little knowledge of the details of his lifestyle.

Subsequently, the Moriarty Tribunal was to hear that in one year alone, 1991, Charlie Haughey spent £15,000 (€19,000) out of the taxpayer-funded 'leaders' allowance' on exclusive Charvet shirts from Paris. A similar sum went to pay a bill at the exclusive Le Coq Hardi restaurant in Dublin where Haughey often entertained lavishly. The other signatory on the leaders' account chequebook was Bertie Ahern.

On 20 July 1999, Ahern himself was called to the Moriarty Tribunal to give evidence. His next appointment on the day was with UUP leader, David Trimble, at the Irish Embassy in London. At the time, Trimble was concerned at remarks made by Ahern that the IRA weapons decommissioning deadline would not be met. The vexed issues shelved in April 1998, however, continue to bedevil the peace effort to this day. On the day, tribunal lawyers asked Ahern about a £25,000 (€32,000) cheque, dated 16 June 1989, from the leaders' account, which had ended up in Charlie Haughey's own bank account. In reply Ahern said he had never signed a cheque for such a large amount but had pre-signed large batches of cheques for administrative convenience and estimated that he had pre-signed as many as 1,600 cheques over a number of years. Furthermore, he told the Tribunal that the other signature on the cheque looked like that of Charlie Haughey. According to Ahern, he had first learnt of anomalies in the leaders' account when contacted by the Tribunal a year earlier. However, he said records for the account over a 13-year period, 1979–1992, were missing.

The year 1999 ended with two more embarrassing revelations about Fianna Fáil TDs. In the first, it emerged that Charlie Haughey had used the leaders' allowance to bail out Sligo-Leitrim TD John Ellis to the tune of £25,000 (€32,000) when facing bankruptcy and disqualification from the Dáil in 1990 after his meat business got into financial difficulty. Clearly, if Ellis had been forced out, Haughey's Government could have fallen. The controversy was compounded by farmers in the West still owed money a decade later for cattle supplied to Ellis. Publicly, Ahern was very slow to act and Ellis continued to chair the Oireachtas agriculture committee. Finally, opposition and media pressure convinced Ellis to quit the committee chair.

The second was the extraordinary story of Kerry North TD Denis Foley who had been vice-chairman of an Oireachtas committee examining tax evasion on DIRT (deposit interest retention tax) by the banks. It transpired that Foley was himself a tax cheat, with £130,000 (€165,000) in bogus offshore accounts. Eventually, with minimal public comment by Ahern, Foley resigned from the Fianna Fáil Parliamentary Party but continued to support the Government from the opposition benches.

~ ~ ~ ~ ~

In spite of all these travails, the Ahern Government continued to enjoy good public support. The public were wearying of tribunal revelations and becoming increasingly difficult to shock. Fianna Fáil had enjoyed good European Parliament and local elections in June 1999 and Ahern's personal popularity ratings remained strong. The June 1999 elections also saw an improved showing for Sinn Féin in the Republic.

The reason for Ahern and his Government's political strength was that the economy was going through an unprecedented boom. Ireland had emerged as second only to Luxembourg in riches assessed in terms of income per head of population. Charlie McCreevy had by now produced three Budgets but, despite the largesse he had to dispense, two of them had generated considerable controversy. In 1997, McCreevy clashed bitterly with the Irish League of Credit Unions – currently boasting 530 branches and 2.5 million members across the island of Ireland –

over plans to tax interest on savings. There was right and wrong on both sides, but McCreevy continued to nurse his wrath much to the embarrassment of Fianna Fáil backbenchers, coming under fire from local Credit Union activists in their own communities.

As noted, McCreevy had fallen foul of Haughey early in his career and was destined to remain a long time on the backbenches. However, the talented chartered accountant was promoted by Reynolds in 1992 and made the transition to the Ahern camp when Ahern was elected leader in 1994, becoming front-bench finance spokesman.

Seeing that he couldn't be a time-serving backbencher, McCreevy had to be radical and active in his role as the second-most powerful member of government. Labour finance spokesman at the time, Derek McDowell, once said that the best way to predict a McCreevy policy decision was to look at his officials' advice and figure out what was the opposite option. Indeed, McCreevy's radical policy decisions were not always unanimously welcomed. Fine Gael finance spokesman, Michael Noonan accused the Minister for Finance of radical action for its sake alone.

'Pol Pot was radical,' Noonan declared.

Critics argued that McCreevy's approach consistently gave most to the highest earners. For his part, McCreevy argued that his approach was to favour priming the economy and encouraging enterprise and cited his decision to halve capital gains tax from 40 to 20 per cent as a good example. In fact, he proudly boasted that revenues had increased as a result.

Above all, McCreevy gloried in his image of being somewhat wayward. In 1998, he told Ógra Fianna Fáil that Irish voters loved flawed politicians who smelt of sulphur. For that reason, he insisted on shunning spin doctors and image-makers.

'They want to sand down the rough bits that make people interesting,' he had said.

McCreevy's biggest row came in his third Budget in 1999 when a move towards so-called 'tax individualisation' was seen to favour two-income families and penalise stay-at-home mothers. Critics spanned the political and social spectrum from the Irish Family Planning Association through the country's biggest trade union, SIPTU, to the Catholic Archbishop of Dublin.

Alarm bells were set off by the Independent TDs supporting the Government, who now numbered four with the addition of Donegal South-West Independent, Tom Gildea. A growing number of Fianna Fáil backbenchers came forward to say that they were feeling the heat, as their constituency offices were flooded with calls and messages of complaint. The Fianna Fáil protesters included Ahern's brother, Noel; Seán Haughey of Dublin North-Central; Batt O'Keeffe of Cork South-Central; Beverly Cooper-Flynn of Mayo and Billy Kelleher of Cork North-Central.

Irish Independent political writer Gene McKenna cited one Fianna Fáil TD as saying the gaffe could cost the party up to 15 seats at the next election. Publicly, the Taoiseach stood by his Minister for Finance, who in turn was slow to give ground. None the less, McCreevy did pledge and implement changes in the enabling legislation that followed the Budget by giving more tax allowances to single-income married couples. In summary, a billion-pound giveaway package had proved a huge political nightmare.

~ ~ ~ ~ ~

As he approached his 50th birthday in September 2001, Bertie Ahern told this writer that he often put in a 35 to 40-hour week grappling with Northern Ireland issues and then turned around to face his regular work running the country. The brutal reality of politics is that there are few votes south of the Border on the Northern issue, beyond a certain national feel-good factor and residual political prestige when things are going well. However, in fairness to the main opposition parties, their support for all-party consensus on the issue also helps insulate the Government from political fall-out in case of reverses.

That said, 400 years of conflict and its attendant antagonisms and mistrust cannot be fully ameliorated in a few years. In the years since 1998 most positive developments were followed by some considerable reverses.

The Good Friday Agreement was sorely tested on 15 August 1998 with a bomb blast in Omagh that shocked the entire world. A total of 29 people died, including grandmothers, pregnant mothers, children and babies. Over 200 people were injured and maimed. The bomb was the work of the so-called 'Real IRA', a dissident group determined on wrecking the fragile peace deal. It was the worst single atrocity in the North's grim history.

All the parties to the Agreement, however, showed considerable fortitude in uniting and condemning the outrage, including Sinn Féin president Gerry Adams. In addition, Ahern pledged the biggest extension to anti-terrorist legislation in 20 years. He also avoided trying to force the pace on IRA arms decommissioning but issued an appeal to Republicans to make a gesture.

'Nationalists have to show a magnanimity that has rarely been shown to them,' he told the International Humbert School in Killala days after the outrage.

The North's power-sharing government was finally established in late 1999 only to be suspended again in February 2000 in the ongoing row over IRA arms decommissioning. Things continued in that vein over the ensuing years with two steps forward and one step backwards – and sometimes the reverse of that process, as a stop-start pattern began to emerge. A similar wearisome blame-game sequence also took shape: the Unionists blamed the IRA's failure to give up weapons and commit to a definitive end to paramilitary conflict; Republicans blamed the Unionists' role in evoking suspensions of the fledgling Belfast parliament and government and demanded a quicker scaling down of the British military presence.

On two occasions, October 2001 and April 2002, the IRA made gestures on weapons decommissioning which were hailed as historic and groundbreaking. Canadian Army General, John de Chastelain, who heads the Independent International Commission on Decommissioning, verified each IRA action. However, ultimately these IRA arms gestures were invariably criticised as belated and too limited in scope to build the required confidence among Unionists.

On 21 October 2003, all of the parties, including Blair and Ahern, again assembled at Hillsborough Castle in an all-out bid to restore the power-sharing institutions ahead of elections to renew the Northern parliament, which had already been postponed. Hopes were high that this effort would succeed. Yet again the question of 'choreography', or sequencing the statements and assurances, loomed large. Ahern was later to confess that he was reluctant to travel that day because he had been unable to make contact with General de Chastelain, apparently busy inspecting weapons dumps.

Belatedly, General de Chastelain arrived at Hillsborough and told the assembled press that he had witnessed a third act of IRA decommissioning more significant than the previous two. However, UUP leader David Trimble announced that he could not accept the assurances because they were not transparent enough. Later Tony Blair told reporters that both he and Ahern knew the details of the decommissioning but could not divulge them because of a confidentiality clause. Rather wearily, Ahern said efforts to find a settlement would continue. But with elections fixed for 26 November 2003, hope was again at a low ebb.

There were two constants: a mix of political suspicion and intransigence amongst the parties and a continuing trust and co-operation between Ahern and Blair. Brian Rowan in his book, *The Armed Peace – Life and Death After the Ceasefires*, aptly summed up the situation which obtained a year previously. As with so much else in the North, the words still applied in October 2003:

> Since the British and Irish elections of 1997, Blair and the Taoiseach Bertie Ahern have become a peace-process double act. With American help, they have steered the Northern Ireland parties through the Good Friday Agreement, power-sharing and the new beginning to policing. They had also watched the IRA move to put some of its arms beyond use, but now the process that London, Dublin and Washington – under two presidents – had devoted so much time to was sinking in political quicksand.

Close observers suggest that the dynamic of the Ahern–Blair relationship may have shifted, however. In their early encounters Blair was extremely confident, riding on the wave of a huge Labour victory and enjoying global notoriety backed by an awesome publicity machine. There is little doubt that Ahern studied his new counterpart and learnt. But more recently, in 2004, Blair is beleaguered, suffering badly at home and abroad for supporting US President George W Bush's misadventure in Iraq. None the less, the Blair–Ahern combination is the most fruitful Prime Minister–Taoiseach collaboration in the history of the Irish State. And now, for the first time, a British leader may need an Irish result more than his counterpart in Dublin. A definitive result from the Northern Ireland peace process is clearly a fillip that Blair badly needs.

~ ~ ~ ~ ~

The Northern Ireland Assembly elections left Paisley's DUP and Sinn Féin as the biggest parties within unionism and nationalism. Henceforth, any deal would have to be brokered between the two extremes that had thus far not even managed to speak to one another. Another review process began in February 2004 only to be stalled again amid further controversy and bickering. This review resumed in June 2004 in the midst of some hopeful signs of a thaw in relations between DUP and Sinn Féin. More all-party talks involving Blair and Ahern were fixed for 15 September 2004 at Leeds Castle in Kent.

Political sources in Dublin attested to Ahern's growing weariness with the Republicans and Sinn Féin, who had taken much throughout the process but given little in return. From the outset, in June 1997, the Taoiseach had assumed the role of keeping the Republicans on side and delivering the assurances they required. As a consequence, Ahern absorbed the fall-out problems such as Republican efforts to import arms from the US and the arrest of three Irish Republican suspects in Colombia on suspicion of training left-wing terrorists.

A week before the October 2003 talks, Ahern had suffered an embarrassment in the Dáil when obliged to admit that his then adviser Dr Martin Mansergh had in fact met leaders of the Real IRA in late 1998 after the Omagh bomb atrocity. Twelve months earlier he had vaguely spoken of contacts with the Real IRA giving the impression that these had taken place before the Omagh atrocity. Outrage and allegations of misleading parliament ensued, but it also again showed the depth of contact with paramilitaries and the lengths gone to in the quest for a settlement.

In October 2003 Ahern had also faced an additional political risk south of the Border. Days after the talks broke down, *Star* journalist, Kevin Farrell, reported that an emerging deal would have involved release for four Republican prisoners held in connection with the killing of Detective Garda Jerry McCabe in June 1996. This was an extremely contentious matter for a number of reasons – not least a personal guarantee by Minister for Justice John O'Donoghue to Garda McCabe's widow, Anne, that the killers would not get early release. The issue was also a considerable potential flashpoint with Ahern's Progressive Democrat Coalition partners. It took until May 2004 for Ahern to admit in the Dáil that Garda McCabe's killers were in line for release. However, he insisted that such a release was contingent on the IRA ceasing all paramilitary activity. Other political sources indicated that a major move on IRA decommissioning would have sufficed and that seven months previously, elaborate plans were being put in place for a release. The issue caused turmoil within the PDs with pressure exerted on their party president and Minister for Justice, Michael McDowell.

A month later in the June 2004 local and European Parliament elections, Fianna Fáil took serious losses and watched Sinn Féin take a major share of their votes. Ahern was given a very good insight into how the SDLP felt north of the Border as their vote share was ruthlessly taken by the Sinn Féin machine. Those within Fianna Fáil say the outcome came as a huge blow to Ahern.

'We lost this election; there is no doubt about that. Sinn Féin won it,' Ahern told reporters as the final counting was done.

The talks in Leeds Castle from 15 to 18 September marked the first time Sinn Féin and the DUP had negotiated together. Even at that, these were indirect or 'proximity talks' without face-to-face meetings, and discussions ended without agreement while still leaving a mood of cautious optimism.

Evidence for that optimism was supported by a surprise visit for talks in Dublin by Ian Paisley and his DUP lieutenants on 30 September 2004. Ahern and Paisley first formally met in Dublin in October 1999 when Paisley visited to discuss attacks on premises belonging to his Free Presbyterian Church in Co Monaghan. There was a further meeting at the Irish Embassy in London in January 2004. As with Trimble before him, Paisley too has learnt to trust Ahern as someone with whom he can do a deal.

By contrast, Sinn Féin–DUP distrust remained intense. Despite this, Blair and Ahern have assured Paisley that the IRA will promptly dispose of all their weaponry and effectively become an 'old comrades' association'. In return, the DUP must guarantee to share power fairly and honestly with nationalists. As 2004 draws to a close, hopes are rising that Northern Ireland's agony will soon be over. Bertie Ahern remains central to that hope.

12

Euro Hero – Local Zero

These days Bertie Ahern generally sees Charlie Haughey only at Christmas time when he visits his old mentor at his classical mansion in Kinsealy, Co Dublin. The passage of time since the first scandalous Haughey revelations in 1996 has reduced the likelihood of any more political harm to the current Taoiseach. The years have also seen Haughey advance in age and decline in health. It is noticeable only recently that Ahern finds he can publicly speak in strident and positive tones again about the man with whom he closely collaborated for 15 years. In September 2004, Bertie Ahern gave this writer the following summation of his current view on Haughey.

> I have huge respect for Charlie Haughey. He gave me a lot of breaks. He never asked me to do anything untoward. Any dealings I ever had with him were always about work – work for the Government, for the country or for the party. Never once did he ask me to do anything that was difficult or something I would resent doing.

> I think history will be kind to him. As far as I'm concerned he made a huge contribution to the State. He got into trouble over a few things and I don't condone those things. A lot of my guys were very annoyed at the time and I said some very hard things at the Ard Fheis in 1997. But I had to say them because you just can't condone that kind of thing.

It did detract from Charlie's reputation, but at the same time, his contribution has been enormous to the country and the party.

He did so much work. When you look back at the things that he did: the reforming legislation, his achievements in justice and family law, the succession acts for women. What he did for culture, Aosdana, the Arts, and some of his initiatives in finance. What he did for the old. You can't take it away from him. He has a huge legislative track record.

Ahern's assessment accords with a view held for some time by writers like T Ryle Dwyer that the medium to longer view on Charlie Haughey will be much more positive than earlier evaluations which focused on his venal side and flawed nature. Some of these more positive assessments draw analogies with the case of former US President Richard Nixon.

Others retain a much stronger view to the contrary, arguing that Haughey's abiding legacy was to play a major role in undermining Irish people's faith in politicians and the democratic system. Some in Fine Gael and Labour argue that Ireland will not move to a 'post-Haughey political era' as long as Bertie Ahern is active in politics.

Down through the years, Bertie Ahern received various legacies from Haughey of a collaboration which began in 1977 and intensified in 1982 when the Gregory deal was concluded and Ahern first walked into the Cabinet room as Government Chief Whip. Ahern acknowledges that Haughey gave him his first breaks and kept him close to the action where he was to learn so much about the practice of politics. Readily, he admits that without Haughey's help he might not ultimately have become Taoiseach.

Haughey also bequeathed Ahern the often-repeated assessment which provides the title for this biography. Again in September 2004, this time in an interview on Lyric FM radio, Ahern recalled how he knew from the moment he heard Haughey's words of effusive praise in October 1991, including the key terms 'most skilful, most devious, most cunning,' that they would haunt him for years to come. As a seasoned politician Ahern accepts that the context, as outlined both in the Introduction and in Chapter 6 of this book, is more usually forgotten. He also reasonably concludes that Haughey could just have said Ahern was 'the best of them all' and left it at that. However, that would not have been Charlie Haughey's style.

It is clear that from early on Ahern learnt to manage his boss and was keenly aware of what happened if Haughey believed you were wasting his time. This was his assessment in the 1986 *Hot Press* interview.

> For one reason or another, you are liked or disliked. If you don't get on well with Haughey, you'll know and he'll know. If you get on well with him, well, he's a very good person. He's straight. I have served under him in difficult times and difficult circumstances. Crises. Several crises. I was probably closer than most people to him. He is just a fantastic worker. He's phenomenally hard-working, from early morning to late at night. He never asks anyone to do anything he wouldn't do himself. He had tremendous style. I'm a great believer in him. He is prepared to take risks. If Haughey thinks it's a good idea, he'll stand on his head, he'll stand the system on its head, to get that to work. If he thinks it's a lot of nonsense, then you'll go out the door knowing that. I think that's a good way to be.

Furthermore, Ahern admitted that he had learnt a good deal from Charlie Haughey and consciously tried to emulate him.

> I have learned an awful lot. I wish I had his ability. I don't think many people in the country have. His means of working is to cut out the nonsense, get on with the job and use the position that you have to the full. I certainly, if not copied, picked up a lot in that I try and approach things in a similarly efficient way.

There is also strong evidence to suggest that towards the end of Haughey's career the pupil–master role was beginning to be reversed. In an angry outburst to would-be Fianna Fáil Parliamentary Party rebels in December 2003, Ahern reminded them of the old days in the party under previous leaders. In a throwaway comment, he said he had kept Charlie Haughey in office.

However, when the extraordinary Haughey revelations came to light in 1996 there were inevitable questions about Ahern's prior state of knowledge. He has persistently insisted that his was a working relationship with Haughey and he had no way of knowing about Haughey's lavish spending, averaging €3,000 per day at its height.

Friends acknowledge that Ahern was a regular at Saturday meetings at the Haughey mansion in Kinsealy. Other regular attendees included PJ Mara and Ray Burke. But equally, these friends insist that these meetings were about work and not intimate social occasions. Indeed, Ahern's contemporaries are extremely protective in rejecting any suggested taint by association with Haughey. One senior member of the current Cabinet, when asked why Ahern did not know about Haughey's antics given their professional closeness, puts it like this:

> Everyone assumed Haughey made big money in the late 1950s and 1960s – sometimes using inside knowledge – which was wrong but somehow acceptable by the standards of the time. People knew about his involvement as a principal in Haughey Boland accountants and assumed that he had money very well invested. Remember that the issue foxed successive Fine Gael and Labour leaders and the vast bulk of the media.

~ ~ ~ ~ ~

Many Fianna Fáil activists see Bertie Ahern's decade of leadership as an effort to move the party beyond the days of sleaze allegations generated by Charlie Haughey and some of his contemporaries. At time of writing, Haughey has made peace with the Revenue Commissioners by paying over some €5m in back taxes, penalties and interest. It is most unlikely that he will ever face charges of obstructing the McCracken Tribunal, as suggested in August 1997. A Circuit Court Judge ruled that prejudicial comments by Tánaiste and Progressive Democrat leader Mary Harney, and a raft of adverse media commentary, have ruined all chances of a fair trial. Meanwhile, the Moriarty Tribunal has yet to pronounce on their investigations into Haughey's affairs. But beyond that, it appears likely that Charlie Haughey just might finally have moved into private life.

Speaking at the International Humbert School in Ballina on 22 July 2004, PJ Mara described his old friend Haughey 'as older and a little shrunken' – but generally in good form and rather bemused by recent social and legislative trends.

'He is somewhat bemused about the whole nanny state thing and certainly doesn't approve of it,' Mara said of his old friend. Indeed, Haughey's observations on his protégé Ahern would make for interesting reading.

As for Ray Burke, he is due for sentencing in December 2004 on charges of tax fraud to which he pleaded guilty in the summer of 2004. Days before his guilty plea on tax charges, Burke had paid over half a million euro to the Criminal Assets Bureau. Currently, the maximum penalty for tax charges is five years in prison. In September 2002, the then Planning Tribunal chairman, Mr Justice Feargus Flood, ruled that Burke had received corrupt payments totalling almost €200,000 in the 1970s and 1980s. The report added that Burke had hindered and obstructed the Tribunal and given it false information. Two years later in September 2004, the new tribunal chairman, Judge Alan Mahon, ruled that Burke was not entitled to €10m in legal costs because he had obstructed the Tribunal's work.

The catalogue of Burke's woes recently caused Ahern to reflect to friends how things might have been for Burke had he answered differently to Ahern's question on the morning of 26 June 1997, when selecting his Cabinet.

'Maybe he could have had a quieter life over the past seven years,' Ahern mused.

Other controversies from the Haughey era however still linger.

In the summer of 2004, Pádraig Flynn was a witness at the Planning Tribunal in which the circumstances of the £50,000 (€63,000) cheque received from builder Tom Gilmartin were and continue to be examined. It is, however, remarkable that Fianna Fáil have made very poor efforts to recover money which appeared intended for the party. Some months earlier in April 2004 Bertie Ahern was back before the Planning Tribunal and faced a five-hour grilling about his knowledge of lobbying by Tom Gilmartin back in 1989. Under repeated questioning from Gilmartin's counsel, Hugh O'Neill SC, the Taoiseach conceded – for the first time – that he may have been among a number of ministers who met with Mr Gilmartin back in 1989. Vigorously, Gilmartin claims that he met up to seven ministers in connection with his plans for two major shopping developments in Dublin in the late 1980s, a period of economic stagnation in Ireland. Moreover, the builder says he was approached shortly afterwards by a man not known to him, who demanded £5m (€6.3m) in return for securing political support for the development projects.

Ahern insisted, however, that any such meeting with the builder would have been a casual enough encounter rather than a formalised 'political' meeting. In fact, most the 1989 Cabinet say they cannot remember such a meeting taking place. The one exception is Mary O'Rourke, who emphatically told the Tribunal that she attended a meeting broadly similar to the one described by Mr Gilmartin. In his testimony, the Taoiseach said he believed he had three meetings with Mr Gilmartin in 1988 and 1989 as well as at least one phone call. However, he admitted that he also put the builder in touch with his friend and political backer, Joe Burke, then a member of Dublin Corporation. The Tribunal continues to consider these matters.

During his five-hour appearance, Ahern was spared the experience of being cross-examined by former Fianna Fáil TD Liam Lawlor, another politician to have created his share of headaches for his former party leader. Lawlor has taken serious issue with the allegations being made by Gilmartin and remains a defiant figure at the Planning Tribunal where he now represents himself.

Amid a welter of controversy and ongoing corruption investigations, Lawlor was obliged to resign from the Fianna Fáil organisation in June 2000. By March 2002 he had been jailed three times, serving six weeks out of a total sentence of three months, for failing to provide all of the required information to the Planning Tribunal. In the spring of 2003, while Ahern was visiting Prague, he shared a bar with Lawlor after an apparent chance meeting.

Like Bertie Ahern, Lawlor was first elected to the Dáil in 1977 and Ahern expressed sympathy on a personal basis with his old colleague when first jailed. There was added embarrassment for Ahern, however, as he had appointed Lawlor to the Dáil ethics committee. Equally, Ahern's Government remained dependent on Lawlor's vote and that of a number of other 'FF exiles', including Denis Foley of Kerry North, who had quit the party because of tax cheating.

There has been only one direct allegation of corruption made against Ahern himself, though this was dismissed in July 2001 by a Circuit Court Judge as 'utterly, completely and absolutely false and untrue'. That finding followed a libel action taken by the Taoiseach after the *Sunday Business Post* published allegations by a Cork businessman, Denis 'Starry' O'Brien, in April 2000. O'Brien had claimed that he had given £50,000 (€63,000) to Ahern in 1989 to help secure planning permission for a shopping development in Dublin. In response, Ahern sued O'Brien only and waived his opportunity to take what could have been a very punitive action against the newspaper. In fact, he interrupted talks about the North at Weston Park, Shropshire, on the Welsh–English border to attend the hearing.

'A politician has to accept that people will often say things about him which are unfair – but no one has the right to spread malicious rumours and direct lies,' Ahern told reporters after the verdict was handed down. He promised to donate the £30,000 (€38,000) award to charity if he received it.

Clearly, it has been hard for Ahern to shake the allegations of sleaze that came with the Haughey legacy. His supporters however point to prompt and decisive action in the case of two more recent incidents, involving Mayo TD Beverly Flynn and Limerick West TD Michael Collins.

In Flynn's case, she was expelled from the Fianna Fáil Parliamentary Party and then from the entire organisation in July 2004. This came after the Supreme Court confirmed a High Court jury verdict that she had been advising the clients of an investment bank, where she worked, to cheat on their taxes in 1990. Initially, the case arose when she took a libel action against RTÉ who first reported the tax cheating allegations. Having resented being expelled from the entire Fianna Fáil organisation, Ms Flynn noted that while the decision was taken by the 104-member Fianna Fáil National Executive, just one person was behind it.

'When Bertie Ahern says you're out – you're out,' she told the International Humbert School in Ballina.

Limerick West TD Michael Collins resigned from the Fianna Fáil Parliamentary Party in September 2003 after it emerged that he had paid almost €131,000 to the Revenue Commissioners in tax, interest and penalties due on a bogus overseas account dating from the 1980s. Investigations into the legality of a declaration of tax compliance he made after the May 2002 general election continue at time of writing.

One veteran Fianna Fáil TD argues that these two cases show that Ahern has worked hard to set a new standard in office. Critics counter that Bertie Ahern's Fianna Fáil still remains close to business in general and the building trade especially.

~ ~ ~ ~ ~

Not all of Ahern's controversies were the products of times past, however. Almost four months after Ahern was elected Taoiseach, a young Dublin architect named Philip Sheedy was sentenced to four years in jail on 20 October 1997. He had been driving his new sports car recklessly while drunk and an accident led to the death of Mrs Anne Ryan and injury to her husband, John, and their two children. His sentence was to be reviewed after two years. Sheedy decided not to appeal the sentence and the review date – which would have obliged him to serve at least two years – was lifted. Distressed at the impact the jail sentence, was having on him, the Sheedy family feared that his mental and physical health would deteriorate. Representations were then made to various politicians including the Taoiseach. He in turn passed a request for day release to Minister for Justice John O'Donoghue. Meanwhile, Cllr Joe Burke, a long-time friend of Ahern's and trustee of St Luke's, who had also worked with Sheedy, visited him at Shelton Abbey open prison in Co Wicklow.

At the same time another connection was made on behalf of the family with a Supreme Court Judge, Mr Justice Hugh O'Flaherty, who agreed to look into the case because of the distress involved. Through his influence, the case was relisted for the Circuit Court. On 12 November 1997 – 13 months after he first went to prison – Circuit Court Judge Cyril Kelly suspended the balance of Sheedy's sentence in very unusual circumstances. The story of this remarkable case swept through the gossipy halls of the Law Library at the Four Courts in Dublin.

Just days following his release, Philip Sheedy was spotted on the street by a relative of the Ryan's, who told the Gardaí and inquiries began. As the Director of Public Prosecutions began appeal proceedings on the sentence suspension, Sheedy returned to prison voluntarily.

The entire controversy led to an investigation by the Chief Justice and the resignation of Mr Justice O'Flaherty and Judge Cyril Kelly along with the Court registrar who had deemed it wise to do a Supreme Court judge a favour. Special legislation was put through the Oireachtas to augment the judges' pensions – but the controversy deepened when they refused an opportunity to explain their actions to a Dáil committee. More crucially, the affair also very nearly ended Ahern's coalition arrangement with the Progressive Democrats. Author Stephen Collins in *The Power Game* notes that Harney boycotted the Cabinet for a day and Ahern had to work hard to repair the damage done.

Inevitably, the Government took a big political blow. Ahern subsequently answered questions in the Dáil and said he had made representations on behalf of Philip Sheedy in the same way as he made representations on the widest range of issues for hundreds of people each week. As his constituency manager Senator Cyprian Brady later told this writer, Ahern's office generates up to 700 representational letters every week.

There followed considerable debate about differing attitudes to middle-class and working-class perpetrators of crime. But there the matter would have rested except that on a sultry Friday evening, 19 May 2000, the Minister for Finance, Charlie McCreevy, announced that he had nominated Hugh O'Flaherty for the vice-presidency of the European Investment Bank (EIB). This EU institution, based in Luxembourg, helps fund large projects across the member states. The job of vice-president carried a salary of £147,000 (€187,000) per year and various perks, including a preferential rate of tax.

Two solid months of political controversy followed, ending only with Mr O'Flaherty withdrawing his nomination in the face of clear hostility from the EIB's other directors. Charlie McCreevy took the political blame saying it was entirely his own idea –

though he admitted he did not know the former Supreme Court Judge at all well. Progressive Democrat leader Mary Harney had been consulted; however, she admitted she should have consulted her parliamentary colleagues. Later she became extremely angry with Bertie Ahern when on radio he announced that it would help if Mr O'Flaherty publicly explained his role in the Sheedy case. In fact, opposition politicians expressed their surprise that the nomination was presented as McCreevy's idea – they argued that it was far more likely to have come from Bertie Ahern who knew O'Flaherty much better.

It was the only issue which really incited the public's anger in the entire first five years of Ahern's first government. Surveys showed that seven out of 10 voters found the decision was wrong – six out of 10 Fianna Fáil voters concurred.

One of Ahern's major projects towards the end of his first term in office, which he approached with considerable dread, was the holding of a referendum providing for an abortion ban in the Constitution. As a practising Catholic, this is a subject upon which Ahern holds strong personal views. The issue remained inconclusive and tangled after various failed attempts to achieve clarity over 20 years during which the public were asked to vote twice on four separate propositions. There were also numerous court cases. Ahern's proposals came after years of consultation and involved putting a law banning abortion into the Constitution.

The only exception to the ban would be when a mother's life was at risk – but a threat of suicide by the mother would not be an acceptable risk. At the same time, the Government set up a Crisis Pregnancy Agency, with a starting budget of €6m per year. The debate proved more civilized on this occasion compared to previous referendums, but it was as deeply confused as the others. On 6 March 2002, Ahern's proposition was defeated by less than 1 per cent of the vote. Not surprisingly, he signalled he had no intention of revisiting the issue.

~ ~ ~ ~ ~

Just after 8 pm on Wednesday evening, 24 April 2002, Bertie Ahern slipped quietly into the Dáil chamber and announced that he would be asking the President the next morning to dissolve the Dáil. Just a handful of TDs were present to see him launch his bid to regain power.

Ahern spearheaded a whirlwind three-week election campaign that was an even better replica of the successful 1997 effort. This time he had Martin Mackin as a very effective Fianna Fáil general secretary and a very similar back-up team. Again the MacSharry Committee had combed through the constituencies and there was a ruthless candidate selection process with highly unpopular instructions issued to veteran deputies to divide territory and vote manage.

Yet again there were occasional appeals for Ahern's intervention, which were sympathetically received without any evidence of action being taken.

'He was a great man for shifting blame to Mount Street [location of Fianna Fáil's HQ] and that was the last you heard of it,' says one veteran TD who was the focus of a bitter territorial row in the south of the country.

Another Leinster Fianna Fáil politician recalls Ahern being called upon to meet three candidates, who were at daggers drawn, during a constituency visit.

'We were led to understand that he would knock our heads together. Instead we got a succession of mumbled 'ah lads' type statements before he was quickly off on his way again.'

A high-profile casualty was Fianna Fáil deputy leader Mary O'Rourke who lost her seat in the three-seat constituency of Westmeath after 20 years' Dáil service. The former Minister for Public Enterprise had been controversial but was well liked by the public. She strongly resisted efforts to vote-share with veteran Fianna Fáil Senator Donie Cassidy, arguing that the party vote was simply not enough to be shared. Though she polled 6,444 first preferences, she lost out to Cassidy.

The view of Fianna Fáil strategists after the event was pretty merciless. 'The votes were there, she simply should not have lost,' one backroom manager told this writer. As one of Ahern's nominators for the party leadership in 1994, O'Rourke successfully demanded a Seanad nomination as one of the Taoiseach's eleven. However, this nomination was only secured after Ahern had asked her to stand in the Seanad election – a suggestion she had peremptorily rejected. Ultimately, she was appointed leader of the Seanad, a post which she has used to harry Government ministers and raise the profile of the sleepy upper house of parliament.

Overall, Ahern and his colleagues had left the Opposition stuck in the traps. Fine Gael had lost much scarce energy replacing their leader of over 10 years, John Bruton, in February 2001. His replacement, Michael Noonan of Limerick East, was a seasoned political campaigner who had often done well in ministerial office.

But rightly or wrongly, a good deal of the blame for the handling of the 'Hepatitis C' scandal about contaminated blood was attached to Noonan. In the months prior to the election, RTÉ screened a fictional dramatisation based on the scandal, which did not help Noonan's case. Yet at the same time Fine Gael were busy making some strange decisions of their own on electoral strategy.

The public reacted with at best indifference, and in many cases hostility, to a proposal to compensate those who lost money buying shares in the privatisation of the national telephone service. A further Fine Gael scheme to compensate taxi drivers hit by deregulation was an even worse non-starter. Above all, it transpired that Noonan had been left with far too little time to revive his party's flagging fortunes.

Fine Gael and Noonan's problems were augmented by Labour's attitude. Their leader Ruairí Quinn would not agree a pre-election pact, which most observers agree was the only means of dislodging Fianna Fáil from power. Conversely, Quinn said they would fight the election independently and see what options were available after the event. Fine Gael had good grounds for suspecting that this was a barely coded message to Ahern that Labour was available for coalition. Later Noonan revealed that he had predicted to Quinn that his stance meant neither of them would be leader of their party within months of the election. Even so, both parties were up against a much simpler reality: Ireland had experienced an unparalleled boom during the five years of Ahern's term as Taoiseach.

Ahern and Minister for Finance Charlie McCreevy were able to ease taxes and increase public expenditure, something which had never previously happened in the State's history. Was Ahern central to its development – or was it largely the product of international events? Beyond a doubt, the debate on that one will continue for some time to come. But recent expert assessments suggest that Ireland's newfound prosperity came from a series of policies followed by successive governments over the previous 40 years. In essence, Ahern was part of these positive developments but not the originator.

Added to that prosperity was the renewal of national consensus with unions, bosses, government and farmers and a certain feel-good factor arising from the continuing imperfect peace north of the Border. Both of these issues had been skilfully handled by Ahern. Against all this, Fine Gael and Labour efforts to raise the shortcomings of an increasingly expensive health service and diminished quality of life made no impact.

Soon it became clear that the real issue was whether or not Fianna Fáil could win an overall majority. This was something few observers would have contemplated even months before the calling of a general election. But it had been quietly discussed within Fianna Fáil with growing conviction for at least two years previously.

Crucially, Progressive Democrat president Michael McDowell took a hand. McDowell had been persuaded to return to politics with his appointment as Attorney General in July 1999. Taking leave from his job as the government's lawyer, he took to the campaign trail with gusto. PD leader Mary Harney had already launched a campaign arguing that the party had achieved much with just four TDs – and would double that achievement with eight. Now McDowell launched a slogan: 'One-Party Government? No Thanks!' He followed up with a personalised attack on Bertie Ahern, likening his ill-starred plans for a National Stadium, the so-called 'Bertie Bowl', as worthy of the vainglorious despots, Nicolae Ceausescu of Romania or Benito Mussolini of Italy.

Former PD leader Des O'Malley's parting shot on his way to retirement was to recall that the last Fianna Fáil one-party administration in 1987 had left a legacy still being examined by the tribunals. However, O'Malley neglected to mention that he had served in Government with much the same team, before and after the Fianna Fáil–PD split, and that his party had spent almost half its existence in coalition with politicians now not fit to govern alone.

The strategy was much commented upon and ultimately successful. But in reality it was just a more distant and noisier version of the 'long-distance' electoral strategy pursued in June 1997. Privately, Ahern himself conceded that McDowell's move was largely instrumental in depriving him of an overall majority. He also insisted that he did not take McDowell's comments personally. 'It's just politics,' he shrugged in a comment reminiscent of what he used to tell his mother 20 years previously when she railed at Fine Gael criticisms of Charlie Haughey.

When the votes were counted on 18 and 19 May 2002, Fianna Fáil had 81 TDs and the Progressive Democrats had eight. The two parties would easily conclude a new coalition 'Programme for Government' deal. Contesting their first election since they merged with Democratic Left, Labour just held their own with 21 TDs. But Fine Gael had a disastrous election dropping from 54 to 31 seats. Even before the election count was completed, Michael

Noonan announced his resignation. Questions were being asked about Fine Gael's survival, though in fact the party had lost seat numbers disproportionate to the decline in its percentage vote. Fulfilling Noonan's grim prediction, Ruairí Quinn quit as Labour leader in September 2002.

The Green Party with six TDs and Sinn Féin with five deputies had made marked advances. There were a total of 13 Independents – including the Fianna Fáil-friendly trio of Jackie Healy-Rae, Mildred Fox and this time Niall Blaney, a son of Harry Blaney and nephew of the late Neil Blaney. There were also a number of other 'FF independents' who successfully bucked the centralist candidate policy, including James Breen of Clare and Paddy McHugh of Galway East. A deal with these could have boosted the 'FF gene pool' to 86 TDs and an overall majority. But for many reasons, including future Fianna Fáil cohesion, it was deemed best to stick with the PDs.

In Dublin Central, Bertie Ahern again easily headed the poll with 10,896 votes, which placed him sixth in the roll of leading vote-getters when measured in numbers of votes. When expressed in quota terms, Ahern was rated second highest with 1.6 quotas. Independent Tony Gregory and Labour's Joe Costello also took seats. But in the final analysis, Ahern's running mate, Dr Dermot Fitzpatrick had just 79 votes to spare over Nicky Kehoe of Sinn Féin. In fact, the Sinn Féin candidate had polled almost twice Fitzpatrick's first preference total of 2,590.

A relieved Ahern got the news during a late-night visit to the party's election headquarters-cum-media centre, which had served them so well through a very successfully orchestrated media campaign. Yet again it was an exemplary exercise in vote management with 81 TDs being returned with 41.5 per cent of the national vote. The PDs also had a good deal of luck as they doubled their number of TDs from four to eight with a fractionally smaller vote share than the previous 1997 election.

However, it was the closest call yet for an Ahern running mate and ironically involved a rival candidate from Sinn Féin, the party Ahern had helped into the political process over a period of five years. It was a sharp lesson in *realpolitik* for Fianna Fáil, right on Ahern's home patch, and more was to come.

To this day Ahern remains extremely sensitive to accusations of hogging the constituency limelight. After the election, he argued that he had written letters advising voters to give precedence to Fitzpatrick and also seconded one of his own best strategists to his running mate's canvass team. But yet again, an Ahern Fianna Fáil running mate in Dublin Central had failed to make any impact in their own right. In fact, not since George Colley, who died in 1983, has a second Fianna Fáil candidate had any decent kind of vote base of their own in Ahern's Dublin Central.

None the less, on 6 June 2002 these things were mere details for Bertie Ahern as he was re-elected Taoiseach for the second consecutive term with the same outgoing team – something that had not been achieved in Ireland since 1969. It enhanced the considerable feat of keeping a minority coalition successfully in power for a full five-year term.

~ ~ ~ ~ ~

'SCREWED BY LIARS' was the page-one headline on the *Irish Daily Star* of 15 November 2002. It was a robust summation of the national mood not quite four months after Ahern's election success. Several opinion polls showed the Government ratings had dropped dramatically in what was the shortest political honeymoon for any Irish government.

The renewed Fianna Fáil–PD Coalition Government's fall from grace was swift and decisive. The weeks immediately after the formation of the new Government had brought a drip-feed of bad news and a number of key and specific election promises were rolled back.

Minister for Justice Michael McDowell announced there was not enough funding for the promised 2,000 extra Gardaí, including a dedicated traffic corps to tackle road deaths. Minister for Education Noel Dempsey conceded that promised refurbishments and rebuilding at hundreds of schools around the country were not all they seemed at election time. His promise to act as honest broker in ordering a new, realistic scheme of priorities did not help disappointed teachers, parents and pupils much.

Publicly, Minister for Health Micheál Martin announced that the aim of ending hospital waiting lists inside two years was not realisable. In addition, the Government said they had no funds to deliver the promised 200,000 extra medical cards. Minister for Foreign Affairs Brian Cowen conceded it would not be possible to reach the promised 0.7 per cent of GNP overseas aid donation promised by Ahern at the UN Millennium Summit in September 2000. Cutbacks elsewhere included the Community Employment (CE) schemes, which kept many social projects operating around the country, and reductions in the forestry budget.

The day the *Irish Daily Star* headline appeared, the Government had just published the spending plans for the year 2003. These included a proposal to end the first-time buyers grant for houses at a time when young workers' struggle to buy a home had become a hot political issue. Dozens of nervous Government backbenchers began expressing their dismay.

Immediately, Bertie Ahern went on the offensive but the public were not receptive to his arguments that there were no cutbacks – merely reductions in the pace of growth in spending. Critics argued that the Government had wildly fuelled spending with two giveaway Budgets in succession before the May 2002 general election. Then Government spending was allowed to increase to a high of 22 per cent – now they were busy hauling that back to a targeted 7 per cent increase.

Behind the scenes, senior Fianna Fáil politicians admitted that they had mishandled a tricky situation. One senior minister admits that the promises before May 2002 were 'excessive in measure and detail' and that they would probably have won the election without them.

'We also took our eye off the ball in the exhaustion and euphoria of winning. We should have explained ourselves more quickly and clearly. We should not have left that drip, drip news about spending reductions go out there like that,' the Minister says.

There were also misgivings inside Fianna Fáil about a written guarantee by Minister for Finance Charlie McCreevy days before polling day that there would be no cutbacks if Fianna Fáil were returned to Government. Even key election strategist, PJ Mara, though reluctant to discuss that issue, gives the strong impression that he felt McCreevy's 'no cutbacks letter' was uncalled for.

None the less, Bertie Ahern also insisted that the 2002 general election was fought against a predicted slow-down in the global economy. He repeatedly argued that election promises were predicated on growth rates which fell short, and spending had to be revised downwards.

In the ensuing months, controversy also grew about 1,300 jobs promised on so-called 'Golden Thursday', 18 April, just six days before Ahern called the general election. Three hundred of these jobs were to go to Macroom at a factory to be set up by the pharmaceutical firm, Elan. However, that autumn it transpired that the board of this firm, by then in deep financial trouble, had not sanctioned the development expected to open in early 2005.

As the political parties prepared for local and European Parliament elections in June 2004, there were widespread fears within Fianna Fáil that the public were waiting for them with vengeance on their minds. An editorial in the *Irish Examiner* in November 2003 cited an old election adage of Fianna Fáil founder Éamon de Valera.

'If you fool me once, shame on you! But if you fool me twice, shame on me!'

In the run-up to Christmas 2003, media speculation was that if Fianna Fáil lost 100 council seats, Ahern's leadership would be in doubt. Previously, Bertie Ahern had dealt with dissent by allowing it to burn itself out in public waves of rebelliousness. In a break with old party disciplines, Ahern tolerated public criticisms by backbenchers such as John McGuinness of Kilkenny and Ned O'Keeffe of Cork East. Ahern's apparent laxness enraged many of the party older guard. Others acknowledged that it was a quietly effective way of marginalising certain people. But at a parliamentary party meeting on 2 December 2003, Bertie Ahern took the offensive. In a very robust outburst he told TDs and Senators that he had seen other ways of operating as party leader, which was taken to be a reference to the more direct style of Charlie Haughey.

'If individuals are trying to undermine me, I will personally spend my time fucking them up. I will fuck ye up,' he told that meeting. In a more humorous aside, caused by the heat of the moment, he also warned that he would not tolerate 'kebabs', a misspoken reference to 'cabals'.

~ ~ ~ ~ ~

Bertie Ahern was chatting casually with EU Commission President Romano Prodi in the Kremlin in Moscow on 21 May 2004. 'Why don't you take the job? You know it's worth a million euro when you add it all up,' the avuncular Italian joked to Ahern.

Ahern and Prodi had just completed a successful EU–Russia summit meeting with President Vladimir Putin, which paved the way for Russia to join the World Trade Organization. Later that same evening Ahern would be knocking on constituents' doors in Cabra urging their support in the local elections.

The job of EU Commission President carries a salary of €300,000 per year and a range of perks including handsome pension arrangements, however, it is all somewhat short of a €1m per year package over the five-year term. But to many people, faced with the alternative prospect of heading back to Cabra to knock upon doors in quest for votes, it might have had its attractions.

Diplomats in Brussels and several other EU capitals rated Ahern as a serious prospect. Like most people he was chuffed by the positive speculation and did not shoot it down as quickly or as definitively as he might. But to anyone who listened closely it was always clear that Ahern was not interested in this job, which could have been his if he showed he wanted it.

Seventeen years of regular visits to Brussels for EU ministerial meetings and seven years of attending leaders' summits have taught him how fraught, and frequently powerless, the task of Commission President really is. Even so, Ahern's lack of French, German or other major European language is no longer the automatic bar it once was in an increasingly Anglophile EU. Brussels officials noted however that Ahern was never entirely comfortable among a group of leaders who frequently switch languages with ease as they try to sound out compromises in informal social discussions. Sources in Dublin suggest that his commitment to completing the Northern Ireland peace process also weighed heavily on him.

Ahern was heading towards the final month of Ireland's six-month EU Presidency, which was to be acclaimed as a major success. On 18 June, he brokered the necessary unanimous agreement of 25 member states on a new EU Constitution which set out a reformed decision-making framework for an expanded bloc of nations. He began these negotiations slowly and cautiously as Italy, having led the previous six-month EU presidency, had left major disagreements behind them. Spain and Poland were insisting on holding on to a stronger weighted voting power in law-making as had been agreed at a summit in Nice on 9 December 2000. The so-called Nice Treaty, for which France had led negotiations, was an incomplete tangle which led on from the 1997 Treaty of Amsterdam, negotiated by the Netherlands, but which also carried inbuilt flaws. The Nice Treaty had brought its own problems for Ahern, requiring two referendums to pass.

Ahern toured the capitals and did a major stocktake on the prospects of a deal before deciding on whether to reopen negotiations. It was only after an interim leaders' summit in March 2004 that he decided it was worth trying again. The circumstances favoured success as all governments knew they must be seen to pull together, given a volatile international situation. But success could not be taken for granted as there was strong disagreement on details.

Ahern benefited from the talents of a small group of able negotiators. The Irish officials steered a middle course between countries like France and Germany – who saw the whole thing as an opportunity to minimise the national vetoes – and Britain and new member states insistent on keeping national decision-making on taxes and welfare policy and maintaining defence links with the USA. The Irish negotiators worked on a principle called 'enhanced cooperation', which allowed groups of like-minded member states to develop common policies between them. But they also built in safeguards to ensure that this did not undermine overall solidarity.

At the two-day leaders' summit, Ahern managed to separate out the issue of choosing a successor to Prodi and concentrated on delivering the constitution. The new EU Commission president, former Portuguese Prime Minister José Manuel Durão Barroso, was chosen 12 days later at a special summit, again chaired by Ahern in Brussels. There were accolades aplenty for Ireland's stewardship which many Irish people found a little difficult to take on board. Veteran French President, Jacques Chirac, a man not known to gush with praise, described the six-month term as simply the best presidency he had ever seen.

~ ~ ~ ~ ~

But being a 'Euro hero' had cut very little ice at home. Some in Fianna Fáil lamented that Ahern's triumphs of negotiation had not occurred a week earlier. On 11 June 2004, the Irish had handed Fianna Fáil their worst election drubbing ever. Historians had to go back to 1927, a year after the party's foundation, to find a worse set of Fianna Fáil results. In the local elections, their vote had slumped to 32 per cent nationally and they lost one in five of their county and city councillors. The European Parliament election also brought bad news as the party dropped from six out of 15 MEPs in the previous assembly to four out of a reduced allocation of 13 MEPs for Ireland this time.

Publicly, Ahern appeared to take the outcome on the chin and promised to listen more to change course and adopt a more socially driven agenda. But Cabinet colleagues say the results had hit Ahern like a hammer blow. One Minister said that a similar return in the general election, due in summer of 2007, would have led to the loss of anything between 10 and 20 Dáil seats. Internal recriminations were bitter with severe criticisms also of the Progressive Democrats.

Fine Gael appeared to have bounced back with 28 per cent of the vote and major seat gains. Sinn Féin also made considerable gains with almost 8 per cent of the vote and nearly 150,000 first preferences. Labour and the Green Party barely held their own.

In the Dublin City Council area, the news was bad for Fianna Fáil who lost eight seats, while Sinn Féin gained six seats. Overall, Fianna Fáil's vote was down 13 per cent on its 1999 result, while Sinn Féin's was up to 18 per cent, an 8 per cent increase on 1999. Closer to Ahern's Dublin Central base, his brother, Maurice, and Mary Fitzpatrick, daughter of Ahern's fellow TD, Dr Dermot Fitzpatrick, had to wait until the 10th and final count to get elected. Sinn Féin's Nicky Kehoe topped the poll with over 3,600 votes, signalling that he will be difficult to beat in the next Dáil election.

Similarly, in the adjoining North Inner City ward Cllr Tom Stafford had to wait until the 11th count to get his seat for Fianna Fáil. Labour took the Fianna Fáil seat held by Royston Brady, who confined himself to running in the European Parliament elections. Indeed Royston Brady's absence and the dual mandate ban on Dermot Fitzpatrick and Senator Tony Kett running may have compounded difficulties. Yet overall the results raised some serious questions about the performance of the much-vaunted Ahern election machine and prompted some soul-searching at a subsequent constituency meeting in late July. A frustrated Bertie Ahern was reliably reported as saying the biggest complainers had done nothing in the run-up to the elections.

Among Ahern's Drumcondra set, Senator Cyprian Brady is the early favourite to become the Taoiseach's running mate in the next election, though nothing is set in stone. It has finally become clear that his brother, Royston, is not a favoured protégé of the Taoiseach. In contrast, Ahern's decision to nominate Cyprian Brady to the Seanad in July 2002 is taken by many as a sign that the elder Brady is on the inside track. Both Bradys are sons of Ray Brady, who was one of Bertie Ahern's most loyal supporters right up to the time of his death in 1997. A native of Sheriff Street in the inner city, Ray Brady was a man whose desire to be different was reflected in the names he chose for his children. Both Cyprian and Royston have worked on Ahern campaigns since they were youngsters.

As a successful Dublin city councillor and high-profile Lord Mayor, Royston Brady clashed openly with Minister for Justice Michael McDowell when he criticised the Minister for failing to meet with him about crime concerns in the city. McDowell's subsequent resignation threat obliged Brady to withdraw his criticisms, however. None the less, Brady went on to run a high profile European Parliament campaign in the four-seat Dublin constituency but ultimately failed to win a seat.

~ ~ ~ ~ ~

Bertie Ahern announced that he would reshuffle his Cabinet and redraw political priorities in the wake of these local election reverses. But he postponed any announcement until the Dáil returned from its summer recess on 29 September 2004. It bought him a summer of peace, as Fianna Fáil TDs hoping for promotion, or fretful of demotion, did not dare show overt signs of dissent.

As well as garnering a quiet summer, it also put the media spotlight on Fianna Fáil as some 10 weeks of speculation had the additional benefit of diverting attention from more pressing political issues such as the future of Aer Lingus and other taxpayer-owned enterprises.

But in the intervening period three important things happened. First, on Tuesday, 20 July, the Taoiseach announced that Minister for Finance Charlie McCreevy had been nominated as Ireland's new EU Commissioner with effect from 31 October. He would resign from Government on 29 September and return to the backbenches for a few weeks before starting his five-year term in the €250,000 per year job. As he went to speak to political correspondents at Leinster House that evening, McCreevy had a desolate air about him, which he attributed to a certain sadness at moving on and the difficulty of deciding on taking the job. The weekend papers prior to his appointment had been awash with predictions that he was going to Brussels. This was in spite of him spending weeks letting it be known that he had no interest in being Ireland's Commissioner. On 28 June, speaking in Cork, he had made it abundantly clear that he wanted to continue as Minister for Finance, a job he had held for seven years.

'I'm not making any arrangements for travel plans, either internally or externally, nor do I intend making them,' he said.

However, the newspapers were used to convey a clear message to McCreevy that his political 'best-before' expiry date in finance had been reached. In the weeks following the 11 June local election disaster, there were persistent reports that Fianna Fáil TDs and Senators wanted a radical reshuffle of Cabinet. Frequently, McCreevy's name was mentioned as having presented a far-right, uncaring image to the public for which voters exacted revenge.

McCreevy's anger at that scenario was made perfectly clear in a *Sunday Independent* interview on 12 September when he said the election canvass yielded no evidence voters felt Fianna Fáil were right-wing, much less that it was his fault. But he was philosophic.

'Live by the sword – die by the sword,' he said. In an earlier interview, McCreevy also indicated that he shared the public's bafflement at what makes Bertie Ahern tick. He said he knew perhaps 25 per cent of Ahern – a good 24 per cent more than most of the rest of the world.

On 13 August 2004, Joe Walsh announced that he was retiring after a successful and distinguished career at the Department of Agriculture which had spanned 17 years. He said he would not contest the next election. The focus then switched to Minister for Defence Michael Smith, who quickly announced that he would not follow Walsh's example. For weeks the pair had been the focus of speculation that they were nearest the door in Ahern's reshuffle plans. It was recalled that both were supposedly to have been dropped in June 2002 when Ahern appointed his second Cabinet. However, both had successfully lobbied colleagues, including McCreevy, to keep them on the team. This time Smith's problems were worsened by his opposition to the so-called Hanly plan for hospital rationalisation, which he had openly opposed the previous autumn because of the impact on his own Tipperary North constituency.

Throughout the summer of limited political news, messages emanating from sources close to Mr Smith repeatedly stated that he would not collaborate in his departure from Cabinet. It was a short step from that to extrapolate that he would oppose efforts to sack him. In fact, he went on television to deny this and say it was the Taoiseach's prerogative to appoint his ministers, but his fate appeared sealed. All the signs were that Ahern was going to be radical and extensive in his shake-up.

When the day finally arrived, however, it was not very radical at all. In fact, it was rather confused in its delivery and predictable in its outcome. The only one told there was no room for him in Cabinet was Michael Smith. The three vacancies were filled by seasoned junior ministers well known for defending the indefensible elements of Government actions, while more senior figures hid over the previous seven years. Veteran Limerick East

TD, Willie O'Dea, became Minister for Defence; Dún Laoghaire TD, Mary Hanafin, was appointed Minister for Education; Wicklow TD, Dick Roche, became Minister for the Environment.

Only three of Ahern's 14 Ministers stayed in their previous jobs. These were PD president and Minister for Justice Michael McDowell; Arts, Sports and Tourism Minister, John O'Donoghue; and Gaeltacht, Rural and Community Affairs Minister, Éamon Ó Cuiv. McDowell used his PD bargaining power to stay and finish controversial work he had started. Ó Cuiv was deemed irreplaceable for gaeltacht and western development issues; O'Donoghue did not move largely because once all other moves were done, there was no better place for him than his old job.

Fianna Fáil deputy leader Brian Cowen moved from Foreign Affairs to Finance, enhancing his credentials as a potential future leader; Dermot Ahern took Cowen's old job at Foreign Affairs; Noel Dempsey took on Ahern's previous job as Minister for Communications and the Marine; Mary Coughlan moved to the Department of Agriculture; Micheál Martin became Minister for Enterprise, Trade and Employment. Most of these appointments had been well speculated about in public. As was PD leader and Tánaiste Mary Harney's appointment as Minster for Health, a department for which funding has trebled to €10bn since Bertie Ahern came to power in 1997, while it continues to be a shambles.

The rationale behind this and the final appointment – a job swop between Martin Cullen and Seamus Brennan – remains a major source of political debate. Brennan had been on a collision course with the various trade unions and other interests in the public transport sector since he took on the job in June 2002. Clearly, there was fierce opposition to his efforts to at least partially privatise Aer Lingus; break-up the airport authority, Aer Rianta, and introduce more private involvement in the bus services.

Brennan strongly resisted efforts to move him and there was speculation that he would be out of Government altogether.

Indeed he is known to resent and reject reports that Mary Harney interceded on his behalf. There was also speculation that his veteran constituency colleague, Tom Kitt, would replace him. In the event, Kitt became Government Chief Whip and Brennan stayed as a rather unlikely Minister for Social and Family Affairs. Martin Cullen, who had been Minister for the Environment, became an equally unlikely Minister for Transport in the circumstances.

The rationale behind these changes is not easy to find. But this writer's understanding is that both Harney's and Brennan's appointments are a deliberate attempt to help both to collude in softening the overall Government image.

'In those jobs they just cannot continue to appear as hardline and free-booting liberals,' one senior Government source said. Each has been assured of extra funds to reinforce this change.

Martin Cullen's appointment remains a further puzzle. Over the years, Seamus Brennan was always accused of being a surrogate PD – but Cullen is a former PD TD whose economic views remain unchanged since joining Fianna Fáil in 1994 and who is decidedly no friend of the unions. Other government sources view his appointment as a signal that Bertie Ahern will call the real shots in government transport policy between now and the next election.

'Brennan's agenda will not be recanted – but it will fall into decline through a benign neglect,' another Government source believes.

For the rest, Ahern sacked just one junior minister, Dr Jim McDaid of Donegal North-East. He confined himself to appointing five new members in all from a group of 17, many of whom were clearly underperforming. Discontent on the Fianna Fáil backbenches continues to simmer.

Ultimately, Bertie Ahern now has only one end in sight to the exclusion of all else – winning the next general election due in summer 2007.

Conclusion

Bertie Ahern's friend, British Prime Minister Tony Blair, says that in another life he would have liked to have been a rock star. Ahern however eschews the prospect of trashing hotel rooms and dumping television sets into swimming pools. His Walter Mitty alternative to leading his country would be to play centre-back for the Dublin footballers and/or Manchester United. But if he were not Taoiseach, odds are that Bertie Ahern could now be giving tax advice to consultant doctors.

In 1978, a year after he was first elected TD, he turned down the job as chief executive of the new Mater Private Hospital. That job paid £20,000 per year (€25,000), with company car, at a time when his TD's salary was £8,901 (€11,300) and some pundits felt he had an unsure political future. He told this writer in September 2001 that at the back of his mind, if politics did not work out, his longer-term plan had been to become a tax adviser to consultant doctors.

Undoubtedly, Ahern's single-minded determination has helped him gain considerable success in politics. Twenty-seven years of involvement have brought the top job of Taoiseach and major recognition abroad. He clearly enjoys his work which he comes at with gusto. Moreover, he enjoys power, certainly not the pomp and circumstance of power, but the ability to be in control, manage and drive an agenda onwards.

In the decade since he took over the Fianna Fail leadership, the two main rival parties Fine Gael and Labour have between them had six leaders. In that period Bertie Ahern has won a general election, defied the odds by leading a minority coalition for a full five-year term and been re-elected with a more secure Dáil support base.

In assessing his work, a number of clear characteristics emerge. First, he is an extremely intelligent and able person who has thrived upon being underestimated for a very long time. In reality, those who doubted his ability were only finally answered after his second election success in May 2002. Ahern's intelligence and ability are augmented by a phenomenal and single-minded work rate, with days that usually stretch from 7 am to past midnight. Even Saturdays and Sundays can average six to eight hours of work. His working methods are clearly effective. In almost 30 interviews conducted for this biography, there was near unanimity about his preparation and about how well informed he was in dealing with the issues upon which he encountered these various interviewees. 'He often knows more about the subject than the person dealing with it,' was a very frequent comment.

Diversions are few and simple. A few pints of Bass with his old friends in Drumcondra, walking his constituency or seen about other constituencies, attending sports events and watching sport on television. In other words, work and hobbies merge. He is a creature of habit; if he travels abroad for work, he likes where possible to be back in Drumcondra before the pubs close. And finally, he likes to spend as much time as possible with his two daughters.

That level of commitment and work rate have certainly come at a price to his personal life. 'No family could stick it,' one veteran Fianna Fáil colleague said simply. Personally, Ahern remains a devout practising Catholic, though he is separated from his wife Miriam and was in a long-term relationship with Celia Larkin. In truth, he is friendly and affable and capable of being extremely charming and warm. But he is decidedly not soft.

'Bertie is tough and very tough and doesn't suffer fools lightly. But he is very humane,' says Senator Tony Kett, a close friend and collaborator of over 30 years.

With a huge clinic operation and considerable voluntary and professional back-up, Ahern is a veritable constituency hound. Furthermore, he is an unrepentant practitioner of the clientelist politics prevalent in Ireland, putting out up to 700 representative letters per week. In his base of Dublin Central he is a decisive and vigorous competitor and no other Fianna Fáil candidate has built a successful base since Ahern achieved ascendancy there over 20 years ago. The ruthless constituency discipline and phenomenally successful vote management, by now applied across the rest of the country by the party, has at best a limited application in Bertie Ahern's home patch.

The quintessential pragmatic politician, Ahern is totally focused on rule number one and those that follow in sequence: get elected; get your party elected; keep it in power. He practised that from the very outset of his career, helping his mentor Charlie Haughey broker a deal with his own deadly constituency rival, Tony Gregory, in 1982 to form a minority government. Some would see his early identification with Haughey and his initial decision to support him 'right or wrong' as further evidence of the Ahern pragmatism.

Later he negotiated with the principals of the Progressive Democrats, whom he had earlier helped Haughey drum out of Fianna Fáil. After that he helped Albert Reynolds deal with the PDs and then broker a new coalition with Labour. Under his own leadership, the relationship with the PDs – bar the occasional notable rows and impediments – has been seamless.

There have been lower-level practical deals with three Independent TDs and talk of many other such potential deals. Most recently, the prospect of a government arrangement involving Fianna Fáil and Sinn Féin has been floated in a scenario where the IRA has abandoned all paramilitarism for good. It is all a long way from Fianna Fáil's 'core value' of never sharing power.

On Ahern's watch, Ireland has moved almost definitively into a mainland Europe model of consensus politics. His conciliatory and inclusive approach to politics has been a major feature of this development. Yet his focus on party matters and his huge personal popularity have also conversely meant that he came within an ace of Fianna Fáil winning an overall majority in May 2002.

Bertie Ahern is at his absolute best when cutting a deal. He was a huge influence in establishing national social consensus, including government, bosses, unions, farmers, and social and charitable organisations. The model was purloined from the Nordic countries and Austria, and worked upon over two decades in Ireland. Undoubtedly, it is flawed and much criticised, but it has persisted to some effect in making Ireland prosperous.

The Ahern deal-making skills have been applied to the Northern Ireland negotiations where he has also shown resilience and persistence and is now close to seeing a lasting and workable agreement. These skills have also been taken overseas to broker agreement on a new European Union constitution and the appointment of a new EU Commission president during Ireland's most recent six-month presidency in the first half of 2004.

Nearer to home, his conciliation has helped rebuild unity within Fianna Fáil since he took over the party leadership in November 1994 and after sporadic conflicts waxed and waned since late 1966. A more hands-off approach to party discipline than most of his predecessors is clearly his preferred style, but has also shown himself possessed of a ruthless streak when required.

His decade of leadership has largely been about coping with the legacy of alleged sleaze dating from the Haughey era and also involving several other big names in the party. In fact, critics have railed against apparent indecisiveness and occasional amnesia on these issues. None the less, he has put through ethics legislation and a code of honour for his own party. He has also clearly done enough to keep the voters' confidence in his integrity and indeed a court has refuted allegations of personal corruption.

Timing has been on his side in certain instances. He inherited a nascent Northern Ireland peace process at a time when the IRA leadership was of an age to think again about a constitutional approach, while Britain's leaders had entered a post-colonial phase. He was tasked with promoting social consensus at a time when union and business leaders were seeking a more practical way of managing their differences. At a European level, he came to EU constitutional negotiations when the various government leaders knew it was time to make compromises after several failures. And perhaps most significantly, the Irish economy was entering an unprecedented boom cycle when he was elected Taoiseach.

However, fortune has not always smiled. He came to the Fianna Fáil Parliamentary Party as their virtual hegemony on government was drawing to a close. Though he got early breaks, he served his time to politics at local council and Dáil level before joining government. He was within 12 hours of becoming Taoiseach when fate intervened and banished him to opposition for more than two and a half years. As a result, he has also shown some grit and persistence.

In essence, Bertie Ahern is extremely cautious, aloof and secretive. Indeed PJ Mara, twice his director of elections, describes him as 'a bit too risk averse'. The summation of a former Cabinet colleague and deputy leader Mary O'Rourke is interesting too.

'Everything Bertie does is for a purpose – ultimately for himself. He's friendly but he's not very warm. I got to know him – and still I didn't get to know him. Sometimes I had the feeling that I met nobody.'

Another Cabinet Minister notes that Ahern rarely admits that he has been researching their areas of responsibility. Any gems of information about their business, which he inadvertently lets slip, are attributed to chance or coincidence. He rarely concedes that he has been reading up on, or speaking with people concerned in the relevant subject matter.

Ahern's conciliatory strengths are also his weaknesses. He shrinks from confrontation and dislikes delivering bad news. Frequent attempts to agree with both sides have wearied people and his attempts to keep his fingerprints away from necessary unsavoury deeds are often seen as an insult to the intelligence of others.

'If you want to be ruthless – be ruthless. Yes, telling people to their face that you're going to screw them – well, they won't like you. But it's not realistic to think that they won't know if you screw them behind their back,' says one veteran party colleague, who actually has benefited from his association with Ahern.

Even the most Walter Mittyish of men would concede that, at 53 years of age, Ahern will not now field for the Dubs or Manchester United. For many years he has identified 60 years of age as his target for quitting politics and trying his hand in the business world, where he certainly would not lack opportunities. This book does not purport to be the definitive word on Bertie Ahern, who at time of writing in late 2004 made it clear that he is far from finished on the political field. Clearly, Fianna Fáil's stocks are low after serious local election reverses in June 2004. However, Ahern, also heads the first unpopular Government in the State's history to have the surplus funds to assuage at least some of the Irish voters' anger. He can also appeal to voters' insecurity as the tried and trusted one. For these and other reasons there is every chance that we will see Bertie Ahern win a third term as Taoiseach.

Index

Index